# The
# Lawn & Garden
# Owner's Manual

# The Lawn & Garden Owner's Manual

## What to do and When to do it

Lewis and Nancy Hill

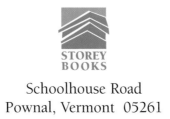

STOREY
BOOKS

Schoolhouse Road
Pownal, Vermont 05261

*The mission of Storey Communications is to serve our customers by publishing practical information that encourages personal independence in harmony with the environment.*

---

**Edited by** Gwen W. Steege and Teri Dunn
**Cover design by** Meredith Maker
**Cover photograph by** © Margaret Hensel, Positive Images
**Text design by** Betty Kodela and Erin Lincourt
**Text production by** Erin Lincourt
**Illustrations by** Elayne Sears
**Photography by** Liz Ball (page 46), © Crandall and Crandall (pages 2, 37, 41, 47, 55, 63, 117, 119, and 124), Carlis B. Grants (page 60), Kevin Kennifick (page 78), Cynthia McFarland (pages 103 and 105), Jerry Pavia (pages 4-5, 24-25, 26, 52, 53, 54, 56, 57, 61, 65, 71, 72, 74, 75, 81, 111, 148, and 158-59), Martha Storey (page 131), and Giles Prett (pages 38, 51, inset 57, 58, 86, 87, 93, 102, 114, 136, 137, 149, 153, 156, 160, and 166)
**Indexed by** Northwind Editorial Services

The information in this book is true and complete to the best of our knowledge. All recommendations are made without guarantee on the part of the author or Storey Books. The author and publisher disclaim any liability in connection with the use of this information. For additional information please contact Storey Books, Schoolhouse Road, Pownal, Vermont 05261.

Storey Books are available for special premium and promotional uses and for customized editions. For further information, please call Storey's Custom Publishing Department at 1-800-793-9396.

Printed in the United States by R.R. Donnelley
10 9 8 7 6 5 4 3

**Library of Congress Cataloging-in-Publication Data**

Hill, Lewis, 1924–
    The lawn & garden owner's manual: what to do and when to do it / Lewis and Nancy Hill.
        p.    cm.
    Includes bibliographical references.
    ISBN 1-58017-214-8 (pbk. : alk. paper)
    1. Gardening. I. Title: The lawn and garden owner's manual.
II. Hill, Nancy. III. Title.

SB453 .H6534 2000
635-dc21                                                    99-047216

contents

# contents (cont'd)

introduction

# This Old Landscape: Taming It and Caring for It

A few years ago we were enjoying lunch at the home of a friend who spends her summers in a house on a Vermont hillside. She mentioned that she and her husband had built their house twenty years ago and surrounded it soon after with foundation plants, a lawn, shade trees, perennial border, herb garden, and a small orchard and berry patch. Now, everything that had once looked so nice was becoming overgrown, and she was unsure what to do about it. "You should write a book on the subject," she commented.

We laughed at the time, but as we talked with others and began to look around, it was obvious that our friend was not alone in her dilemma. Plants rarely stand still, and overgrown landscapes are common. Many homeowners understand how to plan, plant, and care for their young plantings, but are uncertain about how to handle trees and shrubs that have grown too large, perennials that have spread, lawns that have become weedy and filled with holes, flowering trees that don't bloom, and a host of other ills that mature plants are prone to.

So we took her advice. If your landscape has deteriorated, if you have just purchased a property that someone else has not maintained over the years, or even if you only face mature plants that worry you, we hope to help you get your lawn, garden, and landscape back in shape without a lot of work or investment. And, once your plantings are in good condition, we hope to help you keep them that way with pruning, shearing, fertilizing, pest control, and managing other problems that face all growing things. If your lawn and gardens are in tip-top shape already, you have only to understand and implement the ins and outs of good care.

Caring for your lawn and gardens, like caring for anything else, means that you establish a close relationship with them. (It is easiest if you planted and tended for your plants as "babies" rather than met them for the first time as "adults," but we all know that close ties develop then, too.) When you

## CHECKLIST FOR NEW HOMEOWNERS

- Survey the plantings and list any problems you find. Get information from the previous owner.

- Get to know the soil. Check the soil depth with a shovel, and take samples to test for nutrients and pH unless the plantings reassure that all is well.

- If you are living in a different climatic zone from what you've been used to, choose plants that are right for your new home. Your lilac that flourished in Michigan won't do well in Tucson; the forsythia that bloomed well in Connecticut may have its flower buds killed in the winter temperatures in upper New York state.

- Before increasing your plantings or lawn area, look carefully at future maintenance duties an expansion may entail. You may not be up to, or be able to find help for, the work your plan may require.

- To avoid costly mistakes, if it is practical, live with the landscape throughout a growing season or even a year before making major changes.

*Nostalgia is a valid factor to consider when you choose your landscape plantings. The delicious scent of spring lilacs is reason enough to include this old-fashioned stalwart in your garden scheme.*

are intimately connected with your plants, you're interested in their health and welfare and get to know their needs, likes, and dislikes. You recognize immediately when they are not well and try to find out what is going wrong. Above all, you rejoice when they look happy where they are planted and are doing what they are meant to do — thrive, grow, and blossom.

Whether your goal is maintenance of a landscape or a complete transformation, the process of caregiving and its satisfying results are sure to bring you pleasure.

## Assessing Your Yard and Garden

A mature landscape may need a face-lift for many reasons. It may be simply because plants age naturally and need replacing, or because a hard wind, ice storm, or other natural disaster wreaks havoc. A tree's branches may expand and crowd driveways, rub against a roof, or climb into overhead power lines. Its roots can heave sidewalks or sneak into the water lines or a sewage system. Sometimes the lawn is damaged as tree roots grow through the turf. Ferns and weeds may have crept into the perennial bed.

Whatever the reason for the state of the landscape you are faced with rejuvenating, you may be a bit overwhelmed at the challenge. But with a moderate amount of work and expense, you should be able to convert even the most dilapidated land-

---

### FIRST THINGS FIRST: PLANNING YOUR PROJECTS

1. Decide which plants can be saved and which cannot, and tie a colored plastic ribbon on the keepers for easy identification. Remove those that can't be either salvaged or moved to a better location.

2. Move any plants that would be more attractive in another spot. Be certain the new location suits the light and moisture needs of the plant.

3. Improve the remaining plants by pruning and mulching them.

4. Install pathways, walls, fences, pools, gazebos, and other permanent "hardscape" features.

5. Improve or redo the lawn. In areas where it's difficult to maintain a healthy lawn; plant ground covers.

6. Install new trees, shrubs, and other plants you have selected.

scape into a satisfying beauty spot. For inspiration, study photos in home and garden magazines or drive around to check out other yards, noticing what you admire and what you don't.

When you're faced with sprucing up a landscape that has deteriorated, you must decide whether to remodel what is already there or completely redo it. Some experts recommend a complete landscape renovation once every 10 to 12 years, but we feel it is far better to make changes whenever they are needed or desired, rather than on a predetermined schedule. Although some areas may call for complete replacement, most can probably be brought back into shape with a modest investment and a little elbow grease.

Always work your own preferences into your plantings rather than copying others. If you love the smell of lilacs or mock orange in springtime, include them, even though they may not contribute much to the scenery the rest of the year. If they fit into the landscape, you may want to use "nostalgia" plants, such as the yellow shrub roses or heliotrope that you remember from Grandpa's farm or a summer vacation. These, too, give your spot individuality.

## How to Use This Book

This book is divided into three sections. Part 1 is organized by season and designed for quick and handy reference. Thumb through it whenever you have the time or inclination to go out and work on the yard, and you will find a range of tasks you can or should be doing. Consider this section a place to get your bearings. The checklists need not be followed slavishly. Instead, choose what seems to you most important for your yard and the activity that matches your level of ambition and time today.

Throughout part 1, you will be referred to various sections of part 2, which is the heart of the book, the place to turn for detailed information about the hows and whys of garden projects and renovation activities. Everything from how to combat rose diseases, to how much to prune ever-

greens, to how to rescue a weed-infested flower bed is here. If you have trouble finding the information you need, consult the index at the back of the book for faster access.

Last but not least is part 3, with instructions on good gardening habits that lead to successful gardens and yards. You'll save yourself time, grief, and effort by attending to topics ranging from soil improvement to warding off predatory deer. But don't let all the information and problems listed discourage you. Even if the condition of your landscape appears hopeless, it can usually be remedied with careful feeding, pruning, and replacement of some of the plantings. With some attention, "this old landscape" will become a spot of beauty.

### TIPS FOR SMOOTH MANAGEMENT

**Keep records.** Since our property is fairly large, we have found the only way we can keep track of and care for things in an organized way is to have a schedule and keep a notebook handy for jotting down any unplanned items that pop up.

**Be flexible.** In the Northeast, we must continually adjust our schedule because gardening duties depend more on weather than on the calendar. Weekly lawn mowing has long been a tradition, for example, especially by those who do it as a business, but when grass is growing at top speed in the spring, once a week is seldom enough. Then, during a dry spell in August, the grass may not may not need to be cut for nearly a month.

**Consolidate tools and supplies.** Have your tools and supplies arranged in one place, perhaps in a garden house or a corner of the garage. Put up hangers on pegboards or simply drive nails into the wall, and label them so you can hang the tools where you can always find them and they won't clutter the floor. Keep fertilizers and sprays in a cupboard that is secure from children, and place the items you use most often in spots where they are handiest to grab. It is surprising how much time and frustration you can avoid by being able to access these things whenever you need them.

# Part 1

# Lawn and Garden Calendar

By giving your plants the regular care they need, you'll ensure that they won't deteriorate and will reward you with their beauty for many years.

Although caring for plants is not as demanding as caring for a lot of animals, there are some duties that must be done on schedule. Certain chores are weekly jobs, some must be done at the beginning of the season, and others only at certain stages of a plant's growth. If you do not carry them out at the right time, the landscape inevitably begins to look ragged.

There's an old Vermont saying, "The first day of spring is mighty different from the first spring day." No matter where you live, dates are of little use to predict the seasons, which may come early, at the usual time, or late in any particular year. But plants and animals respond to seasonal and climate changes, and their behavior predicts when spring, summer, fall, or winter are imminent. Though our garden calendar cannot give you the exact day or even the month when you should do certain lawn and garden chores, the seasonal cues listed here can help you determine the first spring, summer, and fall days in your backyard.

# Early Spring

*Early spring is the time to listen for sounds of spring peepers and watch the early birds — robins and killdeer. In the North, growth has not yet started on deciduous shrubs and trees, and although the buds may show signs of swelling, the sap is not yet very active.*

**ROUTINE CHORES**

- Inspect all plants for winter damage. Prune out dead and damaged wood on trees and shrubs. ➤ *See page 88*

- Uncover perennial plants, and clean up last year's dead plant material and any debris blown in over winter.

- Spread compost in gardens and on the lawn.

- Prune fruit trees after the wood has thawed but before buds show any green. ➤ *See page 140*

- Prune fruit bushes and grapevines while still dormant. ➤ *See page 145*

- Feed evergreens. ➤ *See page 117*

- Feed deciduous trees. ➤ *See page 125*

- Feed fruit trees. ➤ *See page 141*

- Cut back overwintered ornamental grasses. ➤ *See page 73*

**NOW IS THE BEST TIME TO . . .**

- Plant bareroot roses, trees, perennials, and shrubs. ➤ *See page 109*

- Order bedding plants and grass seed from your local nursery or your favorite mail-order suppliers.

- Move existing plants that you want in a new location. ➤ *See page 50*

- Prune later-flowering shrubs (including roses and broadleaf evergreens such as rhododendrons) while they are still dormant or just emerging from dormancy. (Take care not to remove flower buds.) ➤ *See page 121*

- Prune vines. ➤ *See page 84*

- Prune evergreens while still dormant.
  ➤ *See page 114*

- Reseed the lawn or lay sod. ➤ *See page 33*

- Apply herbicides to your lawn, if needed.
  ➤ *See page 30*

- Fertilize summer-blooming bulbs.

- In the South, fertilize your lawn. In the North, fertilize your lawn only if it appears to need it.

- Prune deciduous trees while they are still dormant. ➤ *See page 129*

## ONGOING PROJECTS TO CHECK ON

- Watch for fall-planted bulbs to emerge. Try to remove any winter mulch before the new growth appears, so that you don't damage young foliage.

- Retrieve hardwood cuttings from storage and prepare to set them in a plant "nursery" outdoors.

## PROJECTS TO START NOW

- Spray fruit trees with dormant oil just as buds swell. ➤ *See page 142*

- Start seeds indoors of plants (vegetables, herbs, and flowers) that you plan to plant out later, in cold climates. Refer to seed catalogs and garden references for suggested planting dates; you don't want seedlings to outgrow their indoor homes and become leggy before being moved to the garden.

- Once the ground has thawed, aerate hard-packed lawn soil (rent special equipment for large lawns). ➤ *See page 29*

- Begin perennial-border rejuvenation project.
  ➤ *See page 61*

- Carry out soil improvement measures in the vegetable and flower gardens. Test your soil, if you didn't do so in the fall, and add appropriate amendments to adjust the pH and nutrients needed by your plants. ➤ *See page 163*

## OPTIONAL TASKS

- If you didn't do so during the winter, clean, sharpen, and oil your pruning tools, hoes, and shovels.

- Consider replacing unwanted shrubs.

# Mid-Spring

*By mid-spring, shadbush, as well as daffodils and many other spring bulbs, are blooming, and grass is beginning to grow. Lilac leaves are forming, grass is turning green, and days are warming.*

## ROUTINE CHORES

• Remove winter covers from bush, climbing, and tree roses, as well as lavender and other plants that are marginally hardy in your area.

• Get a fresh can of gasoline for your mower. Make a routine check that all parts are in working order, and if you neglected blade sharpening and other routine maintenance before winter began, do it now.

• If you haven't already, spread compost and mulches in your flower beds and vegetable garden.

• Pick the lateral buds off peonies to promote larger blooms on the terminal ones.

• Begin weeding. If you use herbicides, apply the preemergent kinds early before new weed seeds sprout.

• Divide overgrown perennial clumps.
  ➤ *See page 49*

• Watch out for pests and diseases.

## NOW IS THE BEST TIME TO . . .

• Fertilize trees, flowering shrubs, roses, hedges, and perennials.

• Install a new hedge. ➤ *See page 101*

• Shear evergreen and deciduous hedges as they begin to grow. ➤ *See page 98*

• Plant containerized roses. ➤ *See page 108*

• Plant balled-and-potted deciduous trees, shrubs, vines, and other perennial plants.
  ➤ *See page 132*

• Stake tall-growing perennial plants, such as delphiniums and peonies, before they reach 12 inches (30 cm). ➤ *See page 57*

## ONGOING PROJECTS TO CHECK ON

• Feed any flowering shrubs that you transplanted last season. ➤ *See page 102*

• Mow new lawns at proper height.
  ➤ *See pages 42 to 43*

- Transplant shrubs that were root-pruned the previous season. ➤ *See page 88*

- Water and fertilize newly planted trees, shrubs, and herbaceous plants. ➤ *See page 96*

- Continue spray program for fruit trees until flower buds appear. ➤ *See page 142*

- Check desirable ornamental grasses you have mowed down to see if they're making attractive new growth. ➤ *See page 73*

**PROJECTS TO START NOW**

- Set lawn mower high for mowing, so vigorous top growth will shade and check the growth of early sprouting weeds.

- Repair bare spots in lawn. ➤ *See page 28*

- Plant new ground cover plants. ➤ *See page 69*

- Begin root-pruning project on shrubs you wish to move later. ➤ *See page 88*

- Start shearing any evergreens that have started growing early. ➤ *See page 115*

- Make a list of bulbs to order for fall planting.

- If you have a leaning tree, start process of straightening it. ➤ *See page 128*

- Plant newly purchased container-grown perennials. Be sure to label everything you plant.

- Take cuttings from the tips of chrysanthemums and delphiniums to start new plants.

**OPTIONAL TASKS**

- Shop for fertilizers and pesticides. (Stores and garden centers usually have a better assortment now.)

- Replace any plant labels that have deteriorated.

- Regrade the lawn; fill in holes and uneven spots, rake, and reseed. ➤ *See page 28*

- Stake floppy rose growth and tie climbers. ➤ *See page 107*

- Fertilize trees, if you haven't already. ➤ *See page 125*

- Install tree guards or deer fence to protect new plants. ➤ *See page 132*

- In mild climates, feed fruit trees. ➤ *See page 141*

# Late Spring

*In late spring the leaves are nearly or fully out, lilacs and many flowering trees and shrubs are blooming, and the lawn is growing vigorously. New growth on evergreens is starting. The soil is drying out enough to till. Birds are nesting and animals are having their young.*

## ROUTINE CHORES

- Prune lilacs and other spring-flowering shrubs immediately after blossoms fade.
  ➤ *See page 88*

- Deadhead perennials as blooms fade. This will direct strength to the roots rather than to seed formation, as well as improve the looks of your garden and avoid unwanted self-sowing.

- Shear early-flowering perennials, such as moss phlox and bachelor's buttons.

- Pinch fall-flowering perennials, such as aster.
  ➤ *See page 57*

## NOW IS THE BEST TIME TO . . .

- Plant or transplant perennials. ➤ *See page 50*

- Set out annual flowering plants, vegetables, and herbs. Check with your Cooperative Extension Service for the average last frost date in your region, so that you don't get started too soon.

- Divide daffodils as soon as they die back if they are too crowded. Do this after the foliage yellows but before it disappears.

- Dig tulip bulbs and store them in a cool closet for fall replanting. Do this after the foliage yellows but before it disppears.

## ONGOING PROJECTS TO CHECK ON

- Mow lawns at proper heights.
  ➤ *See pages 42 to 43*

- Water newly planted shrubs and hedges, if natural rainfall is not sufficient. ➤ *See page 102*

- Keep new ground covers well watered. Pull weeds in the area, so that young plants don't have to compete for space to grow. ➤ *See page 68*

- Continue shearing evergreens while they are actively growing. To maintain size, shear off all new (pale green) growth; to encourage thick growth, shear about half the length of new growth. ➤ *See page 115*

- If you are straightening a leaning tree, don't neglect to water it often and fertilize weekly. ➤ *See page 128*

- Water and fertilize newly planted, trees, shrubs, and herbaceous plants. ➤ *See page 96*

- Weed perennial bed. Vigilance against young newly sprouting weeds will mean much less weeding later in the season when weeds can be more entrenched.

- Be watchful for any insect or disease problems and take steps to control them, if necessary. ➤ *See specific plants.*

- After petals fall off fruit-tree blossoms, continue spray program. ➤ *See page 142*

## PROJECTS TO START NOW

- Take cuttings from perennials you wish to propagate.

## OPTIONAL TASKS

- Aerate any lawn that needs it. ➤ *See page 29*

- Spread mulch where it is becoming thin, if you didn't get to it last fall.

- Plant annuals. Use shallow-rooted annuals to fill spots where bulbs grew and to hide the dying foliage of bulbs and spring-blooming perennials.

- Plant containerized roses, if you haven't already. ➤ *See page 108*

- In mild climates, feed fruit trees, if you haven't already. ➤ *See page 141*

# Early Summer

*In early summer, plants are growing vigorously in the long, warm days and mild nights. Fireflies roam over the damp fields and the first thunderstorms occur. Weeds are competing in the garden with flowers and vegetable plants.*

## ROUTINE CHORES

- Mulch around perennials. Be sure to leave 2 or 3 inches (5 or 7.5 cm) around the base of the plant free of mulch to prevent rotting.

- Deadhead perennials as blooms fade. This will encourage healthier growth and also prevent unwanted self-sowing. Cut back delphiniums after blossom to encourage a fall bloom.

- To moderate soil temperature and conserve moisture, mulch vegetable garden.

- Mow regularly, with lawn mower set for proper height for your particular grass.
  ➤ *See pages 42 to 43*

- Water regularly and often if weather is dry. As a rule of thumb, most garden plants and lawns need about 1 inch (2.5 cm) of water each week.

- Fight weeds: Hand pull; keep weeds from spreading seeds; use organic or synthetic preemergent herbicide to prevent sprouting of new weeds; mulch; use organic or synthetic weedkillers ➤ *See page 51*

- Control insects: Hand pick; use beneficial insects to control pests or spray organic or synthetic insecticides. ➤ *See page 33*

- Deter disease: Remove infected parts or entire plants; plant healthy, disease-resistant plants; spray or dust with fungicide, if necessary. Condition soil to inhibit disease.
  ➤ *See page 163*

## NOW IS THE BEST TIME TO . . .

- Dig up and move early spring bulbs as the plants are going dormant.

- Order spring-blooming bulbs for fall planting.

- Shear late-starting specimen evergreens and evergreen hedges while they are growing most rapidly. One or two trims per year should keep them in shape. ➤ *See page 115*

- Pinch chrysanthemums and other perennials to induce compact growth and larger blooms. ➤ *See page 57*

- Cut off dying bulb foliage and stems. Be sure to wait until foliage is completely yellowed, however, or you will limit next year's blooms. This is also the time to divide bulbs, if needed.

## ONGOING PROJECTS TO CHECK ON

- Water and weed new ground cover area. ➤ *See page 69*

- Water newly planted shrubs and hedges. ➤ *See page 96*

- Continue shearing evergreens while they are actively growing. ➤ *See page 115*

- For a leaning tree that is being straightened, continue to water it often and fertilize weekly. ➤ *See page 128*

- Continue spraying fruit trees that need it. ➤ *See page 142*

## PROJECTS TO START NOW

- Take softwood cuttings from woody plants you wish to propagate.

- Stake tall-growing perennials that will need support, if you haven't already done so. ➤ *See page 57*

- Mark spot where bulbs are growing if you wish to move them later or if you plant annuals over them.

## OPTIONAL TASKS

- Do spot-repairs on lawn; be sure to water well. ➤ *See page 28*

- Deadhead annuals if necessary; plant more.

# Midsummer

*In this season summer is at its peak. Hot, often dry, weather may cause a slowdown in plant growth, especially in warmer climates; plants may become almost dormant. At the same time, weeds and other garden pests may continue to flourish. Deer, rabbits, and other animals now have growing families to feed, and they relish the easy nibbling of country and suburban gardens.*

## ROUTINE CHORES

- Deadhead perennials as blooms fade. This is particularly important for perennials that tend to spread by self-sowing.

- Some plants will offer a second blooming period if cut back at this time.

- Harvest early tree fruits and berries.

- Water all areas of the garden if weather turns dry. Monitor rainfall — most plants need about 1 inch (2.5 cm) per week for healthy growth.

- Keep up with weeding all gardens and foundation plantings.

- If you have climbing and rambling roses, continue to prune them lightly and tie them to their support as they grow. ➤ *See page 107*

- Apply fertilizer to perennials and annuals if plants are actively growing. Do not fertilize in hot weather.

## NOW IS THE BEST TIME TO . . .

- Cut back perennials that go dormant early, such as bleeding heart and leopard's bane.

- Raise the mower blade higher so lawn will better tolerate dry weather. ➤ *See pages 42 to 43*

## ONGOING PROJECTS TO CHECK ON

- Check mulch and add more, as needed, to suppress weeds and conserve moisture. Keep mulch 2 to 3 inches (5 to 7.5 cm) away from the base of plants, to avoid rotting.

- Check staked perennials to see if they need to be secured or tied.

- Most deciduous hedges, such as privet and ninebark, grow over a long season; shear several times during the summer months.
  ➤ *See page 94*

- Deadhead annuals, to encourage continued bloom.

- Water new ground cover, and continue to weed in order to encourage spreading.

- Water newly planted shrubs and hedges.
  ➤ *See page 96*

- Continue fruit tree spraying program.
  ➤ *See page 142*

- Check all trellised plants and tie them to supports, as needed.

- Be watchful for any disease or insect problems and take steps to control them, if necessary.
  ➤ *See specific plants.*

## PROJECTS TO START NOW

- Start seeds for fall-blooming annuals, such as ornamental kale and cabbage.

## OPTIONAL TASKS

- Visit other gardens including public and other botanic gardens, for inspiration and pleasure.

- If you transplant perennials now, be sure to cut them back, water them well, and mulch thickly to conserve water and protect them against weeds.

- Shear yews and other evergreens that are making a midsummer spurt of growth.
  ➤ *See page 115*

- If you will be away on vacation during the next few weeks, arrange to have someone water your plants, particularly container plants.

# Late Summer

*Late summer brings shorter days in northern regions, plant growth slows, and woody plants begin to mature their new growth in preparation for the coming winter. Crabgrass, purslane, and other weeds scatter their seeds before winter.*

## ROUTINE CHORES

• Harvest elderberries, fall-bearing raspberries, and currants.

• Harvest tree fruits.

• In the North, fertilize the lawn. ➢ *See page 39*

• Deadhead late-blooming perennials as their flowers fade.

• Continue weeding, but discontinue fertilizing everything except lawns.

• Be watchful for any disease or insect problems and take steps to control them, if necessary. ➢ *See specific plants.*

• As soon as they fall, rake up leaves. Use whole to mulch perennials and berries, or shred and till into vegetable beds. You can also add them to the compost pile.

## NOW IS THE BEST TIME TO . . .

• Deadhead flowering ornamental grasses before they sow their seeds, except for those you wish to leave in place, to enjoy over the winter. ➢ *See page 57*

• Prune deciduous trees, particularly those that may bleed if pruned in spring (maples, birches). ➢ *See page 129*

## ONGOING PROJECTS TO CHECK ON

• Check all staked perennials to be sure they are still secure.

- Deadhead annuals, and pull out those that have stopped blooming.

- Cut back early- and midsummer-flowering perennials, such as delphiniums.

- Check for unwanted ornamental grasses and, if necessary, spray with herbicide just before they go dormant. ➤ *See page 73*

- Continue to train climbing and rambling roses, clipping and tying them, as needed. ➤ *See page 107*

- Use containers of chrysanthemums or other late-season flowers to fill empty spots in foundation plantings and perennial beds.

## PROJECTS TO START NOW

- Cut back spent perennials. This not only keeps your garden looking neater, but also helps control perennials that spread by self-sowing. ➤ *See page 57*

- Cut out raspberry and blackberry canes that have finished bearing and take to a landfill. Cut back remaining tall canes to 5 feet (1.5 m). ➤ *See page 145*

## OPTIONAL TASKS

- Divide perennials that bloomed earlier in the season and replant them or give them to friends.

- If you plan to create a new garden next spring, choose the location now, mark the area, and begin to prepare the soil (including testing and adding compost and lime or sulfur). ➤ *See page53*

- Cut annual and perennial flowers, as well as ornamental grasses suitable for dried flower arrangements, and hang them in a dry, airy location.

# Early and Mid-Fall

*In early to mid-fall the growing season is winding down, leaves show signs of color, fruiting trees are maturing, and late bloomers, such as chrysanthemums, are in flower. In colder regions, frost protection may occasionally be necessary for tender plants on some nights. Birds are leaving northern regions or have already flown south.*

## ROUTINE CHORES

- Cut down perennials for neatness, disease control, and to prevent self-seeding. Leave a few inches of stem to hold snow for winter protection in northern areas. Divide overgrown clumps of perennials and dig and discard (or give away) any you no longer want. ➤ *See page 49*

- After two or three fall frosts, fertilize perennial beds. ➤ *See page 59*

- Renew mulch on trees and plants, including berry bushes.

- Rake leaves; shred them for compost pile or use them whole for mulch.

## NOW IS THE BEST TIME TO . . .

- Plant spring-blooming bulbs, including tulips, narcissus, hyacinths, crocus, and minor bulbs.

- Fertilize lawn now, if you haven't already. ➤ *See page 39*

- Fertilize established plantings of bulbs.

- Prune deciduous foundation shrubs as they begin to go dormant (some bleed badly if pruned in spring). ➤ *See page 94*

- In cold climates, prepare roses for winter. ➤ *See page 107*

- Seed a new lawn, if you haven't done so earlier. ➤ *See page 34*

- Aerate hard-packed lawn soil (rent special equipment for large lawn). ➤ *See page 29*

- Drain underground sprinkler systems.

- Take in any pool aerators and fountain pumps.

## ONGOING PROJECTS TO CHECK ON

- Continue watering and insect and disease control as long as necessary.

## PROJECTS TO START NOW

- Dig summer bulbs such as dahlias and glads; dry and store for winter.

- Pot up tulips and other spring-flowering bulbs (in cold climates, perhaps lily-of-the-valley); store in the root cellar or other cool place that doesn't freeze, for winter blooms.

- Begin root-pruning any shrubs you wish to move later. ➤ *See page 88*

- Pick ripe fruit. ➤ *See page 138*

- Pot outdoor herbs for indoor growing.

- Clip dried hydrangea blooms for winter bouquets.

## OPTIONAL TASKS

- Prune deciduous trees, particularly those that may bleed in spring pruning (maples, birches). ➤ *See page 129*

- In mild climates, begin perennial border rejuvenation project. ➤ *See page 48*

- Plant or transplant perennials. ➤ *See page 50*

- In mild climates, prune vines. ➤ *See page 84*

- Prepare the soil for any new plantings you are planning for next spring. ➤ *See page 53*

- Undertake any hardscaping projects you've been considering. This may include stone-work, such as walls and walkways, as well as garden lighting or patios.

- Tag your Christmas tree if you live near a "choose-and-cut" operation.

- Set out fall-blooming plants such as chrysanthemums or ornamental kales and cabbages, either directly in the ground or in containers.

# Late Fall

*Days are becoming shorter in late fall. Leaves have fallen from deciduous trees, and evergreens have hardened their growth in preparation for winter. In colder regions, frosts will be more common and harder, and snows more frequent.*

## ROUTINE CHORES

• Attend to the lawn mower: change oil, clean filter, sharpen blades, and empty gas tank.

• Clean out sprayers. Be sure that each is labeled for whatever use it has had.

• Drain and hang up hoses. Turn off water to outside spigots.

• Turn the present compost pile and start a new one.

• Apply compost to flower and perennial beds.

• Do some final weeding in all flower and vegetable beds.

• Mark edges of walkways and driveway to avoid damage from snowblowers or snowplows.

• Protect woody plants under leaves from snow and ice with wooden frames.

• Loosely tie columnar evergreens to prevent damage from heavy ice and snow.

• Put burlap screens around evergreen shrubs to prevent winter sunscald and damage from road salt.

## NOW IS THE BEST TIME TO . . .

• Clean up vegetable garden, removing any diseased material to the landfill.

• Plant cover crop on vegetable garden (in cold climates, winter rye; in mild climates, millet or oats), or protect vegetable beds with a mulch of leaves and staw.

• Dispose of debris such as pruned branches, dead materials, and rubbish. Put herbaceous material on the compost pile.

- Buy tender bulbs such as amaryllis, calla lilies, and paper-white narcissus to pot up for indoor winter blooms.

- In mild climates, prune fruit trees.
  ➤ *See page 140*

## ONGOING PROJECTS TO CHECK ON

- Harvest any remaining fruits and vegetables.
  ➤ *See page 138*

## PROJECTS TO START NOW

- On evergreens, cut suckers emerging from below ground. ➤ *See page 133*

- Seed a new lawn or spot plant to fill bare places in an existing lawn. ➤ *See pages 28 and 33*

## OPTIONAL TASKS

- Clean, sharpen, and oil the pruning tools, hoes, and shovels for easier digging and cutting next summer.

- Clean all other tools, and oil them to prevent rust.

- Take notes on what projects you want to undertake first next year.

- Fill cold frames and hot beds with leaves to prevent the ground from freezing, so you can plant earlier in the spring.

- Begin to study garden and nursery catalogs and study your favorite gardening books, so that you can plan what to order for next year.

- Make a list of garden supplies that are running low, so you can order them in late winter when garden stores are restocked.

- Check fertilizers, peat moss, seed-starting mix, vermiculite, perilite, potting soil, and pesticides, and restock if needed.

- Check your supply of flats, pots, stakes, labels, and marking pens, and order necessary items as soon as catalogs arrive.

- Hunt up the snow shovel. Tune the snowblower, so you are prepared for the first snowfall.

# Early Winter

*Snow falls, and gardeners deck the halls with boughs of holly they have pruned from their hedge. Between the start of winter and the first springlike day, most gardeners relax from their chores and spend time studying garden books and seed catalogs, enjoying the daffodils and tulips that they potted last fall blooming on the windowsill.*

## ROUTINE CHORES

• If you start your own plants, order seeds by early January before seed companies run out of your favorites.

• Care for mowers and other power equipment; sharpen the blades, change oil, clean filters, and drain gas tanks, if you haven't done so already.

• As soon as the ground freezes lightly, cover tender perennials with evergreen boughs. Don't do this too early, or you'll provide an inviting winter home for damaging rodents.

• Prune highbush blueberries.

• Clean and oil the pump on the compressed air sprayer.

## NOW IS THE BEST TIME TO . . .

• Sharpen hoes, shovels, and clippers, and put them in their wintering-over spots.

• Shear broadleaf evergreens that you are growing as hedges. ➤ *See page 121*

## ONGOING PROJECTS TO CHECK ON

• In cold climates, shovel heavy loads of snow off hedges. ➤ *See page 99*

• On deciduous trees and shrubs, cut suckers emerging from below ground. ➤ *See page 133*

## PROJECTS TO START NOW

• Take hardwood cuttings of any shrubs and vines you want to propagate; label and store them upside down in vermiculite for spring planting.

## OPTIONAL TASKS

• In mild climates, prune evergreens while they are still dormant. ➤ *See page 114*

• Read garden books, and sketch out designs and ideas for plantings around your home.

# Late Winter

*By late winter, days are lengthening, thaws are more frequent, and gardeners become anxious to get outdoors. Snowdrops and early crocus may be poking through the dwindling snowbanks.*

## ROUTINE CHORES

- In warm climates, prune dormant roses.

- Remove dead and damaged wood from roses and other shrubs. ➤ *See page 104*

- Mow or cut down ornamental grass area and rake. ➤ *See page 73*

## NOW IS THE BEST TIME TO . . .

- Order plants and seeds, if you haven't done so already. Inspect new tools and equipment in hardware stores and garden centers.

- Start perennial and biennial seeds indoors under grow lights. Consult catalogs and garden reference books for the optimal planting time before last frost in your area.

## PROJECTS TO START NOW

- Begin pruning deciduous trees while they are still dormant. Pruning can begin whenever trees are not frozen. Do not prune trees like maple and birch that bleed heavily at this time of year. ➤ *See page 129*

## ONGOING PROJECTS TO CHECK ON

- In cold climates, shovel heavy loads of snow off hedges. ➤ *See page 99*

## OPTIONAL TASKS

- In mild climates, prune evergreens and fruit trees while they are still dormant. In cold climates, prune fruit trees while dormant. ➤ *See page 140*

- Begin your own garden journal, and resolve to record all routine and unusual events such as weather, new plants, unexpected happenings, plans for future development, and all the many ideas related to your lawn and gardens.

- Line up hired help, if necessary, to handle spring chores. Landscape workers are often busiest during this season and may be booked well in advance.

# Part 2

# Caring for Lawns and Gardens

Because your lawn and gardens are forever changing — sprouting, growing, maturing, and dying — you, as their caregiver, cannot be a passive onlooker. If the plants in your landscape are to succeed, you must keep an eye on them and nurture them in their infancy, protect them as they grow, discipline them, and sometimes make life-and-death decisions on their behalf as they age and deteriorate.

Not every gardening chore is fun, even for die-hard gardeners. No matter whether you balk at such tasks as mowing the lawn, the overall care of your landscape should be rewarding and ultimately bring you pride and many pleasures. It helps to have skill and patience. But more importantly, you need to notice when things go right and make decisions to intervene when something is wrong. Some decisions are as simple as when to cut the lawn grass, but others may keep you awake at night: Can I deal with the giant oak overhanging the roof and driveway? How do I repair the holes in the hedge after the ice storm? Should I start all over again with a new perennial bed? We hope that as you read the upcoming chapters you'll find the answers to whatever questions arise concerning your lawn and garden, so that you can confidently pick up your shovel, pruning shears, fertilizer container, or whatever, and take action.

# chapter 1 Your Ho-Hum Lawn, Attractive Once Again

A lawn sets the stage for everything else in the surrounding landscape. Its greenery and uniformity of cut are background for the shrubs, trees, flower beds, and hedges, as well as the paths, driveways, and especially the home. Whether you have only a tiny patch of grass or enjoy a grand layout, if your lawn is beautiful, it is welcoming and inviting, and makes the other landscape features more attractive. An unkempt, unmown lawn filled with weeds and potholes, on the other hand, is not a happy sight.

Many factors lead to the decline of a lawn. Diseases and harmful insects can devastate grasses and, as anyone who has ever dealt with them knows, moles and skunks are hard on turf. Too much shade inhibits the growth of grass adversely, as does soil that is compacted, too wet or too dry, or lacking organic matter. Deterioration also occurs when someone has planted the wrong kind of grass for the location.

## TIMING LAWN REPAIRS

If you intend to transform many different parts of your landscape, you may wonder whether to put your lawn first or last in the order of your rejuvenation projects. The lawn is the most obvious part of the landscape; if you are making only minor changes, you may want to put it first on the list. But when you are planning major alterations of the general landscape, it makes sense to wait until they are completed, since traffic and digging are likely to be hard on the lawn.

*Growing a superb lawn is actually no different from nurturing any other prized plant. A base of good soil and regular care make all the difference.*

## LAWN TROUBLESHOOTING

| PROBLEM | POSSIBLE CAUSE | SOLUTION | PAGE |
|---|---|---|---|
| UNEVEN GRADE | Holes | Fill with topsoil and reseed. | 28 |
| | Hummocks | Level and reseed. | 28 |
| MAJOR UNEVENNESS | Holes and hummocks | Grade, till, and replant. | 33 |
| PALE, SPINDLY GRASS | Soil lacking nutrients | Add fertilizer. | 40 |
| POOR GROWTH, POOR COLOR | Soil too acid | Test soil and add lime, as needed. | 39 |
| PATCHY GROWTH, DEAD SPOTS | Too shady | Replace with shade-tolerant grass or ground cover. | 41 |
| YELLOWING GRASS, GREENER WEEDS | Low nitrogen | Feed with high-nitrogen lawn fertilizer. | 40 |
| THIN GROWTH, BARE SPOTS | Soil compacted | Aerate, add humus and fertilizer; install paths to divert foot traffic. | 29 |
| SPONGY MATTER AT BASE OF GRASS | Thatch | Dethatch and aerate. | 29 |
| THRIVING WEEDS | Weed seeds blown in or emerged from soil; mower set too low | Set mower higher so grass shades out weeds. | 30 |
| DEAD PATCHES | Pests and/or diseases | Examine grass and soil; treat according to problem. | 32 |

# Lawn Doctor

Minor grading and spot planting are usually more effective and easier to accomplish if done in spring. But you can patch up weak spots nearly anytime during the frost-free season as long as you water well.

## Repairing a Worn Lawn

When faced with a tired, worn-out lawn decorated with bare patches, numerous weeds, hummocks, and holes, you have several options. You can (1) completely remake the area, (2) repair the problem spots, or (3) eliminate grass altogether and grow ground covers or even create a flower, vegetable, or cottage garden. Some people simply give up, pave their yards, and grow plants in large containers. Most of us, however, prefer to have grass surrounding our homes, because it's more beautiful and more practical.

If you decide the problems are minor, repair is the cheaper and less intrusive process. It's not difficult to fill in a few holes with topsoil and reseed. Fertilizer and lime can do wonders for grass that is weak, thin, and pale. Aeration can rid your lawn of thatch. And when the weed problem is not overwhelming, you can get rid of the rascals by hand-weeding or by using selective weed killers.

## MOWING UNEVEN LAWNS

If your lawn is not pool-table smooth, forego a riding mower and choose a mower that's fairly narrow. Wide mowers are more difficult to maneuver on uneven turf.

In cold climates, freezing and thawing in winter can heave the soil, or snowplows can gnaw into it and change the grade of a lawn. Consequently, a bit of regrading may be necessary each spring. As you know if you've ever mowed a grassy lawn that was not level, uneven spots are troublesome because the mower scalps the high spots, while grass in the depressions grows too tall. If the lawn is only slightly uneven, you may need only to buy a few bags of topsoil, fill in the depressions, rake it smooth, and plant seed. Raking it smooth works better than using a roller because it compacts the soil less.

## Spot Plant to Fill Bare Places

**Sowing seed.** The best time to start grass seed is late summer or late fall. The third best choice is spring, when seeds germinate and grow well but also face hot weather and weed competition. Grass species vary in leaf width and color, so when you seed bare areas, look for a variety that matches the rest of the lawn.

First, spade or till up the spot, sprinkle organic fertilizer over it (at the rate recommended on the package), and rake it smooth. Then scatter the grass seed according to recommendations on the package, and rake again. Cover the newly planted seed with a thin layer of hay or straw, and water it often. After the seed sprouts and the grass is well started, remove about one-half the hay or straw. Set the mower about 3 inches (7.5 cm) high for the first two mowings of the new grass.

Sometimes you have to do your spot-patching in midsummer. If you repair then, watering is essential, because the soil tends to be drier then than in the spring. As usual, directly after sowing the seed, mulch the areas with hay. Chopped hay works best.

**Laying sod.** You may decide that you want to repair the weak spots in your lawn quickly, by laying a few squares of sod. Sod is usually available at garden centers. Measure the different spots you want to repair so you will buy the right amount. Since it may be difficult to get sod to match the rest of your lawn grass, dig out a small piece of turf and take it to the center to get as close a match as possible.

Spread topsoil where the new sod will go. Level it carefully, and soak it well, both before and after laying the sod. You will probably find it necessary to cut the sod to fit the areas you are repairing, an easy process with a sharp, square-cornered spade or a large-blade knife. Press the pieces of sod close together, but don't overlap them.

The grass roots of sod are shallow, so water the patch every day until it has become established. Add liquid fertilizer to the water once a week to encourage faster growth.

## HOW TO LAY SOD

▲ To fill weak spots in your lawn with sod, prepare the area first by loosening and leveling it and adding an inch or two (2.5–5 cm) of topsoil. Water well, and then gently unroll the sod.

▲ Fit the pieces of sod closely together in a brick-line pattern. Trim with a knife. To distribute your weight over the area, step or kneel on a board.

## Coping with Thatch

Thatch, a condition that is often hard to spot, can disfigure a lawn. It consists of a spongy mass of grass stems, roots, leaves, and other organic matter not yet decomposed, lying above the grass roots and covering the lower stems. It can form on any lawn grass, but is most common with certain stoloniferous grasses (those grasses that spread by surface or underground stems). Particularly vulnerable are bent grasses and the southern grasses zoysia and St. Augustine. As the thatch becomes thicker, it prevents moisture from reaching the soil and instead traps it near the stems and leaf bases. The trapped moisture encourages disease, which can be especially devastating in warmer climates. Thatch also interferes with grass growth and mowing and creates a generally unhealthy appearance.

**Diagnosing thatch.** Because thatch is often misunderstood, some homeowners spend money buying machines to remove it, or they hire someone to remove thatch that isn't there. To avoid these mistakes, check the lawn yourself by pressing a finger hard into the grass in several different spots. If you can easily touch the soil, thatch is not present; if you cannot reach it, the lawn probably has thatch. Remove it as soon as possible so it does not build up further and become a major job later.

**Avoiding thatch.** Thatch is not usually a problem until it becomes more than ½ inch (1.25 cm) thick. If it is no deeper you can often control it by raking the lawn thoroughly twice each year with a bamboo or metal leaf rake. Also, remove grass clippings after each mowing to prevent buildup, and aerate the area once each season (see below). Fertilize the grass annually with organic plant food to encourage healthy root growth. The best way to prevent thatch troubles is to avoid turf grasses that are likely to develop it, such as bluegrass (especially 'Merion'), Bermuda grass, St. Augustine grass, and Zoysia grass.

**Eliminating thatch.** If the thatch has become too thick to remove by raking, use a dethatching rake or vertical mower to pull it out before the grass begins to grow in spring. This type of equipment is usually available for rent from garden supply stores.

## Aerate Compacted Soil

Lawn soil becomes compacted when there is heavy use of the lawn by people or equipment, lack of humus in the soil, or longtime use of synthetic fertilizers. Once the soil has become hard-packed, earthworms are no longer able to survive there, and the air and moisture that are essential for growth have difficulty reaching the plant roots. To test for compaction, push a long screwdriver into the soil. If it goes in easily, the soil is not compacted, but if pushing takes effort, the area needs your help.

**How to aerate.** There are many ways to aerate the soil and let in air and water. If you have a small lawn, you can use a simple spading fork or special spiked shoes (not golf shoes) to punch holes throughout the lawn. Garden stores sell or rent these shoes as well as various hand-operated and power tools and machines that are more effective for the job, particularly if you have a large lawn. Most have open or hollow tines that pull out cores of soil, leaving behind holes that invite moisture and air to enter. These cores of soil can be left to decompose on the ground.

**When to aerate.** Aerate hard-packed soil in early spring and again in the fall for a couple of years. Then, depending on the condition of the lawn, once every other year should be enough. If possible, do the job following a hard rain or after watering the lawn the previous night, which will make the soil easier to penetrate. For optimum results, after aerating spread a ¼-inch (.63 cm) layer of organic matter, such as sifted compost, dampened peat moss, or dried manure over the soil to add humus.

---

### DISCOURAGING FUTURE COMPACTING

- Install paths where you would prefer traffic. Steer walkers to the pathways with strategically planted shrubs, if necessary.

- Use compost to encourage earthworms.

- Mow the lawn often. You won't need to rake up heavy clippings, and small amounts will decompose, add humus, and encourage earthworms.

## Controlling Weeds

Even if you have given your lawn the best care, some weeds will no doubt find their way into it, and invariably the vigorous types grow faster than grass. Country lawns are almost impossible to keep completely weed-free, since each breeze throughout the season deposits dandelion, milkweed, thistle, goldenrod, and other windborne seeds, often from long distances. Suburban homes may get the same windfall if there are neglected lots, yards, or farms nearby.

If your lawn is small and the grass is vigorous and thick, you may be able to eliminate weeds simply by digging them out with a trowel or dandelion digger. If this operation seems too formidable, however, either an organic or synthetic herbicide can help control them. (See page 67.) If the weeds are scattered, you can get rid of them by spot spraying or by fastening a sponge to a stick or cane, dipping it in herbicide, and touching the weed with it. Such weed wipers are available commercially. Some lawn fertilizers, both chemical and organic, contain weed killers. These control a limited variety of weeds, but they eliminate the spraying of chemicals into the air. In any event, don't expect the first treatment to be your last. Weed control is an activity that never ends.

## Coping with Lawn Diseases

Healthy lawns, like people who are fit, are more resistant to diseases. Many sicknesses occur when grass becomes stressed from circumstances such as poor soil, lack of sunlight, or overuse of chemicals. Adverse weather conditions such as excessive rain, ice, heat, or other factors sometimes incite troubles that are rare when the weather is more normal. The gardener is sometimes at fault too. For instance, a common error is overwatering when the weather is humid, which may cause disease problems.

In many parts of North America, lawn disease is seldom a problem. If you reside where problems exist, however, consider growing only disease-resistant grasses, or use endophytic varieties (see page 36.)

Some lawn diseases are fungal, and others are bacterial or viral. Treat fungal diseases with a registered fungicide if symptoms are widespread, and ask your garden center about the correct treatment for bacterial diseases. There is currently no effective remedy for viruses. See the chart on page 31 for descriptions and advice about the most common lawn diseases.

## TIPS FOR BETTER WEED CONTROL

- Keep the soil pH high, between 6.5 and 7, to discourage ferns, mosses, sorrels, wild strawberries, and other acid-loving weeds.

- Set the mower to about 3 inches (7.5 cm) high for the first few mowings in the spring. Taller grass will shade and discourage sprouting of annual weeds such as crabgrass.

- Eliminate weedy plants in nearby areas that are likely to spread seeds onto your lawn.

- Aerate the soil and add humus to keep it loose.

- Keep the grass growing vigorously so it will crowd out competing weeds.

- Create paths to cut down on traffic over the lawn, which compacts the soil and encourages quack grass, bindweed, and other weeds that grow in hard-packed soil.

- Add lime whenever a soil test indicates it is needed. In acidic soils, lime allows fertilizer to work better, thus encouraging healthy grass growth that chokes out weeds.

# COMMON LAWN DISEASES

| DISEASE | TYPE | DESCRIPTION | CONTROLS |
|---|---|---|---|
| ANTHRACNOSE | Fungus | Reddish brown spots with yellow markings; most common in wet weather; likely to hit grasses stressed by drought or low fertility | Treat with fungicide, either chemical or organic. |
| BLOTCH | Fungus | Dark spots on the leaves | Treat with fungicide. |
| BROWN PATCH | Fungus | Dead plants within a circular area; widespread on bentgrass and warm-season grasses, but may strike others; common in hot weather | Remove thatch, aerate, and sprinkle on compost, dampened peat moss, or other organic matter. Avoid fertilizers before warm periods. Treat with the botanical fungicide neem. |
| CROWN ROT | Bacteria or fungus | A wet rot on the crown of the plant | Treat with fungicide. Consult your garden store for current recommendations about control. |
| DOLLARSPOT | Fungus | Dead grass in small circles on cool-weather grasses; larger circles on warm-season grasses; most common in spring and fall | Use a fertilizer high in nitrogen, aerate the lawn, and spread sifted compost over it. Treat with neem. |
| FUSARIUM BLIGHT | Fungus | Reddish brown grass in irregular patches of wilted turf | Not easy to control, but it helps to aerateand remove thatch. Mow high during the summer. |
| LEAF SPOT | Fungus | Streaks or discolored markings on foliage; common in bluegrass | Mow high and add organic matter. Reduce use of high-nigtrogen fertilizer. Treat with fungicide. |
| MELTING OUT | Fungus | Leaves that wither, turn brown, and die; most common when temperatures and humidity are high | Treat with fungicide. Reseed with resistant variety. |
| POWDERY MILDEW | Fungus | Soft, powdery substance, either white or gray, covering the leaves; common in shady areas with poor air circulation | Treat with fungicide. |
| PYTHIUM BLIGHT | Fungus | Wilted, greasy-looking turf; tan and shriveled or dead grass; most likely to appear when weather is warm and wet; more common on cool-season grasses | Use less nitrogen fertilizer, and don't fertilize at all in hot weather. Remove thatch and aerate. |
| RUST | Fungus | Orange and brown patches on the leaves; thin turf; more common in shady, damp areas | Water only in early morning so the grass can dry quickly. Mow frequently at recommended heights. |
| ST. AUGUSTINE GRASS DECLINE | Virus | Weakens and eventually kills the more susceptible varieties of this grass, as well as centipede grass; produces yellow spots on leaves | No known cure; replacement of the grass may be necessary. Use resistant variety, such as, 'Raleigh'. |
| SNOW MOLD | Fungus | Pink or gray mold covering the turf after the snow melts in the spring | Mow lawn in fall. Avoid early fall fertilizing. Treat with the botanical fungicide neem. |

# Insect Control

Some people panic when they see an insect on the lawn, but only a few are likely to be problems. Many worms and insects reside in any healthy turf. Most are not dangerous, and some are beneficial. Earthworms are particularly welcome creatures because they are so good for the soil, so don't injure them with strong chemical treatments.

Unless a population explosion of bad guys occurs, there is usually little cause for concern, but occasionally your lawn may be invaded by chewing insects. These include grasshoppers, which attack foliage, grubs that devour roots and kill turf, and oth-ers. The large white or gray grubs in lawns are larvae of the scarab beetle family that includes May beetles (dubbed "June beetles" in the North), Japanese beetles, chafers, and others that lay their eggs in grassy plots and attract moles and skunks. Patches of dead grass may be an indication of grubs at work.

Some lawn grass seeds now contain endophytes, which are good fungi that kill aphids, armyworms, billbugs, chinchbugs, sod webworms, and other such creatures. If destructive insects are a problem in your lawn, include endophytic grasses in your seed mixture. The chart below suggests other organic controls, as well as synthetic remedies that may solve your pest problems. Many new products have been thoroughly

## COMMON LAWN PESTS

| PEST | DESCRIPTION | CONTROLS |
|------|-------------|----------|
| ANTS | These spread aphids, invade houses, and sometimes pile up mounds of soil that catch mowers. | Treat with an all-purpose garden insecticide or beneficial nematodes. |
| APHIDS | Tiny insects suck the juices from the leaves and spread viruses. | Destroy ant hills in the area, and spray any infected grass with an all-purpose garden insecticide, such as neem. Use endophytic grasses. |
| ARMYWORMS | Striped catepillars that move in large numbers, eating as they go. | Use endophytic grasses. Apply *Bacillus thuringiensis* var. *berliner* (Btb) or beneficial nematodes. |
| BILLBUGS | White larvae may feed on roots, the brown weevils eat the grass crowns. | Water deeply. Aerate, dethatch, and add organic matter to the soil. Use beneficial nematodes. |
| CHINCH BUGS | Mature bugs are dark brown with white folded wings. The nymphs (immature insects) are red with a white band. Both suck out juice from foliage, turning it brown. | Treat infested areas with a soap-and-water spray or, if that fails to control them, treat with an all-purpose garden insecticide. Eliminate thatch. Use endophytic grasses. |
| CUTWORMS | These worms feed on the base of the plants, especially bent grass, at night. | Treat with an all-purpose garden insecticide. Apply beneficial nematodes or *Bacillus thuringiensis* var. *berliner* (Btb). |
| GRUBS | The immature forms of different species of beetle attack the roots of many plants, including grass. They attract destructive moles and skunks to the area. | Apply milky spore *(Bacillus popilliae)* in midsummer or beneficial nematodes in early summer (such as Scanmask). Apply diatomaceous earth. |
| MOLE CRICKETS | Large, light brown insects burrow like moles with their shovel-like feet and kill patches of grass by feeding on their roots. | Treat with *Neoplectana carpocapsae* (a parasitic nematode available commercially as Nc), or juvenile nematodes. Or, use an all-purpose garden insecticide. |
| SOD WEBWORMS | In early spring, these lay eggs that hatch into night-feeding caterpillars that cut off leaves at the base of the plant. | Treat with *Bacillus thuringiensis* var. *berliner* (Btb), or spray with solution of soap-and-water (be sure to use soap, not detergent). Use endophytic grasses. Apply neem or beneficial nematodes. |

tested and are considered safe, but always use them cautiously. Your garden center can advise the best products to use for your problem. Always be sure whatever you are using will control the pests that are bothering your lawn, and carefully follow application directions on the label. Never apply any pesticide unless it is necessary, because pests often build up a resistance to products that are used casually.

## Animal Pests

If your lawn is spotted with holes, skunks may have been digging there, searching for grubs. When long tunnels break through the grass, moles have probably been burrowing, searching for the same food. To head off these four-legged pests, you'll need to discourage the grubs. See page 32 for suggestions. Soaking the lawn with an organic or mild chemical pesticide helps to eliminate them. Placing mothballs in mole burrows sometimes persuades the moles to move elsewhere. Some catalogs list other mole controls, including wind-activated or electronic devices.

Holes in the lawn may also mean that visiting deer have marred the turf as they walked over it.

A watchdog can do a good job of protecting a lawn from animal invasions. In some areas fencing may be necessary.

# Remaking Your Lawn from Scratch

If you decide to tear out the old lawn and start a new one, you will first need to decide whether to sow seed or lay sod. Both projects require approximately the same amount of preparation, since both need a thoroughly tilled, weed-free, fertile, smooth area. Unless it rains frequently after you seed or lay the sod, both need watering for several weeks to ensure a good start. Watering is especially important for sod because the grass roots are so shallow. Spreading a weak solution of liquid fertilizer with a hose injector once every two weeks will help both sod and seed become established more quickly.

Both methods can be major projects. Unless your lawn is small, you may want to hire a landscaper with the equipment and manpower to handle it quickly and with a minimum of disruption.

Whichever method you choose, the first step you'll need to take is to remove the existing grass. Use a spade, angled quite low to the ground, to remove approximately 1-foot (30 cm) squares of sod from the entire area.

*If you decide to install a completely new lawn, you'll first have to remove the old sod, whether you are laying new sod or reseeding. Use a spade to remove the sod in squares about 2 or 3 inches (5 or 7.5 cm) deep.*

## Sod vs. Seed

Often thought of as "instant lawn," sod can transform your bare earth into green turf in a matter of hours, long before the soil has had a chance to wash or blow away, or be tracked into the house. Sod is expensive, however, and sod farms often supply only bluegrass and other premium grasses. If you plan to use your yard as a recreational area, you may want something tougher. If your climate is likely to experience frequent droughts, you will be happier with a more rugged grass, or a mixture of tougher grasses.

Not only will you have more of a selection with seed, it is less expensive than sod. On the other hand, a seeded lawn must be covered immediately after planting with a layer of chopped hay or straw to protect it from wind and rain erosion. Unfortunately, these products may contain weed seeds, unless you can find a material, such as salt hay, that is weed free. In addition, in windy locations, the mulch must be kept well soaked or it will blow away.

## Six Steps to Seeding a Lawn

If you decide to seed your lawn, here are the steps to follow:

**Step 1. Add organic matter.** If you don't add new topsoil or you can't find fertile soil that is loose and crumbly, spread the surface with a 1-inch-thick (2.5 cm) layer of peat moss, manure, and/or compost. The organic matter will help hold moisture, encourage earthworms, and make the soil loose enough for new grass roots to spread rapidly.

**Step 2. Add sand.** If your soil drains poorly, till sand into it before planting. This will make it easier for grass roots to grow and rains and melting snows will penetrate it better.

**Step 3. Add lime.** Test the soil, and, if necessary, use enough lime to increase the pH to 6.5 to 7 for most lawn grasses. Use a spreader for even coverage. Ten pounds of lime will raise the pH on 100 square feet (9.3 m²) of heavy soil one point.

**Step 4. Till.** Till the soil thoroughly, grade it, then smooth it. Remove any clumps of sod or roots as you till. Mix in a complete organic or chemical fertilizer at the rate recommended on the package or by the store where you bought it.

Step 4. Till

**Step 5. Seed.** Choose the right grasses for your climate and lawn use (see page 32). Plant seed at the rate recommended on the package. You can sow the seed by sprinkling by hand, as shown in the drawing, or use a fertilizer spreader. If you use a fertilizer speader, load the spreder with about half the amount of seed you estimate needing and pass back and forth over the area in one direction. Load the rest of the seed and pass over the area at right angles to your first application. Rake the seed in well, roll it smooth with a lawn roller, and then cover it with a thin layer of chopped hay or straw to prevent erosion.

Step 5. Seed

**Step 6. Follow up.** Water thoroughly and frequently, if it doesn't rain. Continue to water as needed. Grass has shallow roots and dries out quickly. Always apply enough water each time for it to soak into the soil at least 3 inches (7.5 cm). Watering in the evening is most effective because there is less evaporation then, and it has all night to soak in. But water anytime if the soil is so dry that sprouting seeds will suffer, from daily to once every two or three days.

To prevent soil compaction, do not let anyone, even pets, walk on the new grass until it has become well established. Young grass seedlings are fragile and easily damaged. They need loose soil for good root growth and to absorb air and water readily. You may want to install "Please Keep Off the Grass" signs, or enclose the area with a string fence on short posts to protect the baby grasses.

Step 6. Follow up

# CHOOSING THE RIGHT LAWN GRASS

Often a mixture or blend of several different kinds of grasses formulated for your climate, soil, or light conditions is the best choice. (A mixture includes different species of grasses; a blend is a combination of different cultivars of the same species.) Your garden center or Cooperative Extension Service can help you make a good selection.

If you are reseeding a lawn, you have a wide selection, including both cool-season grasses that do best in 60 to 75°F (16 to 24°C) daytime temperatures and warm-season grasses that thrive in temperatures that range from 75 to 80°F (24 to 27°C). Those listed below are perennial except for annual ryegrass. The improved cultivars are usually better choices than the species.

## Cool-Season Grasses for Northern Climates

Bluegrass *(Poa pratensis)*
Fescue, tall *(Festuca elatior)*
Fescue, creeping red *(F. rubra)*
Ryegrass, annual *(Lolium multiflorum)*
Ryegrass, perennial *(L. perenne)*

## Warm-Season Grasses for Southern Climates

Bahia grass *(Paspalum notatum)*
Bermuda grass *(Cynodon dactylon)*
Buffalo grass *(Buchloe dactyloides)*
Carpet grass *(Axonopus affinis)*
Centipede grass *(Eremochloa ophiuroides)*
Gramma grass, blue *(Bouteloua gracilis)*
St. Augustine grass *(Stenotaphrum secundatum)*
Zoysia grass *(Zoysia)*

## Cool-Season Grasses for Overseeding Warm-Season Types

Fescues *(Festuca)*
Annual ryegrasses *(Lolium multiflorum)*

## Drought-Tolerant Grasses

COOL-SEASON
Fescue, tall *(Festuca elatior)*
Wheatgrass *(Agropyron)*

WARM-SEASON
Bermuda grass *(Cynodon dactylon)*
Buffalo grass *(Buchloe dactyloides)*

## Grasses for Shady Areas

No grass grows well in deep shade, but the following do well in spots that get some sunlight and plenty of skylight.

COOL-SEASON
Red fescue *(Festuca rubra* var. *commutata* 'Chewing' and 'Pennlawn')

WARM-SEASON
Fescue, tall *(Festuca elatior)* (in the upper South)
St. Augustine grass *(Stenotaphrum secundatum)*

## Salt-Resistant Grasses

No lawn grass is completely salt-proof, but the following are the most tolerant of salt.

COOL-SEASON
Fescues *(Festuca)*

WARM-SEASON
St. Augustine grass *(Stenotaphrum secundatum)*

The following are especially salt-resistant and although they are not refined enough for lawns, they are useful for holding sand dunes in place:

American beach grass *(Ammophila breviligulata)*
Seacoast bluestem *(Schizachyrium scoparium* var. *littorale)*
Switch-grass *(Panicum virgatum)*
Volga wild rye *(Leymus racemosus)*

## Pest-Resistant

COOL-SEASON
Fescues with endophytes *(Festuca)*

WARM-SEASON
Centipede grass *(Eremochloa ophiuroides)*

## Tough Grasses for High-Use Areas

COOL-SEASON
Fescue, tall *(Festuca elatior)*
Ryegrass perennial *(Lolium perenne)*

WARM-SEASON
Bahia grass *(Paspalum notatum)*
Bermuda grass *(Cynodon dactylon)*
Zoysia grass *(Zoysia)*

## Grasses for Acid Soils

COOL-SEASON
Bluegrass, Canada *(Poa compressa)*
Fescue, Chewing *(Festuca rubra* var. *commutata* 'Chewing')

## Grasses for Alkaline Soils

COOL-SEASON
Ryegrass, perennial *(Lolium perenne)*
Wheatgrass *(Agropyron)*

WARM-SEASON
Bermuda grass *(Cynodon dactylon)*

# Ongoing Lawn Care

To keep your lawn looking nice, you will need to mow, fertilize, and control pests and unfavorable conditions such as thatch.

## Mowing

Mow at the recommended height (see descriptions of grasses, pages 42 to 43) for your type of grass to both aid in weed control and reduce the frequency with which you need to mow. Unless clippings are heavy, leave them on the lawn to fertilize it. Avoid raking unless thatch is a problem.

Mow less frequently during dry weather conditions, and set the mower higher to help keep the grasses green. Taller grasses tend to develop deeper roots.

## Edgings and Other Tricks for a Neat Lawnscape

When renovating a lawn, one way to give it an instant transformation is with edging. Just as a man's handsome thick hair is unsightly if it's shaggy and unkempt, no one will appreciate lush grass if it overgrows flowerbeds and walkways. Edgings that delineate where the grass stops and other plantings begin help to make a lawn look well tended and "finished." In addition to the aesthetic advantage, edgings eliminate hand trimming by letting you mow close to flower beds, trees, hedges, fences, and garden objects such as birdbaths. They also block lawn grasses from creeping into gardens and prevent ornamental grasses, ground covers, and other plants from invading the lawn.

A common edging is a simple trench, from 2 to 4 inches (5 to 10 cm) wide and 4 or 5 inches (10 or 12.5 cm) deep, cut as a border between the lawn and its neighbor. A square-edged spade will cut a soil edging, but a long-handled half-moon edging tool is easier to use and produces a cleaner, straighter cut. Power edgers, either gas-powered or electric, are practical for large lawns. Unfortunately, it is necessary to redo this type of edging at least once a year.

*A good edging not only defines the lawn's border, it also keeps encroaching flowers neatly confined to their beds.*

For easier upkeep, use other, more permanent types of edging, including plastic, rubber, or metal strips sunk vertically into the soil. With their top edges set at ground level, the strips are nearly invisible and won't damage a lawn mower. Be certain they extend deep enough into the soil to stop the rhizomes of your most vigorous plants from creeping under them. Eight inches (20 cm) is usually an adequate depth; the 4-inch (10 cm) ones will not prevent most interlopers. Half-moon and other edging tools work well for installation, but a simple spade can also do the job.

Other useful edging materials include landscape timbers and bricks, which can be set flat, diagonally, or on edge. One gardener we know uses 4-inch (10 cm) soil pipe, the type used for drainage and sewage, painted brown and sunk partially in the ground, as a permanent edging for his straight and slightly raised flower beds. Although we don't usually think of them as edgings, paved or gravel paths also make good boundaries between a flower bed and a lawn, and they have the advantage of being especially low maintenance.

*This type of rubber edging is nearly invisible once it is in place, yet it is wide enough to keep most plants that spread by underground roots and stems from encroaching. In fact, it should keep lawn grasses out of your flower beds, while it also protects your lawn from invasive garden plants. Be sure to keep it vertical when you lay it in the trench.*

## Other Tricks for Neat Lawns

- Plant a border of vigorous perennials against buildings, walls, fences, and hedges. We mow close to rows of foundation perennials such as daylilies (in sunny spots) and hostas (in shady ones) without harming them.

- Set birdbaths, benches, and sundials on flat stones or paving blocks at ground level rather than installing them directly into the soil, so that clipping around them is unnecessary.

- To eliminate trimming around lawn trees or specimen shrubs, encircle them with a thick mulch of bark, shavings, or other organic material, which acts as an edging and also protects the plants from being hit by the mower. Landscape fabric or black plastic laid beneath the mulch will suppress weeds there for a long time.

## Watering

Homeowners seem to be either waterers or nonwaterers. Some people like to have sprinklers running most of the time, and others leave the job entirely to nature. Unfortunately, nature sometimes fails to provide, occasionally for months on end. Even a well-established lawn with deep roots can suffer in a drought. When grass turns brown and withers, you can be sure the lawn is suffering. Avoid watering when it isn't necessary, however, because it not only wastes water, but irrigated grass needs more frequent mowing and is more prone to disease.

**When to water.** In general, it is best to water in the late afternoon or evening, because at that time little moisture is lost through evaporation, as it would be earlier in the day. If grass diseases are prevalent, however, water only in the early morning. This will allow the grass leaves to dry quickly in the sunlight.

**How to water.** When you water, keep in mind that water moves through the soil slowly. A short summer shower, even a heavy one, isn't likely to reach the roots before the moisture has dried and disappeared. Short waterings have the same effect. The best way to water a lawn is to apply ¼ inch (.63 cm) or so, wait 10 minutes, and apply another ¼ inch (.63 cm), continuing until you have applied a full inch (2.5 cm). Set out soup cans or other cans with straight sides to measure. Rotary sprinklers are efficient and helpful because they allow the soil on one side of the sprinkler to absorb water while the other side is being covered. If you use a hose, keep shifting areas so the soil can absorb the water, and always apply enough water so the dampness will be pushed all the way down to the base of the roots by the addition of more water.

**What to do during a drought.** Grass shows stress more quickly than deeper-rooted perennials, shrubs, and trees, and it can take a great deal of water to keep the lawn green during a drought. During dry periods many of us need to ration the water we supply to our lawns so we can keep our flower and food plants growing. In fact, some

municipalities require rationing. When our grass becomes brownish, we are comforted a bit knowing that a dry lawn needs no mowing, even though it is far from attractive. From years of experience we have also learned that the first drenching rain usually revives grasses rapidly, unless they are very delicate or the drought was greatly prolonged.

Remember, too, that if your lawn has adequate fertilizer and soil rich in humus, it will suffer far less during dry spells.

## Adding Lime

Most lawn grasses do best when the soil pH is 6.5 to 7, so try to maintain it at or near that level for optimum growth. Whenever the pH is higher or lower than a plant needs, fertilizer cannot be easily absorbed, and it suffers. The weeds growing in a lawn can be good indicators of whether the soil is too acidic for good grass growth. If your lawn has sheep sorrel, wild strawberries, and ferns, the soil is too acidic. Moss sometimes indicates an acid soil, too, but it can also mean that the soil lacks organic matter.

## Fertilizing: The Route to a Great Lawn

Nature provides wonderful nourishment for lawns in many different ways. We always notice how green the grass becomes after a thunderstorm, when the soil has gathered nitrogen from the air. This is due to the fact that during a lightning strike, nitrogen atoms are released and absorbed by the rain. The plants then benefit from this released nitrogen.

Earthworms loosen the soil and feed the grass with their castings. Most northerners notice that their lawns need less feeding after winters when the earth has been covered with snow for several months. Farmers have long considered snow the "poor man's fertilizer," because the snow protects the nutrients in the soil from erosion by rain, sun, and wind.

Even with Nature's largesse, however, her nourishment is rarely enough, particularly for a tired, worn-out lawn. One of the most neglected aspects of lawn care, and one of the most important, is the simple act of spreading fertilizer when it is needed.

**Amount to use.** Some homeowners use far too much fertilizer and "burn" their grass. The trick is to use enough of the right kind of lawn food to keep it looking nice, but no more. It may take a few years of trial-and-error to discover the amount that is best for your conditions, since moisture (waterings, rain, and snow) affects the amount needed. When you use the right amount, the grass will be healthy and well-fed, and you won't need to mow it any more often.

**What kind to use.** Often a few nutrients can change a poor lawn into a beautiful spread. If your lawn is level and shows no bare spots or thatch, but is simply pale and weak-looking, regular applications of organic fertilizer and lime, if needed, may be all it needs to perk it up. For fastest results, sprinkle either an organic or synthetic liquid fertilizer over it, following the directions on the package. The appearance will improve quickly, but the results won't be as long-lasting as if you were to apply a slower-acting organic fertilizer. Natural fertilizers such as manure, compost, and dried seaweed add valuable humus to the soil, along with the nutrients grass needs to flourish. Because grass roots are close to the surface, a lawn responds surprisingly fast to fertilizer when it also receives irrigation. (For more information about plant foods, see page 162.)

*Organic fertilizers* are usually a better choice than chemicals for feeding a lawn because they promote even, natural growth. When you apply organic plant food in the fall, it can supply nourishment for the lawn throughout the following summer and pose no danger of burning the grass or nearby flowers or shrubs. Another advantage is that organic fertilizers are less toxic than chemicals to the earthworms and good bacteria that keep soil healthy.

*Synthetic fertilizers* give faster results than those with natural ingredients, but they can burn the grass, especially if the weather is dry. Also, they are useful for only a short period because their nutrients leach away more rapidly when it rains. Chemicals can also harm beneficial soil organisms. If you choose synthetic plant foods, use the slow-release types that feed the lawn gradually over a much longer period. For more information about different kinds of fertilizer, see page 162.

**How to apply it.** If you do it carefully, you can spread granular fertilizer by flinging it off the edges of your fingers like sowing grain, but for a more even application, use a drop spreader. We once observed a lawn on which the owner applied fertilizer with a spreader but hadn't overlapped the passes as he pushed it around. The grass had become an interesting series of strips of lush green alternating with strips of yellowish brown. Be sure that you overlap each preceding row as you run the spreader up and down your lawn. Wash out the spreader and be sure it is dry before storing it; the abundance of nitrogen in the fertilizer can cause metal parts to rust quickly.

## TIMING YOUR FEEDING

The best time to feed your lawn depends on where you live and the kind of grass you are growing.

**In the North.** Fertilize cool-season grasses in late summer or early fall. If your growing season is very short and frosts are likely to occur early, fertilize again in early spring if the lawn appears to need more. Spring fertilization on a regular basis is not ideal for most cool-season grasses, however, because at that time you are also feeding the weeds that are sprouting.

**In the South.** It works best to feed warm-season grasses in the spring just as they begin to come to life. If your zoysia, Bermuda, or other warm-season grasses are growing poorly, give them a second feeding in August or September. Feeding late in the fall, however, encourages an undesirable spurt of new growth just as the grasses should be slowing down for winter.

# Places That Don't Love a Lawn

Before you begin to renovate, be certain you are not trying to do the impossible by growing turf in a spot that does not welcome it. Although grass often seems to grow in unlikely places, even where you don't want it, it is sometimes difficult to get a lush lawn where you need one.

**Shady spots.** Most lawn grasses need six or more hours of sunlight each day; they also need adequate moisture. Sometimes shade from your growing trees or those of a neighbor cut off light so gradually that you scarcely notice it is happening. Roots of large trees can soak up the nutrients and moisture necessary for good grass growth. Remove the trees or nurse the grass by watering frequently and fertilizing regularly. Usually, how-ever, a better solution is to grow a variety of grass suitable for shade and/or dry soil (see page 36), or to replace your grass with a shade-tolerant ground cover, such as a bed of hostas, ferns, pachysandra, or vinca, which can grow in a relatively sunless spot with a minimum of care as long as it isn't too dry (see page 70). In moist shady areas, you may wish to try moss as a substitute for lawn grass (see page 46).

**Low spots.** If there is a low spot on your lawn where water sits occasionally, lawn grasses are not likely to prosper there. Fill in the area with topsoil, drain it, or replace the grass with plants that enjoy moist roots (see page 157).

**Steep places.** Because steep slopes are tricky or dangerous to mow, consider using ground covers, either herbaceous or shrubby, in such locations (see page 70). A hillside can also be made attractive with terracing or by growing a rock garden there.

*If the steep sunny slope beside this house were lawn, it would be difficult, even dangerous, to mow. But it's a perfect site for a colorful display of mixed flowers and shrubs.*

# COOL-SEASON GRASSES

| NAME | DESCRIPTION | USES | ADVANTAGES |
|------|-------------|------|------------|
| BLUEGRASS (*Poa pratensis*) | Narrow, upright-growing, blue-green blades; spreads by underground rhizomes. | Considered the best choice for northern lawns that receive plenty of sunlight and moisture. For a more rugged lawn, use a mixture of bluegrass, perennial rye, and fescues, especially those that are endophyte-enhanced and therefore less susceptible to certain diseases. | Looks very nice when mown. |
| FESCUE, CHEWING (*F. rubra* var. Chewing) | Fine-bladed, dark gray grass; forms clumps. | Often included in lawn mixtures. | Stands more erect and has nicer foliage than creeping fescue. |
| FESCUE, CREEPING RED (*Festuca rubra*) | Despite name, leaves are deep green (the bases are red). The upright-standing blades are thin and fine. | Tolerates shade and drought. Best when included in a mixture, since it tends to grow in clumps. In the South it is often mixed with perennial ryegrass and planted on top of warm-season grasses to keep the lawn green after the others brown for the winter. | One of the best grasses to include in a lawn mixture if you have a difficult situation. |
| FESCUE, TALL (*F. elatior* or *F. arundinacea*) | A clump-forming, tough grass with wide, sharp-edge blades. | Can take a great deal of wear and tear (popular for playgrounds). Mix it with other types of grasses for best results. | Grows well in most soils in full sun or light shade; stays green most winters in warm regions. Offers good competition for weeds, provides good erosion control on banks. Is tolerant of heat and salt; among the most drought resistant of all cool-season grasses. |
| RYEGRASS, ANNUAL (*Lolium multiflorum*) | Tends to become clumpy, with rather coarse, light green leaves. | Good for only one season, it is used primarily as a quick "catch crop" until the higher-quality grasses in a mixture germinate. | Grows on a wide range of soils and tolerates either full sun or light shade. Vigorous, germinates quickly, and grows upright. Rugged enough to withstand moderate use. Holds its color well. Is drought, disease, and insect resistant. |
| RYEGRASS, PERENNIAL (*Lolium perenne*) | A bunching grass, light green in color. Its wide leaves make it appear rather coarse. Resembles the annual kind but is winter hardy. | Northern homeowners may find that an all-ryegrass lawn of some of the newer cultivars is the best choice for a truly rugged lawn. | Grows on a wide range of soils; likes full sun but tolerates light shade. Sprouts quickly, controls erosion, withstands foot traffic well. More insect and disease resistant than other lawn grasses. |
| WHEATGRASS (*Agropyron* species) | Perennial grass, usually erect; spreads by creeping rhizomes. | Tough, coarse grass for difficult places. | Quick results; drought resistant. |

| DISADVANTAGES | CARE | CULTIVARS |
|---|---|---|
| Cannot withstand much traffic. | Needs fertile soil. Mow it fairly high (2 to 2½ inches; 5 to 6.25 cm) for best results, keep it watered during dry periods; feed lightly in late summer or early fall. | The cultivars have better color and better disease resistance, are also more disease resistant than the species, although some lack its vigor. 'Merion' is susceptible to rust, develops thatch easily, and needs frequent fertilizing to look its best. Best choices are 'America', 'Bristol', 'Eclipse', 'Kenblue', 'Manhattan II', 'Merit', 'Park', 'Pennstar', 'Princeton', 'Vantage', 'Viva', or 'Windsor'. For best results, use a blend of several compatible bluegrass cultivars. |
| Prone to disease if overwatered in hot, humid seasons; less competitive with weeds if overfertilized or cut too close. | No special care; fertilize only if growth is poor. | 'Centers', 'Highlight', 'Jamestown', 'Longfellow', 'Mary', 'Shadow', 'Tamara'. |
| Not rugged enough to withstand heavy traffic. | For best appearance mow it at about 2 inches (5 cm), and do not over-fertilize; this grass does poorly with too many nutrients. Avoid over-watering, which encourages fungal diseases. | 'Agram', 'Illahee', 'Koket', 'Longfellow', 'Pennlawn', 'Rainier', 'Reliant', 'Scaldis'. |
| A bit coarse for a manicured lawn. So vigorous it can crowd out less thrifty grasses. | Mow it fairly high (2 to 3 inches; 5 to 7.5 cm). In the South keep it watered during the summer to prevent dormancy. | The new cultivars are more attractive, more resistant to insects and disease, and withstand harder use. They also have narrower leaves, tend to be less clumping than the species, and are equally drought resistant. Good cultivars include 'Cochise', 'Falcon', 'Guardian', 'Olympic', 'Mustang', 'Pacer', 'Titan'. |
| Needs frequent mowing. An annual plant, it dies out after 1 year. Avoid lawn mixes with more than 20 percent annual ryegrass in the mix. | Mow at 2 inches (5 cm). Include a perennial grass in the mixture to winter over. Water in dry weather. | None. |
| Not everyone likes the light color. | Plant it either in spring or late summer. Fertilize it sparingly after it is well established. Mow at 3 inches (7.5 cm). | 'Affinity' (recommended for shady lawns), 'Aquarius', 'Commander', 'Fiesta', 'Manhattan II', 'Pennant', 'Pennfine', 'Regal', 'Repel', 'Sunrise', 'Tara'. |
| Can become weedy and spread to unwanted places | Prefers an alkaline soil, though it will grow in acid soils. Needs full sun. Seldom needs fertilizer. | None. |

# WARM-SEASON GRASSES

| NAME | DESCRIPTION | USES | ADVANTAGES |
|---|---|---|---|
| BAHIA GRASS (*Papalum notatum*) | Glossy green grass spreads by underground runners. | Grows where better grasses don't do well, including light shade and sandy or poor soils. | Tolerates foot traffic and shade. Spreads rapidly. Good for controlling erosion on banks. |
| BERMUDA GRASS (*Cynodon dactylon*) | A spreading grass with medium to fine texture. It spreads both by rhizomes and aboveground stolons; its roots go deep. | A high-quality, vigorous lawn grass for full sun in mild climates. | Wears well. Is disease resistant, tolerates both salt and traffic fairly well. The turf is competitive with weeds. Tolerates heat well, and is drought resistant. |
| BUFFALO GRASS (*Buchloe dactyloides*) | Clump-forming, native prairie grass; blue green and fine textured. Forms a gray-green lawn. | Use when a tough lawn is needed. Since it grows to only 4 to 6 inches (10 to 15 cm), it is good for roadsides. | Stands foot traffic and extreme temperature. Tolerates drought. Can stand to be mowed only once a month. |
| CARPET GRASS (*Axonopus affinis*) | Strictly for warm climates, this light green, coarse creeping grass turns brown over winter. | Not for fine lawns, but stands acidic and sandy soils well. | Disease and insect resistant; grows well in spots too warm for other grasses. |
| CENTIPEDE GRASS (*Eremochloa ophiuroides*) | Has a pale green color and coarse texture. Spreads slowly by aboveground stolons. | A good lawn grass where insect resistance and a minimum of mowing is important. | Grows well in a wide range of soils, from sandy to clay, and even in slightly acidic soils where winters are mild. Grows well in full sun when shaded. Grows very dense where other grasses fail. Is insect resistant. Needs little fertilizer. |
| GRAMMA GRASS, BLUE (*Bouteloua gracilis*) | Forms dense clusters of narrow, blue green leaves. | Frequently included in mixtures for lawns in the Southwest, but it is not considered the best choice for a classy lawn. | Grows well in dry soil in full sun or light shade. Tolerates fluctuations of temperature from cold to hot and grows in a wide range of climates. Tolerates foot traffic well. Insects and diseases seldom bother it. |
| ST. AUGUSTINE GRASS (*Stentaphrum secundatum*) | A thick-bladed grass, it grows quickly, spreading by above-ground stolons. | Good warm-season lawn grass. | Grows well in a wide range of southern soil conditions (prefers moist, sandy soil) as long as it has enough moisture. Tolerates both full sun and light shade. |
| ZOYSIA GRASS (*Zoysia*) | Produces a rich, thick turf. Deep-rooted, it spreads slowly by both stolons and rhizomes. | Good for moderate game playing. A nice choice for mid-areas, between North and South. | Grows well on ordinary soil, in full sun or light shade. Drought resistant. Competes well with weeds and other grassses. Stands foot traffic well, and is quite pest resistant except to billbugs. |

| DISADVANTAGES | CARE | CULTIVARS |
|---|---|---|
| Rather coarse and subject to thatch and lawn diseases. | Mow at 2 to 2½ inches (5 to 6.2 cm). Use complete organic fertilizer in both spring and fall. | Choose cultivars for best results; 'Argentine', 'Paraguay', 'Pensacola', and 'Saurae'. |
| Needs edging because it is aggressive. Forms thatch easily. Turns brown after the first frosts and looks dead until spring, even in mild climates; some cultivars stay stay green for longer periods. | Does best in fertile conditions; needs more frequent fertilizing than most other grasses. Mow at 2 inches (5 cm) or slightly shorter. Be careful not to let it dry out. Scatter a cool-season grass seed, such as ryegrass or fescue, over the lawn in fall to keep lawn green all winter. | The seeds of the cultivars don't come true; buy plugs or sprigs and plant them 4 to 12 inches (10 to 30 cm) apart. In certain areas some cultivars are also available in sod. 'Cheyenne', 'Tifdwarf', 'Tifgreen', and 'Turcote' are popular on golf course greens in the South; and 'Tiflawn', a more sturdy grass, is widely planted on playgrounds and athletic fields. 'Tifway' is popular. |
| Seed germinate quickly, but fill in slowly. | Needs full sun; prefers alkaline soil, but can grow in acid soil. Seldom needs fertilizer. Mow to 1½ to 2 inches (3.7 to 5 cm). | 'Bison', 'Prairier'. |
| Not a high-quality grass. Turns brown in winter. Very cold sensitive. | Use fertilizer sparingly; mow at 1½ inches (4 cm) to prevent ugly seed heads. | None. |
| Grows slowly. Not suitable for high traffic areas. Is susceptible to chlorosis (yellowing) if soluble iron is lacking in the soil. | Needs only occasional feeding. Mow only every 2 to 3 weeks to 1½ to 2 inches (3.75 to 5 cm). Needs frequent watering. Apply iron chelate if needed to avoid chlorosis. | 'Centennial' grows on somewhat alkaline soils; 'Georgia Common', prefers acidic soils. |
| None. | A slow grower, it needs little care and infrequent mowing. Mow to 1½ to 2 inches (3.75 to 5 cm). | None. |
| Can't tolerate hard use. Usually browns during winter but stays green longer than Bermuda grass. Not as cold-hardy as Bermuda grass. Susceptible to chinch bug damage and warm-weather lawn diseases. | Plant plugs or sprigs 6 to12 inches (15 to 30 cm) apart or lay sod on newly prepared lawns if seed is not available. Mow to 2 to 3 inches (5 to 7.5 cm). Water whenever necessary. | 'Bitter Blue', 'Floratum', Seville', 'Sunclipse'. |
| Although it may survive fairly cool northern temperatures, it turns brown at the first frost, appearing dead for over half the year. | Plant plugs 6 to 12 (15 to 30 cm) inches apart in thoroughly tilled soil in spring or early summer. (Use annual rye to provide a green lawn until the zoysia becomes established.) Needs less frequent mowing and less watering than other warm-season grasses. | Although seed is sometimes available, better results come from planting plugs or sod of one of the named cultivars, such as 'Bel Air', 'El Toro', 'Emerald Jade', and 'Sunburst'. 'Meyer', the most hardy, turns an attractive yellow shade in winter. |

# Alternatives to a Lawn

If your lawn is large and you have limited time for upkeep, think about shrinking its size by planting part or all of it with something other than grass.

Plant low-maintenance ground covers, perennials, ornamental grasses, or ferns on a portion of it. You can lighten your workload considerably as long as the plantings you choose do not require more maintenance than the lawn. (See pages 59.)

On a practical note, you could grow some food-producing plants in portions of what is now your lawn — a garden of herbs or vegetables, a few fruit trees, or a berry patch. A cottage garden filled with food plants, shrubs, and perennials is another possibility. Admittedly, such projects do not qualify as "work-free," but they make the space useful.

For an area that is almost carefree, consider planting a meadow garden filled with native and ornamental grasses or native wildflowers. These plants keep land open and attractive and usually need mowing only about once a year. You might also include low-growing shrubs, flowering trees, spring bulbs, and ferns in such a planting to make it more interesting. If you use any invasive plants, always install a barrier of some kind to keep them from sneaking into the grassy lawn or flower garden (see page 37).

Since most grasses prefer neutral or slightly alkaline soils, usually it's unnecessary to increase soil acidity (lower its pH) but, strange as it may seem, some people do it for a good reason. When grass will not grow in a very shady spot, they spread enough powdered sulfur over it to lower the pH to 5 or less. (Use 1 or 2 pounds [.45 or .9 kg] of powdered sulfur to lower the pH one point on 100 square feet [9.3 m²].) In only a short time, without planting anything, a rich mossy lawn appears, "planted" by nature with spores that have floated in on the wind. Folks with mossy lawns report that they like them because the mosses are surprisingly durable, withstand light traffic well, and never need to be dethatched, mowed, or weeded. Usually the type of moss that grows will be the right kind for the area, whether moist or dry.

*Dappled shade provides just the right environment for a ground cover of lily-of-the-valley and vinca in lieu of lawn grass.*

# chapter 2

# New Blooms for an Old Perennial Garden

The culmination of a gardener's skill is a perfect perennial garden where the plants are harmonious in color and beautifully spaced, and some are always in bloom. But even a masterpiece perennial border deteriorates quickly without the gardener's touch. Clumps become overgrown. Weeds have a field day spreading in the loose soil, scattering seeds, and overpowering more timid plants. Vigorous perennials crowd out other plants and rob them of light, nutrients, and moisture. Seedlings spread far and wide when seed heads are not removed. Even the soil itself runs out of nutrients and humus.

Facing a neglected, overgrown perennial garden can be discouraging. It also presents some hard questions. Should you simply pull out the weeds and unwanted seedlings, and whittle down the clumps of overgrown perennials so they'll bloom well again? Or would it be easier to plow under the entire bed and remake it from scratch? If you decide to start over, should you plant again in the same spot, or till up that space and plant a lawn there, choosing a "clean" spot for your new flower bed? Should you continue to grow a bed of perennials at all?

The extent of weed proliferation may be the deciding factor in whether to start over in a new place or remodel the current garden.

*A well-maintained perennial garden can be one of the most satisfying parts of your property, but all gardens present certain challenges as they mature, and your "old" garden is likely to need some renewal once in a while.*

# How to Rejuvenate Overgrown Perennials

If you decide to restore your perennial bed in its present location, the easiest time to begin the project is in spring, after the plants have sprouted but before they are too large to move easily and safely. Plants will wilt less at that time because they have less foliage. Another good time to restore a bed is in the fall, after the plants have become dormant and have been cut back. (Gardeners in colder climates should choose spring for this work, however, because their fall season is often too short for dislocated plants to become well established before they face winter.)

First, analyze the garden to figure out what is wrong. Ignore the weeds, overgrown plants, and other problems, and search for the things you want to save, such as attractive perennials that could be divided. Since new perennials take time to become established and you aren't always sure how well something entirely new will enjoy your garden, it makes sense to salvage as many existing worthwhile clumps as possible. They have already

> ## FOR NEW HOMEOWNERS: WAIT AND SEE
>
> If you have inherited an unfamiliar perennial garden, try to live with it through one complete growing season to study the plants. You are likely to find many delightful surprises, and it would be sad to throw away a choice double buttercup or a clump of dainty coralbells simply because you didn't recognize the foliage. If you can't identify the plants when they bloom, ask for help from a knowledgeable neighbor.

proven they are happy in that location and will thrive with a minimum of care.

## 5 Steps to Renovation

**Step 1. Give it a thorough weeding.** Use your favorite method, whether you pull by hand or dig with a trowel, spade, fork, hoe, or dandelion weeder. If you have lots of undesirable weeds and other vegetation, a small power rotary tiller that can maneuver around clumps of perennials will save work and time.

## PERENNIAL GARDEN TROUBLESHOOTING

| PROBLEM | POSSIBLE CAUSE | SOLUTION | PAGE |
| --- | --- | --- | --- |
| OVERGROWN PLANTS | Years of neglect | Divide; give away or otherwise get rid of surplus plants | 49 |
| CENTER OF CLUMP DEAD, DYING, OR BROWN | Natural aging process of perennials | Divide, discarding unwanted parts and replanting clumps of live parts from edges | 49 |
| PERENNIALS WITH SPARSE OR NO BLOOMS | Overcrowding | Divide | 49 |
| | Shade (for sun-loving plants) | Move or trim back whatever is casting shade over them | 88 |
| SELF-SOWING PERENNIALS AND BIENNIALS | Good growing conditions, fertile soil | Deadhead as flowers fade so plants cannot go to seed | 57 |
| LEAVES DISCOLORED | Disease | Diagnose, then treat with appropriate remedy | 56 |
| LEAVES CHEWED OR WEAK LOOKING | Chewing or sucking insects | Treat with garden insecticide | 33 |

**Step 2. Carefully assess your perennial plants.** Save only the best. Do not try to rescue any struggling on their last roots, those that appear diseased, or plants badly mangled by insects. Think twice about keeping many of those that self-seed or otherwise spread rapidly throughout the garden, such as forget-me-not and lily-of-the-valley. Remove any clumps you do not like and those that bloom sparingly or for only a pitifully short time.

When you dig out the pariahs you may want to spread them on plastic sheets to dry where they won't mess up the grass. Then put them on the compost pile, unless you suspect they are infested with diseases or insects. If their health status is questionable, take them to a landfill.

**Step 3. Divide plants.** The clumps remaining should enhance your garden for many years, but if some have become so large that they no longer bloom well, split them into smaller sections to give them a new life. (See Dividing Plants, below.)

**Step 4. Improve the soil.** To add humus to the soil, spade or till a layer of compost or peat moss and manure about 1-inch thick (2.5 cm) into the bare spots left between the plants you have chosen to keep. Then spread a thin layer of a commercial fertilizer, organic or synthetic, over the area and thoroughly mix or till it in. If the soil is acidic, sprinkle lime over it before mixing. Most herbaceous perennials prefer a pH of 6 to 6.5, but some, such as delphiniums, do best when the pH tests above 6.5. If you have doubts about the acidity level of your soil, invest in a small soil test kit. (See pages 166–167 on how to test and adjust soil pH.)

**Step 5. Plant new perennials, annuals, and bulbs.** Set in the new perennials you have chosen to fill in the empty spots. If the spots are large and the new perennials small, include fillers (annuals or bulbs) between them.

## Dividing Plants

It is time to divide your perennials if they are becoming so overgrown that they don't bloom well,

if they are crowding other plants, or if they are starting to die in the center of the clump. In the North, the best time to divide is in early spring when growth is just starting, although poppies and peonies should be separated immediately after they finish blooming. In Zone 5 and warmer areas, you can divide successfully in either spring or fall.

To divide a large plant, if you want several offspring, dig completely around it and slightly under the roots with a rounded spade or spading fork. Then carefully lift the plant out of the ground and cut it into several pieces with sharp thrusts of the spade or a heavy knife. From a large clump you should net four or more divisions that are big enough to bloom the first year after planting. You can probably get even more, if quantity is more important than having fewer, stronger plants.

Note that some perennials, such as gas plant (*Dictamnus*) and peonies, can thrive for many years without needing division. Others, including chrysanthemums, iris, and Shasta daisies, need nearly annual division if they are to continue to bloom well.

### IN-GROUND DIVISION

A good way to divide a large clump is to split it apart while it is still in the ground. Cut straight down through the middle of the clump with a spade, splitting it in half. Then cut again, straight through the middle of one section (or both, if the clump is large enough). Lift out the cut-away portions; if the one remaining is in a good location, leave it in the ground where it can continue to bloom as if undisturbed. Replant the divisions or share them with friends.

*Dividing an overgrown perennial clump*

# 5 Steps for Transplanting

Setting in or moving plants may be frightening for those who think they lack green thumbs. But "green thumbs" consist of brown knees and dirty fingernails plus a little skill, and not some mystical gift. It needn't be discouraging to make a mistake. We all do it, and that is how we learn. Most plant fatalities occur only if you fail to dig the plants carefully and do not get enough roots, or if you let them dry out during the moving process.

**Step 1. Dig a new hole for the plant.** Make the hole larger than the plant actually needs. When you reset it, the plant will have plenty of loose soil around its roots and will be able to start spreading out immediately.

*When you move perennials, be sure to get all of their roots and keep them moist until you get them back into the ground. (Pretend they are goldfish so you don't leave them out in the air any longer than necessary.)*

**Step 2. Provide moisture.** If the earth is dry, soak the soil around the plants you're moving, so you can keep a ball of soil around the roots intact when you lift it out.

**Step 3. Dig up the plants.** Use a spade for large clumps and a trowel for small ones. Try to get all the roots. If you are moving many clumps, place them on a large piece of plastic and sprinkle them frequently with water until you can safely get them back into the ground. If you move plants after they have started to grow, cut off all blooms and flower buds, and trim back the foliage to about 3 inches (7.5 cm). Trim off any roots you have injured while digging.

**Step 4. Water and fertilize.** To give your transplant a good start, mix some compost or dry manure with the soil that you put in the hole around it. Soak it generously with water containing the recommended amount of liquid synthetic or organic fertilizer. Water it every day or so if the weather is dry, and put a box or paper bag over it on sunny days if it starts to wilt.

**Step 5. Mulch around the transplant.** Use shredded bark, cocoa hulls, peanut shells, or other organic material. The covering helps suppress sprouting seeds, retain moisture in the soil, insulate the soil from extremes of temperature, and, when it rots, add humus and nutrients to the soil. Mulch heavily (2 inches; 5 cm) if you have not used a preemergent herbicide; mulch lightly (1 to 2 inches; 2.5 to 5 cm) if you have.

*Mulch around the transplant, keeping the mulch 2 or 3 inches (5 or 7.5 cm) away from the base of the plant.*

## TOO MUCH OF A GOOD THING

Even if your garden-rejuvenation efforts have produced lots of divisions, you may want to refrain from planting all of them. The result will be too many of the same kind of plant. Refer to your garden plan and save some vacant spaces for any new perennials you intend to add. Annuals, spring bulbs, or tender summer plants such as dahlias or gladioli can fill in and supply color when your perennial blooms are scarce.

## Taming Invasive Plants

We often think how wonderful it would have been to garden before so many weeds moved around the globe to our site, but unfortunately we must face the fact that they, like death and taxes, will always be with us.

**Weeds.** If a border has been neglected for some time, the soil will likely be cursed with an abundance of annual weed seeds. You can discourage them by spreading a preemergent herbicide, which inhibits sprouting of seeds without harming established plants. Preemergents are available in both synthetic and natural form, and can save a great deal of future weeding energy. Do not use them, however, if you expect to plant seeds of annuals in that location during the same growing season.

Perennial weeds can be an even worse problem, however, because their roots often go so deep it is difficult to remove them. Quack grass, thistles, and dandelions are particularly pernicious invaders, and if you leave even a small piece of the root, it will grow with renewed vigor. Annual weeds such as purslane, crabgrass, and chickweed that dump their seeds throughout the summer can be problems too, because they always return in the spring, and their germination rate is far better than that of petunias.

**Perennial thugs.** Some of the worst pests in our garden are perennials and ground covers we innocently planted years ago, and found out later that they didn't know how to behave. Among these are ajuga, peach-bells, thyme, and lamb's ears. We have also purchased weeds in the soil of potted perennials and once even acquired some goutweed (*Aegopodium*) roots that way. This plant is high on our list of obnoxious pests and one that is nearly impossible to eradicate once ensconced.

If you have many of these tough characters growing among your good perennials, you will probably save time and trouble by converting the garden to lawn, and starting over in a pristine spot that such plants haven't discovered.

*Even our beloved daylilies can get obstreperous and need controls when they spread out of their territory.*

## SPREADERS THAT TAKE OVER

Although different perennials act differently in various soils and planting zones, the following are among those that are likely to take over a garden, if given their druthers. Some spread by runners that either travel above the ground or just below the surface. Others, including some biennials, scatter their seeds.

Bee balm (*Monarda*)
Daylily (*Hemerocallis*)
Forget-me-not (*Myosotis*)
Foxglove (*Digitalis*)
Lamb's ears (*Stachys*)
Lily-of-the-valley (*Convallaria*)
Lungwort (*Pulmonaria*)
Lupine (*Lupinus*)
Most ornamental grasses

Ground covers, such as ajuga, myrtle, and various herbs, may spread into the perennial bed from elsewhere, and lawn grasses can also invade it. Even such aliens as poison ivy and poison oak have been known to enter garden territory. But weeds are the most common interlopers, spreading from wind-blown seeds of such plants as dandelion, thistle, quack grass, and milkweed.

## Reviving a Neglected Rock Garden

If you have a rock garden that needs remaking, be certain you really want it before going to the trouble of rejuvenation. Rock gardens can be beautiful but they require a lot of hand labor to keep them that way. The gardener must work hard to satisfy the requirements of some of the more popular colorful plants, such as creeping phlox, pinks, and dwarf iris, which can't compete with weeds and grass and are not likely to be happy in the dry conditions of rockeries.

Since such a garden is built among rocks, either in a natural or artificial setting, you may need to reset some of the smaller rocks if they have moved over time, or replace artificial ones. Paths may need to be remade, and since the soil is likely to be limited, you may have to add more humus.

*Use creeping ground cover–type perennials for a colorful rock garden. Play with textures, which can be especially handsome and dramatic in this kind of garden.*

If you decide to renew a rock garden, follow the same steps you would when renewing a perennial bed. Although you may need to enrich the soil somewhat, most common rock garden plants do not need a very rich soil or one with a high pH. Be careful not to overfertilize, which would only encourage the growth of weeds and unwanted grasses.

The plants most often used in rock gardens are creeping, ground cover–type perennials such as sedums and sempervivums, but you may also want to include herbs, ornamental grasses, miniature evergreens, and spreading shrubs, such as cotoneaster, heathers, heaths, and low-bush blueberries.

## Installing a Brand New Border

Before making your final decision about whether to start over from scratch or simply remodel the garden, think about what you really want from it. Above all, a garden should please you aesthetically and give you pleasure as you work there. If you do all the upkeep yourself and suspect you'll feel constantly frustrated with the amount of work, you should do everything possible to make your garden as labor-efficient as possible.

Even if your time, energy, physical ability, or interest is limited, you can have your cake and eat it too. Consider the following remedies:

➤ Reduce the size of the garden area

➤ Keep the bed the same size but substitute new plants that need a minimum of care

➤ Hire a skilled gardener with a strong back

Important as it is to make a plan before you plant a garden, very few that have been established for any length of time still resemble the initial vision. Most borders develop over a period of years because gardeners are notorious movers and shakers. We always seem to be digging out plants we don't like, and juggling the ones we enjoy to get the best effect. And, of course, we frequently add new specimens.

## WHEN TO START OVER IN A NEW SPOT

Starting over, admittedly, is a big project. But if you can answer yes to one or more of the following questions, you should consider it.

❏ Is the current bed filled with weeds and weed seeds?

❏ Do numerous roots or stones fill the soil?

❏ Have trees or structures shaded the area that was once filled with sunlight?

❏ Is the bed too damp, too dry, too near a hedge, or unsuitably located for another reason?

❏ Would another spot be more suitable and attractive?

*For an uncrowded look, mulch heavily between plantings. Repeating the same plant throughout the bed gives continuity to the design.*

## Site Preparation

If you decide to relocate, choose a spot that has fertile, deep soil, and receives full or mostly full sunlight. It should be located away from trees, unless you want a shade garden, and where the soil is well drained and not soaking wet after a hard rain. Till the soil several times deeply and thoroughly to eradicate the grass and weeds and provide loose soil for the plants to grow. Remove any stones or root clumps. Test your soil and adjust it accordingly (see pages 166-167). Smooth the site of your former garden, and return it to lawn, if you wish.

## Planting Day

Move plants early in the spring, if possible, while they have very little foliage on them to dry out. Choose a cloudy, damp day or, if the weather is sunny, do it in the evening. Although we prefer to move our plants in the spring, that season is always busy, and we often have to resort to a mid-summer operation. We've found that if you are careful and either choose a rainy spell or water them heavily and shade them, you can move most plants throughout the season. Oriental poppies and peonies are exceptions and are best moved directly after blooming. When we move a big clump of daylilies, peonies, or similar plants in the summer, we cut back the foliage to about 2 inches (5 cm).

## Clumps and Groupings

Perennials look best when they are uncrowded, and any plan should allow for plenty of space between plants. Actually pulling off this trick is not easy because they quickly expand to fill any empty space, unless you are vigilant. It is tempting to over-plant because usually you start with small plants that look lost in a huge space. To avoid a sparse look, set some annuals between the perennials for a year or two while the perennials grow.

One popular way to keep clumps uncrowded is to plant everything further apart than necessary and surround each clump with a heavy mulch. Since mulch effectively controls the weeds, this method reduces maintenance. You may want to consider this style of planting if you are working with a slope, as the spacing is particularly attractive in such a situation.

A garden looks more integrated and attractive when the same type of perennial is scattered intermittently throughout the space for the eye to follow. In a large border it is common to set the plants in groups of odd numbers, such as 3, 5, or 7, rather than as solitary plants. If the plants are small, such as coralbells or dwarf astilbe, this kind of grouping is attractive and makes large splashes of color throughout the bed. In a small garden, one large peony or one massive delphinium in each spot is enough.

## Coordinating Color

Unlike gardens filled with annuals that appear more or less the same as the season progresses, perennial gardens feature a variety of plants that bloom at different times for shorter periods and provide a varied display throughout the summer. We enjoy checking our perennials each morning throughout the season to enjoy the constant change. Although the frequent transformation makes the garden more interesting, it is also challenging to design a border that appears filled with blooms of complementary colors throughout the entire spring, summer, and fall.

Observing other gardens and perusing perennial books can help you place each plant in a spot where its color will relate well with its neighbors when in bloom. If you find areas without color for long periods, you may want to use annuals or other bedding plants, such as geraniums, as temporary fillers until you find the perfect plants for those "holes."

One of our friends who is a beginning gardener found an easy way to accomplish good color coordination in her garden. She carried around her garden notebook when she visited other gardens and noted the combinations she liked. Gradually, she transferred the information into her plantings, and the garden is now well on its way to becoming a masterpiece of complementary colors.

One final word: Don't despair if colors end up clashing. Good gardeners spend a lot of time and energy moving plants when their color or blooming sequence came out wrong, and if your orange poppies scream at their neighboring red ones, simply make a mental or written note to move one at the proper time.

## Edgings

If the edgings in your perennial gardens have fallen into disrepair, the beds will look ragged. Edgings are the frosting on the cake and provide an important finishing touch to any border, not only delineating the edges, but also preventing lawn grasses from entering the garden. They keep vigorous perennials from creeping into the lawn too.

Depending upon the type of edgings that currently border your beds, you may be able to restore or repair them. Landscape timbers, even treated ones, eventually rot, however, and metal and plastic edging strips sometimes sink so far in the earth that weeds and grass creep over them. If they have greatly deteriorated, it is best to start over.

*When you see a color combination you admire, note the plants (and colors) used, so that you can recreate the scene in your own garden.*

*Purchased edging keeps lawn grasses out of the flower bed and aggressive perennials out of the lawn. Be sure to choose one that is at least 6 inches (15 cm) wide.*

Any work involved in installing an edging is worthwhile. If it is of permanent materials, it can save you much work in future years and make the garden appear more tidy and "finished" immediately.

**Soil edging.** A simple ditch, 3 or 4 inches (7.5 or 10 cm) wide, cut between a flower bed and the lawn, separates them nicely. Cut about 5 inches (12.5 cm) deep with a spade or an edging tool with a flat blade shaped like a half-moon, which is ideal for making a straight cut. This type of edging is labor-intensive and must be renewed frequently; for a large border, you may want to rent a power edging machine.

**Bricks.** Whether laid flat or stood on edge, either straight or diagonally, bricks make an attractive edging. It is difficult to mow close to bricks that are not level with the ground, however, so trimming is necessary. Weeds and grass can creep through the cracks.

**Landscape timbers.** Wooden timbers treated with a wood preservative are attractive. Unless they are sunk in the earth, however, it may be necessary to trim after mowing. Before using old railroad ties for this purpose, check to see if they have been treated with creosote, since that can be toxic to plants.

**Plastic or metal edging strips.** These strips, which range from 4 to 10 inches (10 to 25 cm) wide, effectively separate the garden and the lawn when set vertically along the edge of the garden. If you install them so that the top is at ground level, you can mow safely over them. Choose the widest strips available if you have vigorous grasses or perennials, and to border a shrub bed, since the roots can easily sneak beneath a narrow edging.

**Paved or gravel paths.** Although paths are not always considered edgings, they serve the purpose as excellent borders that require little maintenance.

## The Role of Foliage Plants

To create a well-designed perennial garden that looks nice even when there are few blooms or none at all, keep the foliage in mind. Plant leaves come in a wide variety of hues, and the color green alone may be any one of a multitude of shades, and either dull or glossy. The silvery gray of plants such as lamb's ears and dusty miller can be a beautiful contrast to a garden's greenery, as is the variegated foliage of many hosta cultivars — green on white, yellow over green, and other appealing combinations. The unusual speckled lungwort foliage provides a pleasant change from solid green throughout the growing season.

Textures and shapes also affect the appearance of a garden. The glossy, spreading foliage of peonies contrasts with spiky iris leaves and lacy maidenhair fern, for example. Also, the compact, shrublike form of entire plants such as cranesbill, gas plant, and coralbells, particularly when they are not in bloom, gives shape and interest to a border.

*A variety of foliage colors and textures can create a long-lasting, pleasing tapestry. Here, the tough sturdiness of pachysandra and purple-toned ajuga set off a lacy fern.*

## Ongoing Care

Don't be misled by the word perennial. Gardeners who plant herbaceous perennials under the illusion that they live forever and need little or no care are dismayed to find that they must have regular attention. A once-a-week checkup is desirable, and daily inspection during the growing season, even if it is a fast one, is even better. If you can't spare time to work a bit each day, take along a notebook to jot down the jobs for the weekend.

To keep your renovated garden from falling into disarray, try to avoid the mistakes that brought about difficulties in the previous one. You have now chosen a good location and the right plants, and set them in the proper spots. It only makes sense to give them the very best protection and care so they will stay healthy and confined to their space, and to help them look their best throughout the growing season.

**Control pests.** Guard against the animals that like to chew off young, tender shoots — woodchucks, porcupines, and rabbits. Deer can devastate a perennial garden in only a few nights if you don't take steps to stop them promptly when you first spot the damage. Rabbits, woodchucks, and gophers take only a bit longer. You may even need to provide resting places for birds to encourage them not to roost on and break your tall delphiniums and hollyhocks. Moles tunnel under the ground, letting in air, which dries the roots, and these tunnels provide pathways for destructive mice and voles, which eat plant roots and bulbs.

Pets are not always blameless, either. Male dogs can urinate on expensive plants and cats like to dig in the garden. Ponies and larger domestic animals can easily wreak havoc on a garden.

Insects and diseases present whole new sets of problems, but if your plants are healthy, they are not likely to be seriously affected. Watch for insects and diseases and intervene if they damage the plants.

*Your garden will not only look better cared for, but perennials are actually healthier if you regularly remove faded flowers. If you interplant annuals with your perennials, be sure to deadhead those as well, to encourage continuous blooms throughout the season.*

**Weed.** In most gardens weeding must be a regular chore and it can be either fun or drudgery, depending on your attitude. If you like to be in control and keep your surroundings neat and tidy, you are more likely to enjoy the job. An elderly acquaintance of ours says she thinks of weeding as a battle each week, and even though she knows that the weeds will win the war after she is gone, she savors each victory. She confesses she loves it when dandelions and lamb's quarters invade: "Like a carnivore celebrating a conquest, I promptly dig, cook, and eat them!"

**Deadhead.** Cut off fading flowers regularly. When perennials go to seed they not only look unsightly, but seed production saps the energy of the plant and reduces its ability to bloom in the future. Failure to deadhead may even shorten the life of certain plants. Some types spread rapidly, too, if allowed to go to seed.

**Cut back.** As soon as they turn brown, use clippers or hedge shears to cut off the stalks and foliage of plants that die back after blooming, such as Oriental poppies, delphiniums, and iris. Not only will cutting back improve the appearance of the bed and help prevent diseases and insects from homesteading there, but it will encourage some plants, such as delphiniums, to rebloom later in the season.

**Pinch.** With thumb and forefinger, pinch back plants such as chrysanthemums two or three times in early summer to get them to grow more bushy. If you are growing exhibition mums or peonies, pinch off all the flower buds except those on the ends of a few of the strongest stems. The plant's energy will then go entirely into producing extra-large blooms.

**Stake.** Support tall-growing plants and those with heavy flowers before they fall over naturally or droop from rain or wind. Many types of stakes and other supports are available in various materials, designs, and heights. The tall-growing delphiniums are especially difficult to stake because their hollow stems break easily. Those that grow 6 feet (1.8 m) or taller may need a stake for every spike. If you do not have time to do extensive staking, pinch off the top bud when the plant is about 3 feet (.9 m) high. It will then produce side branches that will bloom, and the plant will stand erect. Naturally, it won't be as dramatically beautiful as if it had taller spikes, but it will stand upright.

Insert stakes and other supports before you need them. Plants grow rapidly in early summer; by staking them early, you will allow the foliage to conceal the stakes as the plants grow. If you use green or brown yarn or cord to attach the plants to the stakes, it will be nearly invisible. Twist ties, a larger version of those you use to close plastic bags, are available up to 16 inches (40 cm) long and are quick and convenient to use.

If you garden in a windy location, you may want to avoid staking by growing only plants that can stand alone through wind, rain, and storms. Many have no need of support because they are short and stout, like chrysanthemums, or tall and sturdy, like lupines and monkshood.

**Water.** Whenever the weather is dry, water your plants. Apply water slowly or intermittently so it can soak deeply into the soil. A weekly watering of an inch (2.5 cm) or more is far better than daily light sprinklings. If dry summers are common where you garden, consider using soaker hoses or drip irrigation in your garden. Lawns usually revive when a heavy rain falls after a drought, but dried-out perennials are less likely to be rejuvenated.

*It makes sense to place taller plants in the back of a garden bed, not only to keep them from blocking shorter neighbors, but to take advantage of the support a hedge or fence can provide.*

## SUPPORT YOUR PLANTS

Commercially available stakes and supports include:

**Upright garden stakes.** Many heights are available in natural or green-dyed bamboo, metal, and wood.

**English-style hoop-type supports.** These are expandable, with supports that slide up as the plant grows. They can be used even after the plant is in bloom to support heavy flowers and foliage.

**Peony hoop supports.** Circular wire hoops hold up heavy blooms.

**Horizontal trellises.** Available in plastic, metal, or nylon, they can be attached to stakes as support for tall, long-stemmed flowers as well as for annual sweet peas, morning glories, and other climbing plants.

**Fencing.** To prevent the necessity of using conventional stakes, some gardeners build a fence at the back of their flower borders. They plant tall-growers such as delphiniums and hollyhocks nearby, and as the plants grow, they tie them to the fence. Rail fences, picket fences, cedar posts, and even chain link types work well for this purpose. If you have a tall hedge as a background, it can be used as an anchor by tying tall perennials to the trees or shrubs.

**Fall care.** Don't neglect to take care of your perennials at the end of the season. Put your perennial gardens to bed anytime after the first hard fall frost when the plants have become dormant. Cut them down to about 2 inches (5 cm) in height and feed the tops to the compost pile. This is also a good time to add a balanced, dry organic fertilizer to the bed, following the recommendations on the package.

---

## THE VIRTUES OF MULCH

Replenish organic mulch in the fall to prevent sprouting of weed seeds that have blown in during the summer. Mulch also helps to protect roots from being heaved out of the ground if the soil thaws and refreezes when there is no snow cover. During the following spring and summer, it will protect the soil from eroding in the rain and baking in the sun.

You might consider piling leaves, if you have them, about 2 inches (5 cm) deep around each plant. We use shredded maple leaves because we have an abundance of them, but those from any deciduous trees will do. (Oak leaves acidify the soil if used in large amounts.) A leaf mulch adds humus to the soil as well as all the valuable nutrients large tree roots find deep in the earth. A small shredder for leaves and garden wastes is a good investment for any gardener. Spread heavier mulches about an inch (2.5 cm) thick, including shredded bark, peanut hulls, shavings, and similar organic products available at nurseries and garden centers.

---

## Less Labor-Intensive Gardens

Garden work should never become a dreaded chore, and if yours is reaching that point, here are some ways to cut back without abandoning the project entirely.

**Control your garden's size.** The Chinese advise us to praise large gardens, but plant small ones. Wise words! Nevertheless, planting more and more is a temptation most gardeners find irresistible. All perennials expand and need dividing sooner or later, which results in extra plants that are difficult to discard. Each year new plant offerings from catalogs and nurseries beckon. Gardeners habitually forget how busy they will be when the sunshine, warmth, and greenery return, yet they can't resist the temptations. A firm stance seems to be the only answer if our gardens are not to become more pain than pleasure.

**Avoid high-maintenance plants.** If your time and energy are limited, when choosing new perennials or replacements for your plantings, beware of those that will cause extra work. If the plants spread too quickly, need frequent division, require replacement often, or are inherently weak, you can save a great deal of time and effort by avoiding them.

**Choose long-lived plants.** It is necessary to replace biennials frequently if they do not self-seed, and certain perennials, such as hybrid delphiniums, are also short-lived in all but the cool planting zones. In our garden, hybrid lupines tend to live only a few years, even though the older kinds are longer-lived. If you are looking for plants known for their longevity, the following are good choices: anemone, astilbe, balloon flower, old-fashioned bleeding heart, coralbells, cranesbill, daylilies, gas plant, globe thistle, hosta, lavender, monkshood, peonies, phlox, sundrops, pulmonaria, salvia, thalictrum, trollius, and yucca.

**Avoid perennials that have been over hybridized.** Certain perennials, including daylily, delphinium, iris, lupine, and others, have been crossed and re-crossed endlessly to get larger blooms, brighter colors, fragrance, or any number of other desirable qualities. Unfortunately, ultra-hybridization has often sacrificed vigor and hardiness. To avoid the necessity for coddling, resist the new, spectacular hybrid flowers offered in catalogs and garden centers until you have researched them thoroughly. Buy a few, if you want, but study new plants at nursery display gardens and public parks to see how they are doing before planting large numbers. Even the well-publicized "All America Selections" aren't always better choices than the easy-care, tried-and-true, old-time favorites.

*With containers, you can create colorful and movable gardens even in small spaces such as decks and balconies.*

## Consider Containers

If bending and working on your knees is difficult, consider placing your garden on a higher level where the plants are easier to reach. Window boxes, stone or concrete planters, hanging baskets, or large pots set on a deck or terrace or beside a pool can solve the problem.

Raised beds framed with timbers several feet high and filled with soil also make "no-bend" gardening possible. You can construct them at any height, making them practical even for dedicated gardeners in wheelchairs.

When filled with perennials, bulbs, or annuals, containers provide splashes of color that brighten the landscape throughout the summer. They are timesavers as well, because if the soil is sterile initially, no weed seeds will sprout.

### A DOZEN EASY-CARE PERENNIALS

You can choose from hundreds of excellent perennials. Your decisions will depend on the size of your beds, the amount of time you have to putter, and, most of all, your personal preferences.

Some that are relatively long-lived in most climates and require infrequent division and minimal pest control:

Achillea (*Achillea* 'Coronation Gold' and others)
Baby's breath (*Gypsophila*)
Coralbells (*Heuchera*)
Cranesbill (*Geranium*)
Daylily (*Hemerocallis*)
Globe thistle (*Echinops*)
Hosta (*Hosta*)
Leopard's bane (*Doronicum*)
Bleeding heart (*Dicentra spectabilis*)
Peony (*Paeonia*)
Pincushion flower (*Scabiosa caucasica*)
Turtlehead (*Chelone*)

# Perennial Border Extras

If your old garden was planted some years ago or seems boring and conventional, it is likely that standard, tried-and-true perennials predominate. To go beyond the basics, you may want to add more unusual and new perennial varieties and cultivars, as well as colorful annuals, biennials, and interesting bulb plants. They can lengthen your garden's blooming season and give it a face-lift with very little additional work.

## Favorite Annuals for Quick, Temporary Color

If you or someone else once grew beds of impatiens, petunias, snapdragons, or other annuals but stopped planting them, the plot was no doubt quickly taken over by weeds and grass unless you planted something else there. To reclaim the area, you may question whether or not to replant annuals. You may also question whether or not they belong in your perennial border.

Annuals can be a bright spot either by themselves or in a mixed garden, because they bloom for most of the summer. They need replanting each spring, however, and most require regular deadheading. If the fading blossoms are not removed, they detract greatly from the appearance, and the plants are likely to stop blooming and go to seed. We like the tall pink, rose, and white lavatera plants, because, unlike many annuals, their spent blooms just drop off without needing to be cut off.

Annuals, also called bedding plants, need time to mature before blooming, so if you want to enjoy them throughout the summer you must either buy the plants in the spring or start your own in late winter. You may decide to plant the seed of certain early-blooming kinds, such as sweet alyssum, directly in the ground where you want them to grow, and thin out the extras. In short growing seasons, however, direct seeding of most annuals means you can enjoy the blooms for only the latter part of the summer.

Most shallow-rooted, low-growing annuals, such as dwarf marigolds and dwarf dahlias, are good choices for planting over deeply planted spring bulbs after their tops begin to die. They not only help cover the fading foliage of plants like daffodils, which must be left to die down naturally for the health of the bulbs, but they eliminate future bare spots in the garden and provide color throughout the season.

## Biennial Citizens: How to Use

A true biennial grows from seed one year, blooms and produces seeds the second year, then dies. But many so-called biennials, such as hollyhocks and sweet William, live for more than two years, in cool climates. Also, if biennials are started indoors in early winter, some are able to bloom the

*Since plants like these foxgloves, as well as Canterbury bells, forget-me-nots, gloriosa daisies, hollyhocks, lupines, pinks, wallflowers, and sweet William reproduce readily each year by self sowing, you can continue to enjoy them in your garden, as long as you stand by to remove the self-sown seedlings you don't need.*

first year when moved outdoors. Such plants are sometimes called short-lived perennials, and for this reason you'll sometimes find them listed in catalogs as "hardy plants."

Biennials are welcome additions to the garden because they usually bloom over a longer season than most perennials. Their short life span may contribute to the deterioration of an aging garden, however, because gaps may appear where they once grew, or the huge number of seeds that some produce may cause the proliferation of a large number of unwanted plants. For instance, foxgloves spread thousands of seeds in our perennial garden 25 years ago, and although we haven't planted them since that time, we still find ourselves weeding out new foxglove seedlings periodically.

If you grow biennials in your remodeled garden, you may want to let a few of them produce seeds so you won't need to replant each year.

## Integrating Bulbs into the Perennial Border

We have learned from experience that it is difficult to grow spring-flowering bulbs successfully in a perennial bed. The first potential problem arises when you are working in the bed, planting annuals or moving other perennials. Unless you have an excellent memory or carefully mark the spots where they are growing, it is easy to dig into the bulbs later in the season after their blooms and foliage have disappeared. Another problem is that bulb foliage should be left standing until it becomes yellow and lifeless, and it often looks grungy for a long time in cool, damp climates where the foliage takes many weeks to die back.

For these reasons, we've found it is more feasible to plant daffodils in their own separate beds. It helps the appearance to plant shallow-rooted annuals around the bulbs as soon as their foliage begins to die back.

Garden author Margaret Hensel describes a type of bulb planting that she says resembles a fruitcake, because it is packed solid with bulbs. A friend of Ms. Hensel's plants spring bulbs among her perennials in tight layers, placing the largest ones deepest, and the smaller ones closer to the surface. By planning the colors carefully, the effect in spring is very pleasing, with snowdrops and scillas coming first, followed later by narcissus and tulips.

## BULB RESCUE

Bulbs in a neglected garden may show foliage but not bloom for several reasons:

- Spring bulbs, including daffodils, tulips, and hyacinths, may be overcrowded, receive too little spring sunlight, or be planted at the wrong depth

- Spring bulbs may lack nutrients, particularly if roots from hedges, large shrubs, or trees encroach

- Hyacinths and most tulips, except for the species types, are short-lived and may be nearing the end of their life span

- Summer bulbs, such as lilies and iris, may not be blooming because they need dividing, or possibly they, too, need fertilizer or are planted at the wrong depth

If the hardy bulbs in your garden have not been neglected for too long it may be possible to get them to bloom again. Dig, divide if necessary, and replant them. Named cultivars are likely to need regular dividing and other care. If you want to grow more carefree bulbs, choose the wild bulb species, the type you'd use for naturalizing, which live for many years with little attention.

Before you set bulbs back into the same bed, till in fertilizer, because the soil will probably be depleted of nutrients. The best time to dig and reset bulbs is in late spring or early summer when you can find them easily, just as their tops are dying down. Replant them at the proper depth.

## Shrubs in the Perennial Border: The Mixed Border

Specimen shrubs, both herbaceous and evergreen, can provide an attractive foundation for the herbaceous perennials in your border. Different types (see chart on page 64) add interesting shapes, textures, and colors to complement the ever-changing perennials. When the garden is dormant, evergreens supply color and form, and certain deciduous types extend the blooming season, from yellow forsythia in early spring to brilliant red burning bush in fall.

Many shrubs, such as mounds of English lavender, heathers, or cotoneaster, can be attractive even when not in bloom and barely indistinguishable from herbaceous plants in the growing season, except for their woody stems. Many contribute significant accents of color to your design. Low-bush blueberries are not only edible but they add deep maroon foliage in the fall. For continuous color, use plants, such as red-leafed barberry, or, plants with golden foliage, such as golden elder or 'Gold Flame' spireas.

Because shrubs are likely to be greedy for food and moisture, which they rob from herbaceous plants, you must pay special attention to a mixed border and add additional fertilizer and water when necessary. Small, dwarf shrubs are preferable because they will not quickly overgrow the space you've allotted to them or become so tall that they shade nearby sun-loving perennials. Be aware that fruit-producing plants may entail clean-up jobs, unless you pick off their fruits.

*The variegated euonymous at the right forms a dependable, richly colored anchor for this small border. This evergreen plant will continue to disguise the low path lighting tucked under its foliage throughout the year.*

## SHRUBS FOR THE MIXED BORDER

| PLANT NAME | ATTRACTIVE FEATURE | HEIGHT | HARDINESS ZONE |
|---|---|---|---|
| BARBERRY, CRIMSON PYGMY (*Berberis*) | Deep red foliage, red berries | 3' (0.9 m) | 4 |
| BLUEBERRY, LOW-BUSH (*Vaccinium*) | Long season of red blooms | 1' (30 cm) and up | 2 |
| BOG ROSEMARY (*Andromeda polifolia*) | Pink-white flowers | 1' (30 cm) | 2 |
| BOXWOOD, 'WINTERGREEN' (*Buxus microphylla*) | Fragrant flowers, deep green foliage | 2–3' (60–90 cm) | 5 |
| COTONEASTER, ROCK SPRAY, OTHERS (*Cotoneaster*) | Colorful berries and foliage | 2' (60 cm) and up | 4 |
| DAPHNE (*Daphne cneorum*) | Heavily fragrant flowers | 2' (60 cm) and up | 4 |
| EVERGREENS (such as dwarf arborvitae, hemlock, spruce, and yew) | Good border plants | Varies | Varies |
| FORSYTHIA (dwarf cultivars) | Early spring yellow flowers | 2 feet and up | 5 |
| HEATH (*Erica*) | Nice blooms and foliage | 1' (30 cm) and up | 5 |
| HEATHER (many kinds) (*Calluna*) | Attractive blooms and foliage | 4" (10 cm) and up | 5 |
| HONEYSUCKLE, 'EMERALD MOUND' (*Lonicera*) | Yellow white flowers, red berries | 2–3' (60–90 cm) | 4 |
| HYPERICUM (many cultivars) (*Hypericum*) | Long season of bright yellow blooms | 2' (60 cm) | 4 |
| KALMIA, DWARF MT. LAUREL (*Kalmia latifolia*) | Nice foliage and flowers | 3' (0.9 m) | 5 |
| LAVENDER, ENGLISH (*Lavandula angustifolia*) | Fragrant rosy-purple blooms | 12–18" (30–45 cm) | 5 |
| RHODODENDRON, AZALEA (Dwarf cultivars) (*Rhododendron*) | Nice blooms and foliage | 2' (60 cm) and up | Varies |
| ROSE (*Rosa*) | Attractive, often fragrant, flowers | 2' (60 cm) and up | Varies |
| SPIREA (dwarf cultivars) (*Spiraea*) | Nice spring flowers; some have good fall foliage | 2' (60 cm) and up | 4 |
| WEIGELA, 'EVITA' (*Weigela florida*) | Attractive foliage, fruits, and fall color | 2–3' (60–90 cm) | 4 |

# Bringing Out the Best in Ground Covers

If ground covers are spreading over parts of your landscape, you may find them either attractive and useful or a pain in the neck. We have a large patch of vinca that thrives on a shady slope near a brook where grass couldn't possibly grow. The rich green foliage is beautiful all season, particularly when its greenery is dotted with blue blooms. But this same plant has become a headache in another spot on our property where it is spreading into an adjacent lawn.

Nature developed ground covers to shield bare spots in the earth created by humans or weather. Their fast-growing habits make them ideal for the purpose, but these same habits can cause problems when they are in the wrong places. At their best, however, they can effectively stop erosion by blanketing poor soil, steep slopes, and other difficult places where lawn grass or other plants are not suitable. They also move quickly into spots where they are eyesores and interfere with the growth of other plants. Many are good at crowding out competing weeds. In addition to being utilitarian, some are quite beautiful; when used imaginatively they add special texture and color to your landscape.

In spite of all their assets, you may be facing problems with certain types of ground covers on your property if the plantings have been neglected. Most likely the problem plants will be those that spread by underground rhizomes, put down roots as they travel (spread by runners), or spread seeds freely. An all-too-common complaint about many covers is not that they don't do their job well, but, like our periwinkle, that they spread outside their designated area to blanket lawns, gardens, paths, and beyond. Our neighbors, superb gardeners, are involved in an unending battle with goutweed, the bane of a gardener's existence once it gets a strong foothold. This attractive cover, planted years before they bought their home, spreads rapidly by seeds and underground runners into every corner of their perennial bed and vegetable garden, crowding out other plants and defying every method of control.

*Confined to the right spot, even a potentially invasive plant like ajuga can be a star.*

## GROUND COVER TROUBLESHOOTING

| PROBLEM | POSSIBLE CAUSE | SOLUTION | PAGE |
|---|---|---|---|
| RAMPANT GROUND COVER ENCROACHING ON ADJOINING AREAS | Naturally aggressive grower, spreading either by runners or self-sowing freely | Cut back and install edging to confine; let animals graze; dig and rip out; apply chemical herbicides to eliminate. | 67 |
| GROUND COVER INVADING LAWN | Naturally aggressive grower, spreading either by runners or self-sowing freely; may also be encouraged by lawn fertilizer | Dig out what you can; spot-treat the rest with herbicide. | 67 |
| SPOTTY GROUND COVER | Weather damage, particularly ice | Mulch in fall. | 68 |
| | Disease or insect damage | Diagnose first, then treat with a pesticide labeled for the problem. | 68 |
| SPOTTY, THIN, OR YELLOWING | Lack of food | Fertilize, and scratch in good organic soil amendments. | 68 |
| | Lack of sun | Remove overhanging vegetation, or replant in a better spot. | 68 |
| GROUND COVER SPOTTY OR THIN | Some dead plants | Fertilize, plant replacements, water well. | 68 |

# Reining In Invasive Ground Covers

Invasive ground covers spread not only by themselves, but by enthusiastic gardeners, happy to share their surplus, who generously give away their bounty without a caveat. Some gardeners over the years have been far too generous with goutweed, Japanese bamboo, ajuga, and other plants, and ended up being personae non gratae in their neighborhoods.

Beginning gardeners who find the plants attractive also buy them without an awareness of their potential. Consequently, if you are a new homeowner, you may have ground covers growing where you wish they were not. If you are faced with a cover that is behaving badly, you may need to outwit it to rejuvenate your landscape.

If you are unable to eliminate a ground cover, you may be able to learn to live with it and keep

it from spreading further by installing edgings (see page 54). One of our friends has made peace with goutweed, letting it substitute for a small lawn in the shade of giant maples on the main street of a small village. It is controlled on four sides by a sidewalk, roadway, stone wall, and their home, and presents a carefree "lawn" that is attractive for most of the summer.

## WHAT DOESN'T WORK

Many ground covers spread by stolons or underground rhizomes that cannot be completely dug out; tilling them only encourages their proliferation. Likewise, pruning back the foliage is likely to stimulate their growth. Digging, cutting, pulling, and tearing out the plants may control them if the bed is small, but in larger areas, hand control may be nearly impossible.

## Eradicating Unwanted Ground Covers

If you decide to tackle an unruly ground cover, you may decide that every plant should go or that a portion of them should be kept in an allotted space. Either way you can accomplish your goal, but you will no doubt eventually conclude, as we have, that a fast-spreading ground cover is much easier to plant than to remove.

➤ Dig out the plants manually if the patch is small.

➤ Smother them by laying black plastic or black building paper over them. Be patient, this may take a season or two.

➤ Cover them with clear plastic to burn them in the sun.

➤ Bury them under a layer of topsoil. This may not work if the plant is a fighter.

➤ Torch plants with a propane gas weed burner. We don't recommend this method of killing off unwanted vegetation, because it can be dangerous. If you decide to use it, take these precautions: Aim the flame at the base of the plant, use it only after a rain when surrounding vegetation is wet (or thoroughly water entire area with a hose), and avoid using it near flammable materials. Wear a heavy jacket, pants, and thick gloves. Weed burners are available from garden suppliers and hardware stores.

➤ If you live in a rural area, let goats, sheep, pigs, or chickens loose in the spot. Be sure no toxic plants, such as horsetails, are in the vicinity. Also, check your local zoning laws.

➤ As a last resort, carefully use a synthetic herbicide containing glyphosate, generally regarded as one of the safer synthetic herbicides. The area may require more than one treatment. *Important:* Make sure the product works on the foliage rather than the roots. Those that work on the roots may leave a toxic substance in the soil that could remain for some time and prevent replanting in that spot. An overdose of a strong synthetic fertilizer can often kill unwanted plants, but it, too, can leave the soil sterile.

➤ Hire professionals to eradicate the miscreants, but make sure that the products they use are safe.

## AGGRESSIVE GROUND COVERS

Allen Lacy has called English ivy "a Trojan horse in a garden," and the same phrase could be applied to many other plants. A daylily grower once told us that she had been advised by a nurseryman to plant ajuga among her daylilies as a protective mulch. Within two years she had to abandon the entire bed and start over again because the ajuga choked out her daylily plants.

Think twice before planting the following invasive ground covers. If you already own them, keep an eye on them and notice if they are spreading. They could be ideal solutions for a spot that they will cover quickly and never cause trouble, but be aware of the potential. Since certain plants become invasive in some soils and climates but not in others, you may find some of the plants listed here are noninvasive on your property, and others that are not listed could be problems in your landscape.

Bugleweed *(Ajuga reptans)*
Creeping bellflower *(Campanula rapunculoides)*
Creeping Jennie *(Lysimachia nummularia)*
Creeping lilyturf *(Liriope spicata)*
Crown vetch *(Coronilla varia)*
English ivy *(Hedera helix)*
Gold moss, stonecrop *(Sedum acre)*
Goutweed, bishop's weed *(Aegopodium podagraria)*
Horsetail *(Equisetum)*
Mazus *(Mazus reptans)*
Periwinkle *(Vinca minor)*
Prickly pear *(Opuntia humifusa)*
Pussy-toes *(Antennaria dioica)*
Snow-in-summer *(Cerastium tomentosum)*
Spotted dead nettle *(Lamium maculatum)*
Sweet violet *(Viola odorata)*
White evening primrose *(Oenothera speciosa)*
Yellow archangel *(Lamiastrum galeobdolon)*

## Control Measures

If you have a vigorous-growing ground cover and you want to keep it, there are ways to manage it so it looks attractive and doesn't cause trouble.

➤ Mow around herbaceous types frequently to keep them in place

➤ Surround them with edgings

➤ Pruning and chopping may successfully control the woody, vinelike types

After you have pushed back invaders to where you want them, keep an eye out for any new plants that spring from roots deep in the earth or from sprouting seeds. It may take several years of vigilance before you can celebrate victory, but you will win the war if you are persistent. After six years we finally eliminated the last "wild" daylily on our property.

---

### SAVE WHAT YOU WANT, GET RID OF WHAT YOU DON'T WANT

If the aggressive ground cover has intermingled with plants you like, first dig out all those you want to save. Wash off the roots and heel in the "keepers" in a safe place, such as an unused portion of your vegetable garden, until you can replant them. Then you can undertake the bed-clearing methods described on page 67. Just remember to think twice about using any herbicide if you want to return the "good plants" to the spot later.

---

# Spotty Ground Cover Areas

Most ground covers are so vigorous that compared to other plants they seldom need much attention. When a portion of a ground cover expires or becomes ragged because of weather damage, disease, or insect infestation, however, it is extremely noticeable. In cold climates, ice is often the culprit. It usually makes our ground covers look spotty and unkempt in the springtime, but fortunately, within a few weeks the vigorous plants always revive and cover the dead areas.

If yours don't recover on their own, it may not be winter damage, and you may need to replace those that are in bad condition. If weather is not the villain, the plants in a spotty area may be diseased, overcrowded, or undernourished. Try to identify what may be affecting them and take appropriate action by treating the condition.

Like all plants, ground covers need nutrients. Although they don't require as much fertilizer as other plants, if portions seem scraggly it may be time to give the ground cover a light feeding. You also may need to replace a few of the plants to renew the planting.

## Repair Strategies

First, remove those plants that are struggling and scraggly. Then separate some of the healthier specimens and plant them where needed.

When weeds intrude on the area, you can usually remove them by hand. If that is too mammoth a job you may need to resort to spot spraying with chemicals or use mechanical means to dig them out. Sometimes spreading a light helping of fertilizer over the ground covers helps revive them so they are better able to fight off grass or other competition.

## Prevention

Although ground covers are attractive when a single species is used, a mixture of compatible species also works well if the plants are nearly the same height. Thyme, sedum, and similar plants look nice when different species are mixed, and the different colors and textures make the patch more interesting. As with lawn mixes, this tactic also helps assure that something is always thriving at any given time.

# INSTALLING A GROUND COVER

If you decide to replace a ground cover you don't like or start a new planting, you may want to choose from the list of well-behaved ground covers, depending on your location and purpose (see Recommended Ground Covers, page 70). Keep in mind that even these can go rampant in the right location.

Use a liquid fertilizer to get the plants off to a good start. Then water your transplants every other day until they are well established. After that, feed them only if growth is slow. Install edgings (see page 54) to keep the new planting in its place if there are no natural barriers to contain plant growth.

**Step 1.** Till the ground thoroughly before planting to get rid of existing vegetation, and loosen the soil for setting the plants. If you have really tough plants growing there, you may first want to get rid of them by spraying a herbicide containing glyphosate.

If you don't want to use chemicals, till more deeply. Mix in some compost, manure, and organic balanced fertilizer for the less vigorous ground covers such as bleeding heart, candytuft, daylily, geranium, hosta, iris, and lavender. The especially vigorous herbaceous ground covers, such as forget-me-not, lily-of-the-valley, mint, pachysandra, sedum, thyme, vinca, and similar plants do not need extra fertilizer or special care in planting. Nature created these ground covers to clothe bare earth quickly and protect it from the elements.

**Step 2.** Plant small herbaceous low-growers 6 to 10 inches (15 to 25 cm) apart in every direction. For those that grow larger, plant a bit further apart. If your soil is well tilled, just set the plants so the roots are well covered and the leafy crown is just about ground level. Leave a slight depression around each plant to catch waterings.

*Step 1. Before planting, clear the area of weeds and rocks to a depth of several inches.*

*Step 2. Space new plants widely, unless you want dense growth or don't mind thinning later.*

# RECOMMENDED GROUND COVERS

| PLANT NAME | BEST FEATURE | LIGHT NEEDED | SPREAD AT MATURITY | PLANTING DISTANCE | HARDINESS ZONES |
|---|---|---|---|---|---|
| ASTILBE (*Astilbe chinensis* var. *pumila*) | Pink flowers, fernlike leaves, drought resistant; mat forming | Sun/partial shade | 1–2 feet (30–60 cm) | 1–2 feet (30–60 cm) | 3–8 |
| BLEEDING HEART, WILD (*Dicentra eximia*) | Fernlike foliage; long season of pink blooms | Sun/light shade | 1–2 feet (30–60 cm) | 1 foot (30 cm) | 3–8 |
| CANDYTUFT (*Iberis*) | Attractive white blooms; low spreading growth | Sun/light shade | 2–3 feet (60–90 cm) | 1 foot (30 cm) | 3–9 |
| CRESTED IRIS (*Iris cristata*) | Neat, dwarf iris; lavender blooms in late spring | Partial shade | Unlimited | 12–18 inches (30–45 cm) | 3–9 |
| FERNS, DWARF (*Dennstaedtia punctilobula*) | Hay-scented fern and other low growers; good on poor soil | Shade/sun | 2 feet (60 cm) or more | 2–3 feet (60–90 cm) | 3–11 |
| GERANIUM, CRANESBILL (*Geranium sanguineum* and other species) | Clumpy plants; nice flowers | Sun/light shade | 2–3 feet (60–90 cm) | 2 feet (60 cm) | 4–7 |
| HERBS OF VARIOUS KINDS | Attractive blooms and foliage; fragrant and useful in cooking | Sun/light shade | Varies | 1 foot (30 cm) | Varies |
| HOSTA (*Hosta*) | Massive plants with large leaves; blooms in midsummer | Shade | 2 feet (60 cm) and up | 2–3 feet (60–90 cm) | 3–8 |
| LAVENDER (*Lavandula*) | Fragrant purple to lavender flowers in summer | Sun | 1–2 feet (30–60 cm) | 2 feet (60 cm) | 5–7 |
| JAPANESE PRIMROSE (*Primula japonica*) | Attractive flowers in many colors | Sun/light shade | 18 inches (45 cm) | 1–2 feet (30–60 cm) | 3–7 |
| MOSS PHLOX (*Phlox subulata*) | Pink, purple, or white flowers in spring; evergreen foliage | Sun | 8–12 inches (20–30 cm) | 1 foot (30 cm) | 2–9 |
| PACHYSANDRA (*Pachysandra terminalis*) | Attractive, low, evergreen | Shade | 2 feet (60 cm) and up | 8 to 12 inches (20–30 cm) | 4–8 |
| PERIWINKLE (*Vinca minor*) | Shiny evergreen leaves; vigorous cover for woodlands; blue flowers in spring | Shade | Unlimited | 2 feet (60 cm) | 3–9 |
| ROCK SPEEDWELL (*Veronica prostrata*) | Deep blue flowers in late spring to early summer | Sun/light shade | 18 inches (45 cm) | 2 feet (60 cm) | 3–8 |
| SANDWORT (*Arenaria montana*) | Wide, white flowers with yellow eye | Sun | 1 foot (30 cm) or more | 1 foot (30 cm) or more | 4–8 |
| STONECROP (*Sedum spurium*) | Tough spreader for dry soils | Sun | 2 feet (60 cm) | 1 foot (30 cm) | 3–9 |
| SUNDROPS (*Oenothera speciosa*) | Pink and white flowers in summer; nice foliage | Sun | 2 feet (60 cm) and up | 2 feet (60 cm) | 5–9 |
| TAWNY DAYLILY (*Hemerocallis fulva*) | Vigorous grower and spreader; tawny-colored blooms in midsummer | Sun/shade shade | 2 feet (60 cm) and up | 3 feet (90 cm) | 2–9 |

# ALTERNATIVES TO TRADITIONAL GROUND COVERS

When you have a spot where you think an herbaceous ground cover might spread too much, consider planting woody shrubs instead.

**Evergreens.** Many low-growing shrubs, particularly spreading evergreens such as junipers and yews, offer attractive year-round greenery and are ideal for landscaping a slope. Set them 3 to 6 feet (0.9 to 1.8 m) apart, depending on their ultimate spread.

Common juniper *(Juniper communis)*
Creeping mahonia, dwarf Oregon grape
   *(Mahonia repens)*
Sargent juniper *(J. chinensis* var. *sargentii)*
Siberian carpet cypress *(Microbiota decussata)*
Spreading juniper *(J. horizontalis);* cultivars
   'Bar Harbor', 'Nana', 'Plumosa'
Spreading yew *(Taxus cuspidata)*

**Deciduous.** Low-growing deciduous shrubs also make excellent covers and many add colorful blooms and berries.

Bayberry *(Myrica pensylvanica)*
Bramble *(Rubus pentalobus)*
Euonymus *(Euonymus fortunei)*
Heather *(Calluna vulgaris)*
Japanese quince *(Chaenomeles japonica*
   var. *alpina)*
Lace shrub *(Stephanandra incisa)*
Low-bush blueberry *(Vaccinium angustifolium)*
Rock spray *(Cotoneaster horizontalis)*
Shrubby cinquefoil *(Potentilla fruticosa)*
Slender deutzia *(Deutzia gracilis)*
Spring heath *(Erica carnea)*
Three-toothed cinquefoil *(Potentilla tridentata)*

*Low-growing shrubs, such as this juniper, make ideal evergreen ground covers, especially on slopes.*

# Gardening with Ornamental Grasses

Spreading ornamental grasses, like other ground-covering plants, stimulate strong responses from homeowners who have them. You may feel enthusiastic or more than a little upset when they are mentioned, depending on your experience with them.

If you are unfamiliar with the type of grasses growing on your property, first try to identify them accurately so you will better understand their growth habits. Use them in perennial beds or as specimens, like small shrubs. When they are isolated in this way it is easy to control them by mowing closely around their perimeters.

The more invasive grasses can make good ground covers, but watch out for their eager growth and plant them only where they won't interfere with your other plantings. Although some kinds might be perfect for a meadow, a wet area, or a spot so dry that little else would grow, in the perennial border they can rival the worst weeds.

*The more refined ornamental grasses grow in neat clumps, meriting places in the perennial bed or foundation planting, where they are no more threatening than any other moderately vigorous perennial.*

# Salvaging an Overgrown or Damaged Planting

Although most ornamental grasses cast off and absorb their old foliage as mulch, the area looks better early in the season if you mow them before new growth has started and then rake up the litter. In fact, you may be able to salvage an overgrown planting this way. Spring is the usual time to do this, because the blooms on many grasses are attractive well into the winter. If the grasses bloom early, or they were chosen for their leaf color rather than for their bloom (golden variegated hakone grass, for instance), you can do this mowing in the fall. As the grasses regrow, examine them closely. If there is decided improvement in their appearance, mowing the area once a year may be all the attention that is necessary.

It may also be necessary to get rid of plants that don't belong there, such as weeds or other species. Climb in and dig them out, or kill them off by spot treatment with an organic herbicide or a chemical that is considered safe by most experts, such as a product containing glyphosate. Unless there are a lot of unwanted plants, the remaining grasses should quickly fill in the bare spots.

# Starting Over

If it is clear that trying to improve the planting would not be worth the work and time involved, the best option is to get rid of the plants and start over. Ornamental grasses are likely to have deeper roots than lawn grasses or ground covers, so they could present a challenge if you decide they have outlived their usefulness.

Most foliar herbicides work best when sprayed on the plants as they are growing rapidly. This will be when the grasses start to grow again after being cut down, or as they start growing in the spring. Wait until they are about 5 inches (12.5 cm) tall before the first application; apply as a fine mist, and, if necessary, apply another spray at the end of the summer just before the plant begins to go dormant. Then it will carry the herbicide into the roots where it usually effectively kills the plant.

## ORNAMENTAL GRASS TROUBLESHOOTING

| PROBLEM | POSSIBLE CAUSE | SOLUTION | PAGE |
|---|---|---|---|
| PLANTS RUNNING WILD | Neglect, poor choice of planting site | Thin out, cut back, plant elsewhere, or dispose of in a place where they cannot grow | 73 |
| WEEDS INVADING GRASS PLANTING | Neglect | Tear out as many weeds as possible by the roots; the rest can be spot treated with an herbicide | 73 |
| PALE, YELLOW, OR BROWNING LEAVES | Site too wet or too dry | Improve site drainage, or water more often; move to a more suitable site | 75 |
| BROWN-TIPPED LEAVES | Nutrients lacking, site too shady | Apply liquid fertilizer; provide more sun | 75 |
| ENTIRE PLANTING RATTY OR ILL-LOOKING | Neglect | Clean up, water, and fertilize; if severe problems, mow to the ground in spring and allow the plants to start afresh | 73 |
| PLANTS DON'T RETURN AFTER THE WINTER | Not hardy in your zone; waterlogged site | Mulch in fall; try to improve site drainage or transplant in drier ground | 74 |

## Choosing an Ornamental Grass

So many ornamental grasses are available that you have a number of choices among those that are well behaved and unlikely to pose a future threat to your landscape. They range in size from low, compact plants to huge giants. Some are showy all season and others add color to a home landscape in late fall and winter when the scenery is otherwise drab. Look for the one that will be appropriate for your area. A collection of 12-foot (3.6 m) pampas grass can be a gorgeous traffic-stopper in a park, but quite out of place in a small backyard.

A few grasses are suitable for northern gardens, but most grow best in Zones 5 and warmer. In cooler zones, cutting back those that are half hardy and mulching them with evergreen boughs offers winter protection, but then, unfortunately, you lose their attractive fall and winter color. Nearly all ornamental grasses become dormant in the winter in cold regions, but many of them are evergreen in mild climates.

To avoid planting species that you may not like later, visit a nursery where display beds of the plants are growing and see how they look when they are mature. If you buy a variety and don't know its growing habits, isolate it for a year before giving it space in your garden.

## Right Plant, Right Place

Ornamental grasses, depending on their habit of growth (clumping or spreading), can be used in many areas of the yard. The key is making a good match, so you are not constantly reining them in or wishing you'd planted more.

Generally speaking, they need plenty of sun. It's also a good idea to give ornamental grasses plenty of elbow room on all sides, so they can grow freely and be admired from various angles (the ones that produce great flower plumes are spectacular when backlit by the sun).

**Slopes and banks.** Ornamental grasses are a good choice for stabilizing steep or uneven ground or for preventing erosion. They can grow in places you cannot or don't wish to mow, and their deep roots will anchor the soil. Once established, they should also crowd out weeds or other unwanted plants.

**Curb strips.** These grasses make a tough, eye-catching planting, if you don't want to maintain lawn grasses there, or if you consider flowers or shrubs too vulnerable or too high-maintenance.

**Perennial borders.** Choose candidates with care, or plant lusty growers in containers, before introducing ornamental grasses to a flower bed. They can look wonderful in the company of plants with casual profiles and similar requirements for sun and soil. A popular combination, with good reason, is fountain grasses with black-eyed Susans, coreopsis, and other domesticated wildflowers.

*If you plant ornamental grasses in a perennial bed, make sure to give individual specimens elbow room on all sides so they can look their best.*

**Containers.** Aggressive but handsome grasses look terrific in large containers. A pair set in formal iron or terra-cotta pots flanking a doorway, stairway, or garden entrance can be very dramatic. You can either set a container on the ground or submerge it partway or completely. Whatever you decide, be sure to site it first, because a pot full of soil and plants may be too heavy or unwieldy to move around. One last note: If the grass you want is not hardy in your area, potting it (and bringing it in during the winter months) might be worth trying.

## Culture

Most ornamental grasses like full sun, but some tolerate partial shade. Most prefer good to average soil that is well-drained, but some like it boggy. Unlike lawn grasses, fertilize them only if growth is poor. Mow or cut back annually in late winter or early spring.

*Some of the most beautiful grasses can be too vigorous. The solution? Grow them in large containers.*

---

## ORNAMENTAL GRASSES FOR SPECIFIC SITES

### Fast Spreaders by Rhizomes or Seeds
Blue fescue (*Festuca glauca*)
Blue lyme grass (*Leymus arenarius* 'Glaucus')
Fountain grass (*Pennisetum*)
Giant reed (*Arundo donax*)
Golden wood millet (*Milium effusum* 'Aureum')
Indian grass (*Sorghastrum nutans*)
Northern sea oats (*Chasmanthium latifolium*)
Pampas grass (*Cortaderia selloana*)
Prairie dropseed (*Sporobolus heterolepis*)
Tufted hairgrass (*Deschampsia caespitosa*)
Velvet grass (*Holcus lanatus*)
White-striped ribbon grass (*Phalaris arundinacea* 'Picta')

### Best for Dry Areas
Blue hairgrass (*Koeleria glauca*)
Blue oat grass (*Helictotrichon sempervirens*)
Indian grass (*Sorghastrum nutans*)
Little bluestem (*Schizachyrium scoparium*)
Prairie dropseed (*Sporobolus heterolepis*)
Ravenna grass (*Erianthus ravennae*)
Side oats gramma (*Bouteloua curtipendula*)

### Best for Wet Areas
Bowles' golden sedge (*Carex elata* 'Aurea')
Bulbous oat grass (*Arrhenatherum elatius* var. *bulbosum*)
Feather reed grass (*Calamagrostis* x *acutiflora* 'Stricta')
Japanese silver grass (*Miscanthus sinensis*)
Quaking grass (*Briza media*)
Switch-grass (*Panicum virgatum*)
White-striped ribbon grass (*Phalaris arundinacea* 'Picta')

### Best for Shaded Areas
Bottlebrush grass (*Hystrix patula*)
Golden variegated hakone grass (*Hakonechloa macra* 'Aureola')
Northern sea oats (*Chasmanthium latifolium*)
Sedges (*Carex*)
Snowy woodrush (*Luzula nivea*)
White-striped ribbon grass (*Phalaris arundinacea* 'Picta')

# RECOMMENDED ORNAMENTAL GRASSES

| NAME | BEST FEATURE |
| --- | --- |
| BLUE FESCUE (*Festuca glauca*) | Silvery blue evergreen foliage |
| BLUE HAIRGRASS (*Koeleria glauca*) | Blue green blooms on 18-inch (45 cm) stems that change to buff color later |
| BLUE OAT GRASS (*Helictotrichon sempervirens*) | Showy, narrow, blue, pointed leaves; 3- to 4-foot (0.9 to 1.2 m) stems bearing bluish white oatlike flowers that later turn gold |
| BOTTLEBRUSH GRASS (*Hystrix patula*) | Bushy, green spiked blooms that hang on for most of the summer; brown seedheads that fall apart in the fall |
| FOUNTAIN GRASS (*Pennisetum alopecuroides*) | Creamy white to pinkish flowers in midsummer in long clusters |
| FROST GRASS (*Spodiopogon sibiricus*) | Purplish flowers that turn wheat color; attractive when covered with frost |
| GIANT REED (*Arundo donax*) | Wide 2-foot (60 cm) leaves; can be invasive |
| GOLDEN VARIEGATED HAKONE GRASS (*Hakonechloa macra* 'Aureola') | Yellow, bamboolike leaves striped with green |
| INDIAN GRASS (*Sorghastrum nutans*) | Green-blue leaves that turn yellow, then bronze, and hold their color all winter long; rosy blooms in late summer, turning gold and orange |
| JAPANESE SILVER GRASS (*Miscanthus sinensis*) | Silver to purple flower plumes from midsummer to early fall on 6- to 10-foot (1.8 to 3 m) spikes; silver-colored foliage that turns brown later, then changes to various hues of red, rust, and yellow |
| NORTHERN SEA OATS (*Chasmanthium latifolium*) | Flat green blooms, with seeds that turn copper colored in fall and last into winter; light green foliage that turns copper colored in fall and brown in winter |
| PAMPAS GRASS (*Cortaderia selloana*) | Showy 3-foot (0.9 m) white or pink plumes in midsummer |
| PRAIRIE DROPSEED (*Sporobolus heterolepis*) | Shiny, coarse leaves 12-inches (30 cm) long, short gray tassels, and large green seeds that turn white or black when ripe |
| RAVENNA GRASS (*Erianthus ravennae*) | Silvery flowers with purple tones that become a creamy color; blooms in fall, lasts into winter |
| VELVET GRASS (*Holcus lanatus*) | Gray green semi-evergreen leaves; white flowers on tall spikes bloom for most of the summer |

| GROWING CONDITIONS NEEDED | HEIGHT AT MATURITY | HABIT | HARDINESS ZONES |
| --- | --- | --- | --- |
| Full sun in cool climates; light shade in hot climates; moist, well-drained soil | 8–12 inches (20–30 cm) | Clumping | 4–9 |
| Full sun, well-drained, somewhat alkaline soil | 6–12 inches (15–30 cm) | Clumping | 6–9 |
| Sun or light shade; well-drained, fertile soil | Up to 2 feet (60 cm) | Clumping | 4–9 |
| Full sun; moist, fertile, well-drained soil | 2–4 feet (60–120 cm) | Clumping | 5–9 |
| Sun, light shade, fertile, moist, well-drained soil | 3 feet (90 cm) | Clumping | 5–9 |
| Full sun, light shade in hot climates; moist, fertile, well-drained soil | 2–3 feet (60–90 cm) | Clumping | 5–9 |
| Full sun in cool climates; shade in hot areas; moist, well-drained acid soil | 6–20 feet (1.8–6 m) | Vigorous and spreading, invasive | 6–10 |
| Light shade; moist, well-drained, fertile soil | 2 feet (60 cm) | Clumping, noninvasive | 6–9 |
| Sun or light shade; deep, rich, loamy, moist soil | 3 feet (90 cm) | Clumping | 4–9 |
| Full sun; moist, humus-rich soil | Foliage height 3–5 feet (0.9–1.5 m); flower spikes are 6–10 feet (1.8–3 m) | Clumping | 5–9 |
| Full sun in cool climates; part shade in warm areas; moist, fertile soil | 3 feet (90 cm) | Clumping | 5–9 |
| Full sun; rich, well-drained soil | 5–12 feet (1.5–3.6 m) | Clumping | 6–10 |
| Full sun; dry, poor soil | 6 feet (1.8 m) | Clumping | 5–9 |
| Full sun; well-drained, moist, fertile soil | 5 feet (1.5 m) | Clumping | 5–10 |
| Sun or light shade; fertile, moist, well-drained soil | 1–2 feet (30–60 m) | Spreading | 5–9 (may go dormant in late summer in warm areas) |

# chapter 5

# A Face-Lift for Vines

Our friend Flora Philbrook, a stalwart gardener, decided at age 80 that she would eliminate some garden beds to cut down on her work. She planted ivy instead and, now 93, she reports with alarm that the ivy has covered everything in sight — stone walls, shrubs, and trees — and is heading rapidly toward her front porch.

Ivy growing over a cathedral or large university building is attractive and not likely to be a problem, but the same vine clambering over a small cottage, trellis, or pergola can quickly bury its support in foliage. Climbing vines can damage buildings, both wooden and stone, and some actually girdle trees, slowly choking them to death.

Left to their own devices, perennial vines such as woodbine, ivy, and some honeysuckles can romp over lawns and even up tall trees, utility poles, and buildings. Though *vine* is defined in our dictionary as "a weak-stemmed plant that derives its support from climbing, twining, or creeping along a surface," we find it sometimes difficult to use the word *weak* in connection with the aggressive tendencies of many of them.

An attractive vine with the right stuff, well cared for, can be a great asset to your property. The fast-covering types provide good erosion control on banks and are useful for covering eyesores such as old stumps and rocks. The wrong vine, however, or a fine vine that has grown out of bounds or in the wrong place, can be a liability.

*A spectacular vine is a well-managed plant — wisely sited from the start and trimmed regularly. Clematis makes an especially dramatic focal point for porches, decks, and gazebos.*

## VINE TROUBLESHOOTING

| PROBLEM | POSSIBLE CAUSE | SOLUTION | PAGE |
|---|---|---|---|
| VINE DRAGGING DOWN SUPPORT | Overgrown, top-heavy | Prune off overhanging portions anytime. | 84 |
| YELLOWING LEAVES | Lack of sunlight, disease, lack of nutrients | Remove overhanging neighboring plants. If leaf disease is present, use fungicide. Add fertilizer. | 85 |
| VINE DYING OVER THE WINTER | Species or cultivar is not hardy in your area | Choose another hardier type. Remove from support and mulch for overwintering. | 82–85 |
| VINE FLOWERING POORLY OR NOT AT ALL | Not receiving enough sun or nourishment, frost-damaged flower buds | Cut back encroaching plants; thin; fertilize. | 84–85 |
| SUDDEN WILTING OF CLEMATIS CANES | Disease or dry conditions | Water heavily, if soil is dry. If it doesn't revive, prune off wilted portion. | 84 |
| LEAVES CURLING UP OR BEING CHEWED | Sucking or chewing insects | Spray or dust with a garden insecticide. | — |

# Reining In and Revitalizing Overgrown Vines

Attacking a vine that has become weedy is not exactly a job for the faint of heart. The first step is to identify the vine. Too often new homeowners discover that the attractive glossy green vine they acquired is poison ivy. If that is the case, eradicating it should probably be your first order of business, but we hope you won't start ripping it out without protecting your hands and body. This may be a job for the professionals.

If a vine has spread only mildly out of bounds, some cutting back may be all you need to do to get it under control. Prune it back to 6 or 8 feet (1.8 to 2.4 m) from the ground when it is dormant, in fall or early spring. Then steer the new growth to cover only its territory — trellis, arbor, pergola, wall, or fence — and prune it frequently to keep it from going farther astray. You may find that electric clippers are the best way to accomplish this.

## Moving an Existing Vine to a New Spot

If your vine is small, you can move it. In early spring, just as it emerges from dormancy, or in fall, dig it carefully.

It is difficult to move a huge, overgrown vine, because its root system is massive and it is unlikely to survive. Instead, start a new plant by layering or digging a cane that is already rooted near the main vine, being sure it has live top growth and roots. Replant the transplant or new vine in its new location where you have prepared the site by digging a large hole near its support.

*If you would like to move a large vine to a new location, look for young shoots. These are better candidates for transplanting than worn-out or overgrown "mother" plants. Use a spade to dig all the way around the shoot, taking as much root as possible.*

## Killing a Vine

When a vine has gone really wild, the best solution is to get to the roots of the problem. If you don't want to save the plant, cut it off at its source.

When one has spread widely, it has probably rooted at various places, so you will need to cut off all of these sources as you find them. Cut just above the roots and, for ease in handling, let the canes wilt a few days before you remove them from any structures they are covering. To prevent regrowth, use an herbicide on the stumps or new sprouts as they emerge, or cut off all new growth until the plants give up.

# Planting a New Vine

Before you plant a new vine, be sure that the proper type of support is in place to hold it (see below). Each vine moves in a specific way. Some twine around a support and others cling, either by tiny holdfasts that grip smooth surfaces or with spring-like tendrils that wind around a narrow support.

**Step 1.** Remove potted vines from their containers and plant with the soil ball intact. Or, cut back the tops of bare-rooted vines by about half to encourage new growth quickly.

**Step 2.** Set the vine into the hole you have dug, fill the space around the plant with some new topsoil, or with the soil you removed from the hole fortified with compost and a balanced organic fertilizer, such as 5-5-5. Mix a cupful of lime into the soil for vines that need a high pH, such as clematis.

**Step 3.** Soak thoroughly with water containing liquid fertilizer (follow directions on the package).

**Step 4.** Mulch around the plant with shredded bark or grass clippings.

**Step 5.** Water every two or three days until the plant begins to grow well.

**Step 6.** After the new vine is well established, fertilize it only when it fails to grow well. If you want the vine to grow thicker and wide, pinch back the new sprouts from time to time.

## HOW VINES CLING AND CLIMB

Vines have various ways of climbing and clinging. Choose your supports according to the vining habit of your plant. Grape (A) has tendrils; Dutchman's pipe (B) twines; and Boston ivy (C) has holdfasts.

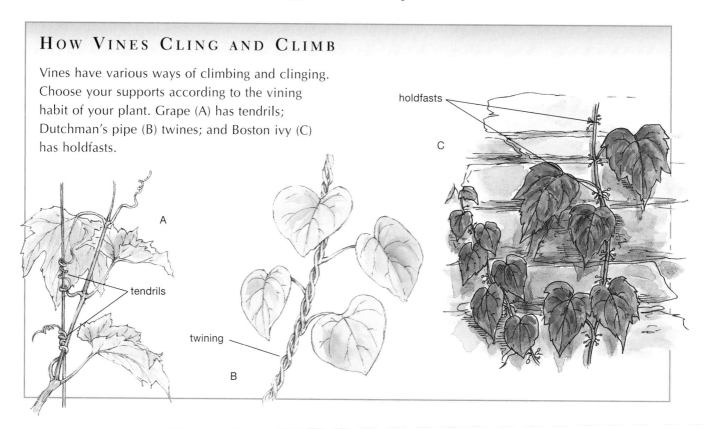

## Appropriate Locations for Vines

Be sure to choose a favorable spot for your new vine:
➤ Never plant a vine directly under the drip line of a building, where rain and falling snow could damage it, and rain from the roof will wash fertility from the soil quickly.

➤ Be certain there is enough light for flowering vines, or you may get only foliage and sparse or no flowers.

## Appropriate Supports for New Vines

If the vine is to grow next to a wooden building, install a trellis or wire fence to hold it about 6 inches (15 cm) away from the building, rather than placing it tight against it. This will allow air to circulate between the vine and structure, while protecting the building from rot and mildew.

A support should be strong, because many vines — so small and unassuming at first — become large and heavy or top-heavy. Wooden supports are sometimes not up to the job in the long run, which is why metal or iron stakes, trellises, and arbors are popular.

Play it safe and plunge a vine support deeply into the ground, or otherwise anchor it firmly.

## Training

When your vine doesn't begin on its own to twine or cling to the support you have provided, tie it to the trellis or fence until it gets well started. Plant twist ties (available from garden supply catalogs in many lengths or in rolls that you can cut into the lengths you prefer), green yarn, brown string, or even torn strips of old sheets or nylons can help vines get started on a trellis before they begin to cling naturally.

Watch to see that a vine on a building is not growing under clapboards or into crevices where it could cause damage.

## AN EASY WAY TO GET A NEW VINE: LAYERING

Bend a portion of the vine down to the ground and cover it with soil. Keep it watered, and when it forms roots, cut it from the mother plant and transplant it.

*Climbing hydrangea* (Hydrangea anomala *subsp.* petiolaris) *is a handsome and reliably hardy vine with large white flowers in summer and an interesting light-brown, peeling bark even in winter when the vines are bare.*

# RECOMMENDED VINES

| NAME | BEST FEATURE |
|---|---|
| AKEBIA (FIVE-LEAF), CHOCOLATE VINE (*Akebia quinata*) | Purple flowers early, followed by edible, elongated purple fruits |
| BITTERSWEET (*Celastrus scandens*) | Heavy crop of red berries with a yellow husk |
| BOSTON IVY (*Parthenocissus tricuspidata*) | Scarlet autumn color |
| BOWER VINE (*Actinidia arguta*) | Large, heart-shaped, slightly variegated leaves, and fragrant white flowers |
| CHINA FLEECE VINE, SILVERLACE VINE (*Polygonum aubertii*) | White to greenish white flowers in late summer when few other woody plants bloom |
| CLEMATIS (*Clematis*) | Large range of sizes bloom in a variety of colors |
| CLIMBING HYDRANGEA (*Hydrangea anomala* subsp. *petiolaris*) | Small, white fertile flowers and larger sterile ones in large clusters |
| CROSS VINE (*Bignonia capreolata*) | Orange red flowers in spring; reddish green autumn color` |
| DUTCHMAN'S PIPE (*Aristolochia durior*) | Large, glossy green leaves; interesting pipe-shaped flowers |
| ENGLISH IVY (*Hedera helix*) | Evergreen foliage; small, inconspicuous flowers and black berries |
| EUONYMUS (*Euonymus fortunei*) | Shiny evergreen leaves |
| GRAPE (*Vitis*) | Both ornamental and edible |
| HONEYSUCKLE (*Lonicera japonica*) | Many honeysuckle species and cultivars with a wide variety of bloom colors; some have a heady fragrance |

| GROWTH | HARDINESS ZONES | CLIMBING METHOD | COMMENTS |
|---|---|---|---|
| Vigorous, reaching 40 feet (12 m) | 5 and warmer | Twining | Likes sun or light shade. Control by heavy pruning. Evergreen in the South, but leaves darken and hang on over the winter in the North, giving it the common name. Cut to the ground in late fall to control, and mow around it to suppress the suckers that grow from underground runners. |
| 25 feet (7.5 m) | 2–7 | Twining | Thrives in sun or light shade, and in most soils. Berries appear on the female plants, but both sexes are needed to ensure fruiting. |
| To 60 feet (18 m) | 4–11 | Holdfasts | Similar to English ivy but hardier and better for the North. Stands city conditions well. Several cultivars available with different leaf sizes and shapes. |
| To 30 feet (9 m) | 4–8 | Twining | A good choice for screens. Male and female blossoms are on separate plants. Closely related to the hardy kiwi fruit. Few pest problems. Cut back in the fall for heaviest blooming. Needs good soil and full sun. |
| 20 feet (6 m) or more | 5–8 | Twining | Grows well in sun or part shade, but likes rich soil. |
| To 12 feet (3.6 m) | 3–8 | Tendrils | Needs to have cool roots, shaded lower stems, and a soil with a pH of 6.5 or higher. The roots thrive under a cool mulch of lawn clippings or similar material. Most do best in a location where they do not get hot afternoon sun. |
| To 75 feet (22.5 m) | 5–8 | Holdfasts | Likes slightly acid soils rich in organic matter. Due to its heavy weight, it often needs some cutting back to keep it from pulling away from a building. |
| Can reach 50 feet (15 m) | 6 and warmer | Tendrils | Evergreen in South; semi-evergreen elsewhere; attractive leathery leaves. |
| To 30 feet (9 m) | 3–8 | Twining | Good choice for heavy summer shading over terraces and decks. Grows in sun or light shade, and in ordinary soil. Needs a strong trellis to support it. |
| To 90 feet (27 m) | 5 and warmer | Holdfasts | The vine most used for covering buildings. Likes sun and is also used as a ground cover. Many cultivars are available. |
| To 20 feet (6 m) | 6 and warmer | Holdfasts | Provides rich, green blanket for a building or a ground cover. |
| 20 feet (6 m) or more | Varies by cultivar | Tendrils | Cut back heavily for fruit. Otherwise, prune to keep under control and to remove old wood. |
| 15 feet (4.5 m) or more | *L.j.* 'Halliana', Hall's honeysuckle, Zone 5; species vary | Twining | Good for arbors, bowers, trellises, and pergolas, and as a colorful ground cover. The invasive *L. japonica* needs close control where it is hardy. |

| NAME | BEST FEATURE |
|---|---|
| MOONSEED *(Menispermum canadense)* | Dense, attractive, ivylike foliage |
| PORCELAIN BERRY *(Ampelopsis brevipedunculata)* | Yellow green berries that change to yellow, then to bright blue with a crackled look resembling porcelain |
| TRUMPET VINE *(Campsis radicans)* | Two-inch (5 cm), orange red, trumpet-shaped flowers in midsummer that last well into autumn |
| VIRGINIA CREEPER, WOODBINE *(Parthenocissus quinquefolia)* | Blue black berries, rich red fall color |
| WISTERIA *(Wisteria)* | Many species and cultivars for a wide selection of blooms in pink, violet, reddish violet, and white; some are fragrant |

# Vine Maintenance: Keep It Looking Good

After your vine reaches the size you want, cut it back regularly. Mow frequently around any vine that sends up suckers or drops seeds. Pruning in summer and early fall results in less vigorous regrowth than pruning when dormant. Regular pruning will prevent future problems and avoid heavy chopping or replacement.

## Pruning

By snipping away the new growth throughout the summer with clippers, you can train your vine to grow the way you want. Cut back the tops to encourage thick, lush side and bottom growth; prune the sides to encourage more upward development. Prune all vines in the spring to remove winter injury, and anytime to cut out dead or diseased portions. Do any heavy pruning to renew the vine when it is dormant, in spring or fall. In Zones 7 and warmer you can cut the entire vine nearly to the ground to renew it when necessary, but be more cautious in cooler climates and cut back only a portion to the ground each year until the entire vine is replaced.

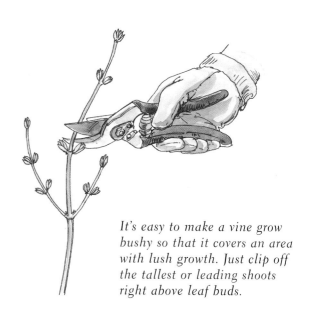

*It's easy to make a vine grow bushy so that it covers an area with lush growth. Just clip off the tallest or leading shoots right above leaf buds.*

| GROWTH | HARDINESS | CLIMBING METHOD | COMMENTS |
|---|---|---|---|
| To 12 feet (3.6 m) | 5–8 | Twining | Grows best in shade on poor, moist soil. Dies to the ground each winter in the North, but grows back rapidly. Can be invasive, spreading by underground rhizomes. |
| Grows rapidly to 20 feet (6 m) | 5–8 | Tendrils | Likes an eastern exposure that is free from afternoon sunlight. Needs little pruning, and some fertilizer in the spring. |
| To 40 feet (12 m) | 4 and warmer | Holdfasts | Does well in sun or light shade, and in well-drained soil with plenty of moisture. Cut back severely to control. |
| 20 feet (6 m) or more | 2 and warmer | Tendrils | This vigorous vine can cover just about anything in time, so choose its spot with care. |
| To 25 feet (7.5 m) | Most are hardy in, Zone 4 but bloom reliably only in warmer areas | Twining | Good on trellises, arbors, and pergolas, but the heavy vines need strong support. Prune out old and winter-injured vines in late winter to within bounds. Don't overfertilize. |

## Culture

If your vine is not growing well or leaves are pale green, apply an organic or synthetic balanced fertilizer, such as 5-10-10, in the spring or early summer. Start with a small amount, and add more if you don't get results. If growth is satisfactory, avoid fertilizing or mulching, because both are likely to encourage a rank growth that may be hard to manage.

## WEEDY VINES — BATTLE TACTICS

Even some of the recommended vines become overgrown in time. We know of a century-old grape vine that, by layering itself, now covers about an acre, and bittersweet can become just as rampant. Schedule hard annual cutbacks as part of your cultural program, keep weedy vines separated from less aggressive plants, and don't fertilize the lawn or other shrubs growing near them. Some plants, including the following, probably should not be planted at all except where their aggressive tendencies will never become a problem.

Dutchman's pipe
Boston ivy
Japanese honeysuckle
Kudzu
Moonseed
Virginia creeper (woodbine)

# chapter 6

# Good-Looking Shrubs and Hedges

The condition of the shrubs in your landscape depends a great deal on which kinds you have and how they age. The old-fashioned lilacs can survive without care for decades and still bloom prolifically. Other bushes, however, quickly and dramatically indicate when they haven't been pruned, fertilized adequately, or protected from insects, animals, diseases, and weeds.

A few shrubs (such as potentillas) produce blooms throughout the season, while others provide colorful fruits (viburnums, for instance) or blazing foliage (notably burning bush, *Euonymus alatus*) in the fall. But most, including lilacs, honeysuckles, mock oranges, and spireas, bloom for only a week or two, depending on the weather and temperature. Then they fade into the background and provide only greenery for the rest of the season. So no matter what kind of shrubs you have and why you want them in your landscape, it is important to keep their foliage healthy and attractive.

## Flowering Shrubs

If your flowering shrubs show signs of deterioration due to age or damage from lawn mowers, deer, insects, or disease, you may want to start over again with something new. Chances are good, however, that you can rejuvenate a neglected shrub with a little care. If you're a new homeowner, don't be impatient, because it may be worthwhile to live with an unfamiliar plant through one growing season before deciding whether to keep it.

Do not feed a shrub for at least a year after you have cut it back severely because it will then have more roots

than top, and fertilizer will force a fast spurt of limb regrowth. It is not desirable to stimulate too much soft new growth because it could either break off easily in the wind or become winterkilled. After the shrubs have recovered and are growing normally, feed them each spring unless growth is already satisfactory.

*Thoughtfully designed and well-cared-for foundation plantings can dramatically enhance the value of your property. Here, even with deciduous foliage gone, evergreens in gold and varying shades of green, from dark green to blue green to gray, provide year-round color.*

| PROBLEM | POSSIBLE CAUSE | SOLUTION | PAGE |
|---|---|---|---|
| WEAK, SPINDLY, UNHEALTHY GROWTH; PALE LEAVES; SPARSE BLOOMING | Malnourishment | Begin feeding a balanced fertilizer (5-10-10) at regular intervals (consult label; use more for mature plants). | 165 |
| SHRUBS THAT DON'T BLOOM | Wrong soil pH (too acid or too alkaline) | Take a soil test; adjust with amendments according to information that accompanies the results. | 166–67 |
| | Not enough sunlight | Prune back overhanging or encroaching vegetation, or transplant to a sunnier spot. | 88 |
| | Excessive seed production weakening the plant | Cut off faded flowers before they go to seed. | 87 |
| BADLY OVERGROWN | Years of neglect | Undertake a several-season renewal pruning program. | 87 |
| WEAK OR DEFORMED GROWTH, NIBBLED LEAVES | Pest problems (Japanese beetles and aphids are most common) | Get correct diagnosis before treating. A variety of tactics may be required, including spraying (either organic or chemical pesticides). | 110 |
| DAMAGED LEAVES | Leaf miners, blight, other pests or diseases | Get correct diagnosis before treating. A variety of tactics may be required, including spraying (either organic or synthetic pesticides). | 110 |
| SHRUBS NIBBLED ON OR DECIMATED | Deer or other animal pests | Identify culprit. A variety of tactics may be required, including spraying either organic or chemical repellents. In our experience, the only truly effective measure is erecting a fence. | 172 |

## Renewal Pruning

Neglected shrubs are likely to need considerable thinning and pruning back of their old wood to rejuvenate them. The best time to prune most shrubs is late fall or early spring when they are dormant. Exceptions are those that bloom in spring and early summer. Prune these immediately after blooming so they will have time to grow new flower buds for the following year's blossoms before winter. (See chart on pages 89–92 for requirements of individual shrubs.) It is difficult to know the best time to prune those shrubs that produce both ornamental fruits and flowers, such as the viburnums and amelanchiers, because you will always sacrifice some of either the blooms or the berries. With viburnums, cutting out some of the berries for decorations in late fall is as good a method as any of pruning them.

*Prune spring-blooming lilacs immediately after they bloom. This gives them time to grow new flower buds for the following year. When pruning, always use a sharp tool that is the right size for the job.*

*You can remove up to one-third of an overgrown plant's growth in a single season without damaging the plant.*

**Pruning young deciduous shrubs.** When deciduous shrubs are young they usually need only enough trimming to shape them and to make them grow bushy. If that has been neglected and they have become too large or lopsided, you can safely cut back the sides of most spreading shrubs if they are too wide, and shear off their tops if they are too tall.

**Pruning mature deciduous shrubs.** To keep a mature flowering shrub youthful, cut two or three of its oldest limbs to the ground when they are dormant each year. Younger limbs will quickly replace them. Most deciduous shrubs can tolerate a heavier cutting back than evergreens, but even so, do not remove more than one-third of the branch area in any one year. It may take several years of light, careful pruning after that initial cutting to return the shrub to a beautiful shape.

There are always exceptions to the rule. In frost-free or nearly frost-free areas, it is possible to cut back many shrubs almost to the ground. The result will be a new, youthful bush that will bloom well again. If your shrub seems hopelessly overgrown and you elect to replace it, a little pruning each year on the new one will prevent the need for heavy cutting in the future.

## IS IT ALIVE?

If you examine your grounds when the plants are dormant, many woody plants and trees may look dead to you. Whenever you are uncertain, bend a small twig. If it snaps back readily it is probably alive. If you still aren't sure, break off a twig. A green cambium layer under the bark is a good indication the bush will soon show signs of life.

## Root Pruning

If you want to move a large shrub that you are especially fond of, you may want to make the job easier and safer by delaying the operation for a year while you cut off the outside roots. Any time of the year, with a sharp spade and the additional aid of some sturdy, sharp loppers if necessary, slice all around the plant just outside the branch spread, or "drip line" as some call it. The shrub will then grow a compact set of new roots within the cut area and a year later will be easy to dig, and with its new root system, will almost certainly survive and grow in its new location. Root pruning is also a technique often used to keep a shrub small by constricting its root area.

*Root pruning a season prior to moving a plant makes the move much less work for you and much less traumatic for the plant. To root prune, use a sharp spade to slice into the soil all the way around the plant just outside its branch spread.*

# RECOMMENDED FLOWERING SHRUBS

| NAME | BEST FEATURE(S) | DIMENSIONS AT MATURITY | HARDINESS ZONES | WHEN TO PRUNE | COMMENTS |
|------|-----------------|------------------------|-----------------|---------------|----------|
| ALPINE CURRANT (*Ribes alpinum*) | Handsome red berries, beloved by birds, not people | 7' (2.1 m) tall, 4' (1.2 m) wide | 2–7 | In late fall, prune out old wood to renew. Let it grow naturally to get the most berries, or shear throughout the summer for a tighter form. | Excellent for hedges. |
| BARBERRY (*Berberis*) | Thorny hedge plant with either red or green leaves | 2–5' (0.6–1.5 m) tall and wide | 3–11 | Take out dead and old wood, and shape if you want a tightly clipped hedge. | Can spread and become sprawling if left unpruned. |
| BAYBERRY; SOUTHERN WAX MYRTLE (*Myrica pensylvanica*) | Fragrant semi-evergreen leaves | 2–9' (0.6–2.7 m) tall and 9' (2.7 m) wide | 5–7 | In early spring, prune mostly to neaten the bush and remove winter injury. | Because it has different sexes on different plants, at least one of each is necessary to get fruit. Grows well on poor soil. |
| BUCKTHORN (*Rhamnus*) | Stately, makes a fine specimen plant; an excellent choice for sheared or unsheared hedges | 10–15' (3–4.5 m) tall, 3–5' (0.9–1.5 m) wide | 3–7 | When dormant, prune mostly to shape. | The berries attract birds. |
| BURNING BUSH (*Euonymus alatus*) | Vivid pink red leaves in the fall | 4–20' (1.2–6 m) tall, 5–8' (2.4 m) wide | 4–8 | Prune tall-growing kinds heavily to shape and to renew the bush, in fall or early spring. | Dwarf varieties also available. |
| BUTTERFLY BUSH (*Buddleia davidii*) | Blooms of various colors attract butterflies; may die to ground in cold climates, but grows back and blooms same year | 5–10' (1.5–3 m) tall, 4–6' (1.2–1.8 m) wide | 5–9 | Take out old wood or any that has been injured by cold. | Many different cultivars available. |
| CHOKEBERRY (*Aronia arbutifolia*) | White flowers, followed by dark edible berries | 6–10' (1.8–3 m) tall, 3–5' (0.9–1.5 m) wide | 4–8 | Late fall, mostly to remove old wood and to keep within bounds. | Cultivars available with better fruiting habits than species. |
| COTONEASTER (*Cotoneaster*) | Red berries and attractive glossy small leaves; some have pretty white or red flowers in spring | Vary in size and form | 4–8 | Needs little pruning, except to shape, which can be done anytime. | Good bird attractors; tall cultivars can be espaliered. Spreading types are excellent on banks and in rock gardens. |
| DAPHNE (*Daphne*) | Early-blooming shrubs, with an abundance of pink flowers, many of which are fragrant | 3–5' (0.9–1.5 m) tall, 3–4' (0.9–1.2 m) wide | 4–9 | After blooming, mostly to shape. | A neat shrub that looks nice even when not in bloom. |
| DEUTZIA (*Deutzia*) | Low-growing shrub with white or pink flowers | 2–6' (0.6–1.8 m) tall, 3–5' (0.9–1.5 m) wide | 5–8 | After blooming but before the flowers are completely gone so new growth can get started quickly. Prune heavily if you want a bushy shrub. Remove all suckers as they form. | Many species and cultivars offer a variety of flowers and bush sizes. |

| NAME | BEST FEATURE(S) | DIMENSIONS AT MATURITY | HARDINESS ZONES | WHEN TO PRUNE | COMMENTS |
|---|---|---|---|---|---|
| FIRETHORN (*Pyracantha*) | Brightly colored orange berries | 6–12' (1.8–3.6 m) tall, 6–10' (1.8–3 m) wide | 5–9 | Prune sparingly to avoid injuring either the flower buds or forming berries. Late fall is the best time to cut out old wood and shape bush. | 'Kasan', with bright red fruit, is hardier than most other cultivars (Zone 5). |
| FLOWERING ALMOND, CHERRY, PLUM (*Prunus*) | Lovely spring-flowering shrubs | 3–20' (0.9–6 m) tall, 5–20 feet (1.5–6 m) wide (depending on variety) | 3–11 | Do any necessary light pruning just after they finish blooming, and any heavy cutting when they are dormant. | These ordinarily need little care. Susceptible to black knot disease. Cut out immediately, if visible. |
| TARTARIAN DOGWOOD (*Cornus alba*) | Beautiful white fruits in early summer | 4–10' (1.2–3 m) tall and wide, depending on cultivar | 3–7 | Prune in fall to shape and remove damaged wood | Many interesting cultivars; 'Elegantissima' has variegated green leaves with white margins. |
| FLOWERING QUINCE (*Chaenomeles*) | Orange red blooms for a long season in spring, followed by green fruits in late summer | 3–7' (0.9–2.1 m) tall, 3–6' (0.9–1.8 m) wide | 4–8 | After blooming, to shape; remove any twigs and limbs damaged by weather. | Green fruits used for preserves. |
| FORSYTHIA (*Forsythia*) | Bright yellow flowers arrive before the foliage; to many, the first true sign of spring | 3–10' (0.9–3 m) tall, 6–10' (1.8–3 m) wide | 4–8 | Immediately after the blooms fade so that new flower buds can form in time to bloom the following year. Prune to keep in shape and to remove old, broken branches. | Although the shrub is hardy, flower buds can be killed by low winter temperatures. |
| FRENCH HYDRANGEA (*Hydrangea macrophylla*) | Has pink blooms in neutral soil, blue in acidic soil | 3–6' (0.9–1.8 m) tall, 2–5' (0.6–1.5 m) wide | 6–11 | Prune to shape, and remove old damaged wood when dormant. | Less hardy than other hydrangeas; often grown as potted plant for Easter. |
| HEATHER (*Calluna vulgaris*) and HEATH (*Erica*) | Low-growing, colorful summer-blooming shrubs. Flowers range from white to pink and purple; foliage comes in many shades. | 6–24" tall (15–60 cm) | 4–7 | Early spring, to encourage bushiness; remove any damaged wood. | Short-lived, but good choice for banks, borders and for lining paths; prefers acidic soil and climates that are not too cold. |
| HIGHBUSH CRANBERRY and others (*Viburnum*) | Attractive blooms; red berries that often hang on the bush all winter | 2–12' (0.6–3.6 m) tall, 8–12' (2.4–3.6 m) wide | 2–8 | In late fall or early spring, sparingly, so you do not cut off the developing flower buds. Cut out some of the oldest wood from time to time to keep the plant youthful and vigorous. | The American species, *V. trilobum*, has edible, tart berries; those of the European (*V. opulus*) are more showy, but inedible. The snowball (*V. opulus sterile*) has attractive white blooms in large round clusters but no berries. |
| HILLS-OF-SNOW (*Hydrangea arborescens*) | Mounds of white blooms in midsummer | 3–5' (0.9–1.5 m) tall and wide | 3–9 | Prune after blooming to remove faded blooms and to shape. | Very adaptable to soils of different type and pH |

| NAME | BEST FEATURE(S) | DIMENSIONS AT MATURITY | HARDINESS ZONES | WHEN TO PRUNE | COMMENTS |
|---|---|---|---|---|---|
| HONEYSUCKLE (*Lonicera*) | Abundant flowers and berries that birds love | 3–10' (0.9–1.5 m) tall, 6–8' (1.8–2.4 m) wide | 4–8 | Immediately after the flowers have faded. Cut out old and damaged wood. Take off only as much as is necessary so you don't sacrifice colorful berries. You can prune plants as a tight hedge, but blooms and berries will be scarce. | Many cultivars offer a variety of flower and fruit colors. |
| HYPERICUM (*Hypericum*) | Flowers in various shades of yellow | 1–4' (0.3–1.2 m) tall, 3–4' (0.9–1.2 m) wide | 4–8 | Do any necessary pruning when the plant is dormant; usually necessary only to neaten the plant. | Nice compact shrubs for border or foundation planting. |
| LILAC (*Syringa*) | Beautiful fragrant flowers; very long-lived | 8–15' (2.4–4.5 m) tall, 6–8' (1.8–2.4 m) wide | 3–7 | Do light pruning after they flower. Remove faded blooms before seeds form to get full bloom each year. To renew old bushes, cut some of the largest stems to ground each year and thin out the young ones. | Few shrubs, other than roses, have parented so many cultivars. Lilacs do best in soil that isn't acidic. |
| MOCK ORANGE (*Philadelphus*) | Single or double white blooms, some of which are fragrant; a springtime favorite | 3–10' (0.9–3 m) tall and wide | 4–8 | Early spring, to remove old wood, winter injury, and to keep it from sprawling. | Blooms just after lilacs. |
| NINEBARK (*Physocarpus*) | White to bluish flowers in early summer | 8–35' (2.4–10.5 m) tall, 2–6' (0.6–1.8 m) wide | 2–7 | After blooming, to shape; or shear throughout the summer for a tight hedge. | Good accent plant. |
| PEEGEE, TREE HYDRANGEA (*Hydrangea paniculata* 'Grandiflora') | White flowers in autumn, turning pink and then bronze, clinging for months | To 12' (3.6 m) tall, to 8' (2.4 m) wide (both tall and dwarf forms available) | 3–8 | Prune in fall or early spring | Shrub often pruned into tree shape. Adaptable to urban environments; very hardy. |
| POTENTILLA (*Potentilla*) | Golden yellow or white blooms for most of the summer | 2–4' (0.6–1.2 m) tall, 3–5' (0.9–1.5 m) wide | 2–7 | Prune in the fall to remove old seed heads if you wish. To renew, every three or four years, in late fall cut shrub back to 1' (0.3 m) in height. It will grow into a new a bush and bloom the following year. | Plant stays compact and has almost no insect or disease problems. White, pink, and reddish blooming cultivars also available. |
| ROSE OF SHARON, SHRUB ALTHEA (*Hibiscus syriacus*) | Single or semidouble flowers in a variety of colors in late summer | 10–12' (3–3.6 m) tall, 4–6' (1.2–1.8 m) wide | 5–8 | In spring before growth starts. If unpruned, plant will be fine but flowers will be small. Early spring pruning promotes much larger flowers. | One of the last shrubs to leaf out in spring. Good late-flowering shrub. Grows well near the seashore. |

| NAME | BEST FEATURE(S) | DIMENSIONS AT MATURITY | HARDINESS ZONES | WHEN TO PRUNE | COMMENTS |
|---|---|---|---|---|---|
| SHADBUSH, SERVICEBERRY (Amelanchier) | Famed for its very early white spring blooms that appear before leaves are obvious and edible berries in early to midsummer that attract birds; certain species have bright yellow to red leaves in autumn | Depends on species; some grow to 40 feet (12 m) tall | 3–9 | Needs little pruning. | Few pest problems. |
| SMOKE TREE (Cotinus) | Plumy, foamy lavender or smoky pink flowers; green or purple leaves | 8–15' (2.4–4.5 m) tall, 8–10 feet (2.4–3 m) wide | 4–8 | When dormant, to keep it the size you want, and to eliminate old or injured branches. | Prune off faded flowers in midsummer. |
| SNOWBERRY, CORALBERRY, INDIAN CURRANT (Symphoricarpos) | Attractive berries; the white ones are unusual and attractive | 6–8' (1.8–2.4 m) tall and wide | 3–7 | Late winter to early spring. | All species provide good indoor winter bouquets. |
| SPIREA (Spiraea) | Some species have an abundance of small white flowers in early spring; others, pink flowers in summer | 2–8' (0.6–2.4 m) tall, 3–6' (0.9–2.7 m) wide | 4–8 | Trim off the dead flowers after they bloom, and do any necessary shaping at that time. | Many of the large number of species of this plant deserve a choice place in the landscape, including foundation plantings and as unsheared, natural hedges. |
| VERNAL WITCH HAZEL (Hamamelis vernalis) | Bright yellow fall foliage; tiny, very fragrant flowers that begin to open in late winter | 6–10' (1.8–3 m) tall, 6–8' (1.8–2.4 m) wide | 4–8 | Immediately after flowers fade, to control size and shape. | Not commonly planted, but always creates interest because of its early blooms. |
| WEIGELA (Weigela) | A neat, low-growing colorful plant with red or pink blooms in early summer | 3–7' (0.9–2.1 m) tall, 4–8' (1.2–2.4 m) wide | 5–8 | Prune after flowering, to shape the plant and to remove any broken or weather-damaged branches. | Good choice for an unsheared flowering hedge. |

# Foundation Shrubs

When we began to look carefully at the foundation plantings around homes in our part of the country, we found an astounding number of overgrown shrubs hiding windows, overhanging limbs narrowing the passage to front doorsteps, and tall evergreens leaning against walls and drooping over rooftops. Most of the homeowners were probably unaware of the encroachment of the landscape because it had happened so gradually. Healthy plants are not static. They keep growing and growing, and even compact evergreens and flowering shrubs can become untidy if they go without care for a few years.

**Problems caused by overcrowding.** Foundation plants outgrow the space allotted to them if they are not pruned and sheared. They may have been the wrong plants for the location originally, or possibly they were planted without consideration for their growth habits. They may have been set too close together when the plants were small in an effort to make the landscape look attractive immediately. Consequently, within a few years those plants became overcrowded, even if someone had been tending them regularly.

**Environmental problems.** Struggling plants around a foundation are another kind of problem. If fertilizing has been neglected, plants suffer, especially under eaves because the extra water from the roof washes nutrients from the soil at a fast rate. In cold climates, plants there are also more likely to encounter damage from heavy loads of snow or ice falling from the roof.

Originally, the reason for surrounding a house with plantings was to obscure an unsightly stone or concrete foundation. Although most new homes these days have more attractive bases, foundation plantings are still an important part of the home landscape and, ideally, connect the structure with the surrounding land. An attractive planting serves an aesthetic and decorative function similar to that of houseplants indoors — making a building more welcoming and friendly.

But foundation plants can struggle for other reasons. If they have become overgrown or disheveled and are in a weakened condition, they may be attacked by pests or diseases. Depending on their condition, you must either repair your planting or dig out all the plants and start over.

## Placement of Foundation Plants

Plants that are in good shape but in the wrong location should be moved. Foundation plants should never be located directly under the drip line of a building if there are no eave spouts. In cold climates, as we have mentioned, they should not be growing where heavy loads of snow or ice could fall on them. If a house has a low, wide roof overhang, plants beneath it will not get enough light to grow well or enough rain to keep them healthy (unless you water them regularly).

Be sure to leave enough space between your shrubs and your house. Plants too close to the foundation will become misshapen as they lean outward to get more light. Tall specimens growing against a building may also retain moisture there, causing wooden surfaces to rot.

*So that your foundation shrubs aren't damaged by heavy rains, ice, or snow, avoid placing them directly under eaves. In this planting, an interesting-looking rock is located to deflect run-off from where the two roof angles join, while it also provides continuity with the shrubs in either side.*

## Upgrading the Design

Even if your plantings are in good shape, you may be ready for a change. Many homes were originally landscaped in the style that was popular in the 1950s, the housing-development look. It usually consisted of a row of evergreens stretching across the front of the house; a pyramidal arborvitae or juniper on each corner, globe specimens flanking the front steps, and spreading dwarf yews or junipers beneath the windows.

The old rules can be helpful in planning a foundation planting even if you don't want to copy the older design of using all evergreens. Use tall plants at the corners of the building to frame it; small, spreading ones beneath the windows where they will not block the light; and slightly larger plants, depending on the height of the house, at each side of the doorway to invite guests to the entrance.

The wide variety of available plants gives you almost unlimited choices. Since most flowering plants are less expensive than evergreens, you can also change the design from time to time, if you desire.

Most of us don't want to entirely forego planting evergreens around our foundations. In much of North America, most deciduous plants are colorless and uninteresting during the winter months, but evergreens provide welcome color. Both coniferous evergreens (yews, arborvitaes, junipers, spruces, hemlocks, and firs) and broadleaf evergreens (boxwood, camellias, hollies, laurels, mountain laurels, and rhododendrons) brighten up a winter scene, especially in areas where there is no snow.

**Add edible plants.** Some people are now including food-producing plants in their landscaping. They use dwarf blueberries, currants, gooseberries, even vegetable plants and herbs instead of flowering shrubs for foundation plants. Sometimes they set dwarf fruit trees at the corners of a building.

**Add color.** More colorful and imaginative landscape designs often include flowering shrubs, perennials, annuals, and ground covers. Spring bulbs are also an important part of the scheme, because they are attractive and herald the beginning of spring. After they finish blooming, bedding annuals that flower all summer can take their place.

Perennials and annuals that are out of sight during the winter are good choices for spots where snow or ice might ruin evergreens or deciduous shrubs. We use a great many daylilies around our home and outbuildings in sunny spots, and grow hostas on the shady north-facing side. Other attractive shade-loving herbaceous plantings include ferns, lily-of-the-valley, astilbe, and monkshood.

**Add a variety of shrubs.** If you prefer shrubbery, low-growing plants such as potentilla, dwarf viburnum, bayberry, and weigela are good choices for sunny areas, and dwarf hemlocks and dwarf peegee hydrangeas thrive in light shade.

## Pruning and Shearing

Wherever necessary, use your pruning shears. If the evergreens and flowering shrubs surrounding your foundation are dwarfs, they probably have not grown too large or unshapely, and you should be able to cut them back enough to restore them to good form. If they are full-size species and have never been pruned or sheared, however, it may be difficult to salvage them.

Begin by cutting back branches that are too long, those that overhang steps and pathways, and those that rub against the house or another plant. At the same time, trim any branches that are broken or damaged by disease, insects, or weather.

With hedge shears, give your evergreens a haircut. Cut off the soft new growth when the plants are growing in early spring. Shear your deciduous plants throughout the summer to keep them in shape.

### WHEN AND HOW MUCH TO PRUNE

**When.** Prune off live woody branches only when the plants are dormant in fall or early spring so they won't bleed badly.

**How much.** The generally accepted rule is that you can remove up to a third of the plant in one year without harming it, although in some cases it is safe to take off more if it doesn't disfigure the plant too badly.

## Removing an Old Planting Entirely

If you decide to remove a shrub that appears to be past reviving, you can do it anytime, either by cutting it to the ground, or by digging or pulling it out. The latter options are best choices if you decide to plant another shrub in its place. When you take out part of an old overgrown planting, the plants that remain will look better and be more healthy since there is space for air to flow among them. More light will enter your home too, and you will no longer need to fear damage from every windstorm.

First check to see what is salvageable. There are advantages to saving any plants that still look good. You are sure they are likely to grow well there, and they won't have the acclimation shock that new ones might. Any shrubs that aren't suitable where they are now located may be perfect for another part of your yard. If you move such shrubs, early spring is the best time.

A professional arborist can cut and shred large plants into a pile of organic mulch in a short time; but most foundation plants are likely to be small enough for you to cut them with a saw. Cut each tree as close to the ground as possible; if it isn't too large, you may be able to dig out the roots. Faced with a whopper, however, you'll probably need to hire professionals who also have the equipment to grind up the roots in the ground.

It is possible, though not advisable, to plant small shrubs or perennials among any roots still remaining, as long as there is enough good soil to support the roots of the new plants. If you do this, provide additional nutrients on an ongoing basis to nourish the new plants, since decaying roots absorb a great deal of nitrogen.

Even if you can get out most of the roots, the soil in the area is likely to be depleted from years of use, so it is important to add new topsoil and fertilizer before setting in new plants. Either an organic or a slow-release synthetic fertilizer will provide nutrients continually and avoid burning the roots.

When you are grading the new soil, slope it away from the foundation, so that moisture will not flow toward the building and damage the foundation.

If you have decided to do your own landscaping, consider doing the job in stages by adding only a few new plants each year. This will give you a chance to shuffle them around to see how they look best. Whether you begin anew or remodel, as always when landscaping, start by drawing a plan. It is far cheaper and less labor-intensive to make mistakes on paper than in the ground.

## HOW DO YOU DECIDE?
## A CHECKLIST

Deteriorated foundation plants should be removed when they are:

❏ Crowding other plants
❏ Covering windows
❏ Threatening rooftops
❏ Grossly overgrown

## CHOOSING THE RIGHT SITE

When you start a foundation planting from scratch, you have a sterling opportunity to avoid mistakes that lead to later trouble.

**Give plants enough space.** Set the plant far enough from the foundation so it will not be under the drip line if there is one, and be sure it is not so far back under a low, wide overhang that it will suffer from lack of sunlight and rain. Allow space enough away from the house too, so the plant will have plenty of room to grow. Concrete foundations attract heat, so keep plants a short distance from these as well, and, as always when working near a foundation, slope the soil away from it.

**Avoid utility lines.** Be extremely careful when digging near buildings because electric and telephone wires, as well as gas and plastic water pipes, are often buried close to the surface. Hitting one can obviously be dangerous as well as inconvenient, so try to find where all utility lines are located and work around them. (Most utility companies will be glad to pay a free house call to help you determine the areas to avoid.)

## Starting Over

An overgrown or sickly foundation planting may necessitate a remodeling, but even when a planting is not in critical condition, you may enjoy a change. By removing the existing planting and starting afresh, you can select the plants you like and not be stuck with someone else's choices or an unfortunate choice of your own in years past. Starting over also enables you to train and shape small plants the way you want them to grow.

To transform your exterior decor, you can either buy new plants or transplant small specimens from elsewhere, preferably in the early spring. Always take into account the ultimate size of the plant and don't try to make a planting look complete the day it goes in the ground.

The shrubs listed on page 97 are ideal for planting around buildings. Please check these charts for more information on the characteristics of individual shrubs.

## Planting a Shrub

**Step 1.** Dig a hole at least 12 inches (30 cm) wider and a few inches deeper than the rootball of the shrub so there will be loose soil all around it (this enables new roots to grow easily). Mix in a pint or more of dried manure, depending on the plant's size, plus (.5 L) a quart or two (1 to 2 L) of compost or peat moss. Put discarded subsoil in your compost pile. If you are setting a new plant, remove the plastic wrap or burlap from the rootball before planting.

Step 1

**Step 2.** Add a layer of enriched soil to the base. Then pour a pail or more of water containing some liquid fertilizer into the hole and carefully set in the plant so the rootball stays intact. Set it at about the same depth it grew originally, or slightly lower. Pack the enriched soil mixture around the rootball, letting it soak up the water so no air pockets will be left, which could dry out the roots.

Step 2

**Step 3.** You may want to lay landscape fabric around the plant to suppress the growth of grass and weeds. Over it, add a 2-inch (5 cm) mulch of organic material such as wood chips or shredded bark. This will protect the roots and help keep them from drying out rapidly. A visible mulch also helps to keep the lawn mower away from the trunk and protects the landscape fabric from deterioration by sun and weather. Leave a slight depression around each plant to catch future waterings and rainfall.

Step 3

### CARING FOR A NEWLY PLANTED SHRUB

Unless it rains hard, water new foundation plants thoroughly every two or three days. Mix liquid fertilizer with the water (follow the directions on the package) once a week for two or three weeks. This treatment helps plants recover from moving shock and encourages new growth.

## Protecting Foundation Plants When Painting or Remodeling

All your plants, particularly those around a foundation, are vulnerable and need protection when you or others are working around your home — painting, digging up plumbing, installing a new lawn, deck, or terrace, repairing windows or a roof. Any work involving ladders, heavy equipment, or vehicles can be hazardous to the shrubbery. Before painting or

### Deciduous

**Cotoneaster.** Attractive berry-producing plant that can be kept compact by shearing.

**Daphne.** Good, low grower that needs little pruning.

**Firethorn.** Nice red orange berries are an added bonus. Shears nicely.

**Flowering quince.** Good flowering plant, but needs heavy shearing to shape.

**Hydrangea.** Many different kinds are good for flowering hedges. Prune to shape in spring or fall.

**Potentilla.** Good, easy-care shrub that blooms for many weeks. Prune heavily every four or five years to renew bush.

**Rose.** Many species and cultivars give wide choices for flowering foundation plants. Prune in fall or early spring to renew and shape.

**Spirea.** Good flowering shrubs. Many species from dwarf to tall, compact to spreading. Prune after blooming.

**Weigela.** Nice summer-blooming hedge. Cultivars grow from 3 to 6 feet (0.9 to 1.8 m) in height. Prune after flowering.

### Evergreen

**Arborvitae, Eastern white cedar.** Conifer with leafy foliage instead of needles. Many cultivars of various shapes and heights.

**Hemlock.** One of the best ornamentals because its fine-textured, needle foliage is attractive and easy to shape. Cultivars in different heights.

**Holly.** Popular broadleaf. Choose from many species and cultivars, and be sure to get at least one male and one female plant if you want berries.

**Rhododendron, azalea.** Flowering broadleafs. Many species and cultivars. Vary greatly in size, hardiness, and bloom colors, so get help in choosing if you aren't familiar with them.

**Spruce.** One of the hardiest needled evergreens. Species grow very tall, so choose dwarf cultivars for foundation plants.

**Yew.** A beautiful needled evergreen for foundation planting. Buy both male and female plants if you want red berries. Many species are available, so choose the right one for your location and climate.

construction begins, cover valuable plants with tarps or plywood "tents" to avoid any destruction. You may even want to dig and heel in elsewhere any that are particularly delicate.

# Hedges

Hedges not only decorate your landscape, but they can be extremely functional, serving as windbreaks, screens, fences, barriers, or background for a garden. We love our backyard arborvitae hedge borders, but they need annual shearing.

A neglected hedge is likely to have become too tall and fat and perhaps developed openings where one tree or shrub died or became injured. The lower branches of some plants may have died because the top of the hedge became too wide and shaded them. Lawn mowers, dogs, children, or nibbling deer can change the shape of a hedge. Vines, weeds, or brush often sneak into its foliage and spoil its appearance.

When a hedge has become much taller and wider than you'd like, you must question whether it can stand a severe cutting back and still survive. Let common sense guide your decision. If your hedge has become 20 feet (6 m) tall, it is unlikely to survive if you try to cut it back to 6 feet (1.8 m). But if it is only 10 feet (3 m) tall and you'd prefer an 8-foot (2.4 m) size, you may be able to reduce the height that much when the plants are dormant, provided they are healthy. More than that might be risky, but if you'd like to take a chance, you may get lucky. Some folks do.

A hedge may be an eyesore for reasons other than being overgrown. If it is suffering from malnutrition, wrong pH, lack of moisture or sunlight, disease, insect attacks, or just old age, something besides cutting is necessary. Check out what might be wrong (see page 112 for evergreens, 87 for deciduous shrubs.)

## Repairing an Overgrown Hedge

Whenever it is difficult to decide whether to repair or replace a hedge that has grown out of bounds, it is usually better to replace it. But if you decide to repair the problem, use the directions that follow. The worst that can happen is that you may need to remove your mistake and start over.

**Pruning.** If you decide to do the surgery, you are sure to wonder how it will it look afterward. Deciduous plants in a hedge can survive a heavy pruning operation better than evergreens because the greenery of evergreens is concentrated on the outer ends of their branches. When you cut them back extensively, you are likely to expose unsightly bare limbs. Arborvitae recovers from severe pruning more readily than other evergreens, but there are limits as to how much you can cut them, too. If you have serious doubts, get professional advice.

Cut out injured branches on a deciduous hedge at any time, but remove aged wood only when plant is dormant.

Don't prune flowering hedges too tightly, or they are not likely to bloom well. Prune them immediately after

flowering so the buds for the next year's blooms have time to form. By doing it annually you don't need to remove much at any one time.

**Shearing.** The cutting off of the soft new growth of evergreen and deciduous plants, called shearing, is essential to the upkeep of a well-mannered hedge. Plan on shearing an evergreen hedge at least once every year when it is growing — that is, in the spring and summer months — unless it is a dwarf variety and you want an informal appearance. Shear a deciduous hedge as often as necessary to keep it in the shape you want.

You can tighten up a loose-growing hedge by shearing it heavily, and forcing growth inward, but this may take a few years. The tightest plants are created by annual shearing, beginning at a young age, which forces growth to become thicker.

For shearing short hedges, long-handled hedge shears work well, but for large ones, power clippers are faster and make it easier to do a neat, straight job. They are lightweight and easy to handle. One of the hazards of electric clippers is that it is very easy to cut off the cord, which results in lots of sparks, tripped circuit breakers, and a tedious repair job. (Just ask us!)

Some of our friends use gasoline-powered clippers to shear hedges far from power sources. They are better for extensive work than battery-powered ones, which need frequent recharging.

*If you want a deciduous hedge to grow thicker, cut it back nearly to the ground, provided it is not more than 4 feet (1.2 m) tall. Do this work only when the plants are dormant, ideally in early spring when they are naturally generating new growth.*

## Tips for Shearing Evergreens

- Shear most hedges when the plants are growing so the cut ends will heal over quickly. (A) Broadleaf evergreens, however, can be sheared in early winter, which will provide a supply of holly, boxwood, and similar clippings for gifts and holiday decorations.

- Always shear to keep the bottom slightly wider than the top so light will hit every part of the plant (B).

- If you live where heavy snow is likely, keep the hedge narrow and the tops rounded or pointed to prevent snow and ice from crushing the plants. Shovel off any heavy loads of snow to avoid limb breakage.

- If some unfamiliar insect or disease shows up, don't attack it with a powerful spray immediately. Get advice as to what is causing the damage and how to stop it. Much damage can be caused by overuse of strong pesticides.

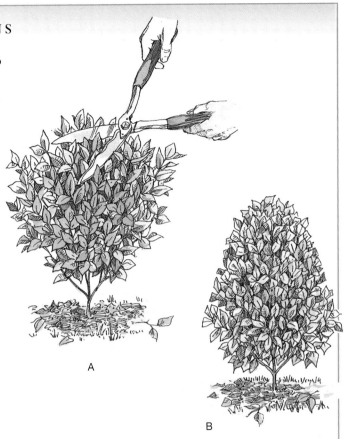

A

B

Whatever you choose, if you have more than a tiny hedge, don't buy cheap clippers, because you will never be happy with them. Also, be sure the ones you choose open wide enough for the foliage you plan to tackle. For boxwood and privet, the width of the opening is not important, but for arborvitae and most other evergreens it must be wide enough to make smooth cuts.

Clipping a tall hedge from a ladder can be dangerous, and depending on its height and your agility, it may be much wiser to hire a professional with the proper equipment, insurance, and expertise.

### Filling Gaps

Your hedge may consist of a row of coniferous evergreens such as yew, hemlock, or spruce; broadleafs such as holly or boxwood; flowering shrubs, including hydrangeas, lilacs, and roses; or deciduous and leafy specimens such as privet or ninebark. The fact that the plants are planted in a tight row makes any variance more obvious.

Consequently, when a sick, damaged, or dead plant is removed for any reason, the continuity is lost and attention is focused on the gaping hole, as if one front tooth were pulled out.

One of our neighbors encountered a hole in her beautifully sheared 6-foot (1.8 m) arborvitae hedge after her neighbor's horse decided to practice steeplechase there. She was about to remove the damaged tree and replace it, when someone advised her to feed the injured plant and wait. She did, and in three years the hole was completely closed again. Things don't always work out this happily, but nursing existing plants along is certainly a method worth following if the damaged ones aren't completely ruined. Finding a suitable replacement for a hedge tree can be difficult.

Even when a hedge plant dies, sometimes the adjoining plants can be encouraged to fill in the space, if it isn't too wide, by giving them extra fertilizer. You may also be able to shift a full-size plant from the least conspicuous end of the hedge as a replacement.

Good-Looking Shrubs and Hedges **99**

# RECOMMENDED PLANTS FOR HEDGES

## Evergreens (Conifers)

If you want a tall-growing evergreen hedge or screen, avoid pines and firs, as they tend to lose their lower branches as they get taller. Arborvitae, false cypress, hemlock, spruce, and yews are better choices.

Many of the evergreens listed below come in various species and cultivars that mature into different sizes and shapes. Choose dwarf cultivars for low-growing hedges that need a minimum of shearing. Choose native species, instead of the narrow or dwarf cultivars, if you want a full, tall hedge. Shear when the plant is growing for best appearance.

**Arborvitae (*Thuja*).** A good hedge for Zones 3 to 6 and ideal for alkaline soils. Easily sheared to any width and height.

**Cypress (*Cupressus*).** For warm zones (mostly Zones 7 and warmer), this is a fine hedge and easy to shape. Italian cypress (*C. sempervirens* 'Stricta') is excellent for a narrow hedge.

**False cypress (*Chamaecyparis*).** Hardier than true cypress (to Zone 4). *C. lawsoniana* has many varieties, some with feathery blue foliage and some with silvery white foliage.

**Hemlock (*Tsuga*).** Outstanding evergreen that is easily sheared to any height. Dwarf types especially good for low hedges.

**Juniper (*Juniperus*).** Junipers are not as popular as they once were because they have many pest problems. Choose upright kinds for hedges, and since hardiness varies, choose those that are right for your climate.

**Pine (*Pinus*).** The foliage of most pines is coarse and difficult to keep sheared to an attractive shape. Choose dwarf cultivars of the various pine species for a hedge.

**Spruce (*Picea*).** Extremely hardy choice for cold climates. Dwarf types make good low, tight hedges.

**Yew (*Taxus*).** Yews have long been the aristocrats of the garden and make beautiful hedges that can be sheared to any height. In addition to the popular Japanese yews, other upright types are also popular, including 'Hicksii' and 'Hatfieldii', which are hardy to Zone 4.

Spreading yews make good low hedges, including *T. baccata,* the English Yew, hardy to Zones 5 to 7, and *T. canadensis,* Canadian yew (hardy to Zones 3 to 6; grows well in both sun and shade, but the color is best in shade).

## Broadleaf Evergreens

Like other evergreens, species and cultivars vary in hardiness and ultimate size, and all need a soil pH of from 5 to 5.5.

**Boxwood (*Buxus*).** Makes one of the best tightly sheared, formal, evergreen hedges.

**English laurel (*Prunus laurocerasus*).** Very popular hedge west of the Rockies; attractive shiny foliage. Needs frequent clipping.

**Holly (*Ilex*).** Makes a spectacular hedge. Species and cultivars vary greatly in leaf shape, berries, and size. Choose both male and female plants to have fruits, and shear only lightly to get the heaviest crop of berries. Need a soil with a pH of about 5 to grow well.

**Rhododendron, azalea (*Rhododendron*).** Some azaleas and rhododendrons are deciduous, some evergreen. Some evergreen species are deciduous in the North.

## Flowering Hedge Plants

**Barberry (*Berberis*).** Deciduous thorny shrub producing red berries. Prune to keep it from becoming rangy and unattractive.

**Pacific wax mrytle (*Myrica californica*).** Fragrant deciduous shrub. For berries, choose both male and female plants.

**Cotoneaster (*Cotoneaster*).** Nice flowers followed by colorful fruits. Good for sheared or unsheared hedges.

**Forsythia (*Forsythia*).** Forsythia is hardy to Zone 3, but the flower buds are easily injured by cold winter temperatures, sometimes even in Zone 5. Choose the dwarf kinds for a lower hedge, and shear lightly after blooming.

**Hibiscus, Shrub althea (*Hibiscus syriacus*).** Not often used as a hedge, but since it has an upright growth habit of from 8 to 12 feet (2.4 to 3.6 m), it can make a tall screen in Zones 5 and warmer. Prune in late fall or early spring, since the flowers appear on new growth. It will bloom even if kept short.

**Honeysuckle (Lonicera).** The tall species of honeysuckle make good tall hedges or screens; the more dwarf kinds are good for shorter ones. All shear well, and the berries attract birds.

**Lavender (Lavandula).** Semi-evergreen shrub. Growing to 3 feet (0.9 m), lavender makes a nice, aromatic hedge. Spreads a bit over a foot (30 cm), and is hardy in Zone 5 or, with protection, even in Zone 3.

**Mock orange (Philadelphus).** Several species and cultivars of this popular fragrant shrub are available. White flowers in late spring, most of which are fragrant. Heights of the various cultivars range from 3 to 8 feet (0.9 to 2.4 m).

**Privet, California (Ligustrum ovalifolium).** Grows to 12 feet (3.6 m). Once a popular hedge plant, it is still grown somewhat because it shears well, although frequent clipping is necessary to keep it tight. Other species are hardier, and some grow to shorter heights.

**Rose (Rosa).** Roses are best in unsheared or lightly sheared hedges so their blooms will not be affected. Shrub roses are best for the colder zones, and the teas and other garden types are ideal in Zones 5 and up. Most need spraying to control pests, and pruning to keep at a uniform height.

**Viburnum (Viburnum).** V. trilobum, the American highbush cranberry, and V. opulus, European cranberry, are good choices for tall, berry-producing hedges or screens. The more dwarf cultivars are better for shorter ones.

**Willow (Salix).** The willows shear nicely, but choose the dwarf species to make the job easier. Heights vary, so consult a catalog or your garden center to find the kinds that are best for you. Their catkins are good harbingers of spring. Arctic willow, with its fine, bluish leaves, is a good choice for hedges.

## Eradicating an Unwanted Hedge

From a practical point of view, it is better to replace a hedge if it has become extremely overgrown. One way to remove the plants is to cut the tops back partially and pull out the remains with a chain attached to a tractor or truck. Such an operation is likely to mess up the lawn, but by removing the roots, it will be considerably easier to replant in the same location.

On the other hand, if you do not plan to plant anew in that location and a mass of roots in the soil won't be a problem, get out the chainsaw and cut off the tops at ground level, or hire someone to do the job. Cover the remaining stems with topsoil and plant grass seed there. Keep after any sprouts that manage to poke up and eventually the spot will no longer be obvious.

## Installing a New Hedge

Before you set out a new hedge, look around at others, or visit nurseries to see samples of mature shrubs. Your choices are almost unlimited, because if you are willing to shear heavily, you can create a hedge of just about any plant material. You might choose needled or broadleaf evergreens, flowering plants such as shrub roses, or deciduous leafy forms such as privet.

### Site Selection and Preparation

Most plants that are suitable for hedges need a well-drained, moderately fertile soil, and do best in full sun. Hemlocks grow well in light shade, however.

After buying the plants, don't cut the planting job short, because you won't want to replace any part of it later. Usually it is easier to dig a long trench rather than individual holes for each plant, especially if you want a straight hedge. For a long hedge, a backhoe will save many hours of hard work.

For a low, tight hedge, choose dwarf plants, and set them 2 feet (60 cm) apart on their centers. Space taller, more spreading plants 3 to 5 feet (0.9 to 1.5 m) apart. For a tall hedge or screen,

*Arborvitae makes a handsome, dense hedge that's easy to shear at any height. We created this living arborvitae arch by tying together the top branches of two adjacent plants to encourage growth across the top. We shear it regularly to maintain the archway. If you decide to do this, be sure that the foundation plants are spaced wide enough to keep an opening for clear passage.*

determine the planting distance by how quickly you want the hedge to "close up." (See listing of evergreen shrubs in chapter 8, page 123, and deciduous shrubs in this chapter for characteristics of the individual plants.)

Spring is usually the best time to plant, but balled or potted material can ordinarily be safely installed anytime the ground isn't frozen. Follow the usual planting rules for the type of plant you are using. Mix peat, compost, and fertilizer with the soil.

### Ongoing care

Be generous with water at planting time and every three days for at least two weeks. Add liquid fertilizer to the water once each week, following the directions on the package.

## FEEDING HEDGES

Overfertilizing your hedge, especially a deciduous one, can result in having to shear it more often. When the plants are small you may want to feed them frequently to hasten growth, but once they are growing well, feed them only once a year in the spring, with a complete organic or chemical fertilizer with a formula of about 5-10-10. Give them extra nutrients only if the color and growth are poor. If a soil test indicates a lack of lime, apply the amount necessary to correct the pH.

# 7 Revitalizing Roses

When it comes to flowers, there is nothing like a rose . . . nothing in this world. Whether it is a solitary, elegant, long-stemmed hybrid tea, a rambler cascading over a garden fence, or a nosegay of fragrant old-fashioned shrub blooms, the rose is irresistible. For centuries horticulturists have worked with wild roses and successfully transformed them into thousands of gorgeous cultivars, some of which are ideal in practically every climate.

You may have found some long-neglected roses on your property. Whether it's a single bush or an entire garden, untended roses are probably in desperate need of attention. Shrub roses, especially, are likely to be overgrown and require heavy pruning. Other types may need only minor pruning and nourishment, but they could have more serious problems if they are infected by diseases or insects. Grafted tops may have died and wild roots sprouted and taken over. They may have stopped blooming entirely, a victim of increasing shade from growing trees. Or crowded by weeds, they may be starving for space and nourishment. Although tough types, such as certain shrub roses, are competitive and can survive some encroachment by other plants, more

refined roses will need a rescue operation whenever shrubs or weeds are threatening them.

Before you take corrective actions, know the rose types you have (see page 106). If you need help with identification, visit a nursery or public garden where rose displays are labeled.

*Few plants are more satisfying to restore to their glorious promise than roses. Even long-neglected roses can be brought around with proper pruning and fertilizing. This 'Queen Elizabeth' rose combines beauty with a hardy nature.*

## AN INVALUABLE RESOURCE

Sometimes you simply need advice from a more seasoned gardener. The American Rose Society (ARS) has a national network of "consulting rosarians" who can help you with everything from choosing a trouble-free rose for your area to identifying and combating a pest or disease. For this free service contact the ARS national headquarters (see Sources for address).

| PROBLEM | POSSIBLE CAUSE | SOLUTION | PAGE |
|---|---|---|---|
| VERY OVERGROWN ROSES THAT HAVE SMALL, WHITE FLOWERS | In Zones 3 or 4, probably a wild multiflora rose rootstock that has remained after less hardy grafted-on rose expired | Wild multiflora rose is not worth saving; cut the bushes down and dig out the roots. | |
| VERY OVERGROWN ROSES OF UNKNOWN QUALITY (VARIOUS TYPES OF FLOWERS) | Neglect (in Zone 5 or a warmer climate, both the desirable rose and its rootstock out of control) | Undertake renewal, if you have a good one, it will be worthwhile. | 104 |
| SPINDLY GROWTH AND FEW OR WEAK BLOOMS EVEN AFTER RENEWAL EFFORTS | Old age. Modern hybrid tea roses have a shorter life span than species roses and their hybrids. | Take them out and replace them with new plants. | 108–9 |
| FEW BLOOMS, LACKLUSTER APPEARANCE | Not enough sunlight | Nearby plants may have grown up around the rose and shaded it. Either cut back surrounding vegetation or move the rose to a sunnier location. Early spring, as it is emerging from dormancy, is the best time. | |

# Renewing an Old Rose Garden

No matter what types of roses you have, cleaning them out and pruning back the plants should be the first order of business. You can begin the cleaning at any time of year by removing grass and weeds and any wild bushes that have invaded the rose's territory. Reserve any heavy cutting of live rose wood, for when plants are dormant. In most planting zones, late winter or early spring is the best time to prune because you can snip off any winter damage at the same time.

Cut off all branches that look sick or were injured, and thin out any growing too close together. By keeping branches a few inches apart, you will get larger blooms and the air will be able to circulate freely throughout the plant, which helps to prevent disease. When you are finished, burn all pruning debris or otherwise dispose of it, so no pests can lurk there to reinfect the plants.

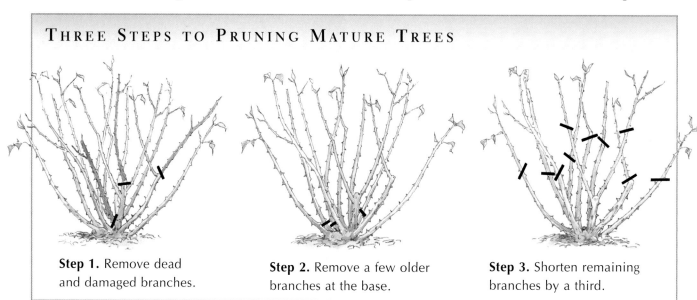

## THREE STEPS TO PRUNING MATURE TREES

**Step 1.** Remove dead and damaged branches.

**Step 2.** Remove a few older branches at the base.

**Step 3.** Shorten remaining branches by a third.

## Heirloom Roses vs. Modern Roses

The debate over the merits of modern versus heirloom roses rages on in the gardening magazines, at rose shows, and among rose experts. It's true that many of the old-fashioned roses are breathtakingly beautiful and sport heady fragrances, but many also bloom only once a summer. Also, their growth habit, left to its own devices, can result in a rambling, ungainly plant, fine for a lush, informal garden, but maybe not what you had in mind for your formal rose display. Modern roses, on the other hand, may repeat-bloom wonderfully but lack strong fragrance and need spraying to ward off pests and diseases. If you want the best of both worlds — beautiful form and intense fragrance plus modern repeat-blooming — consider the rising stars of the rose world, the so-called English roses, bred by crossing the old and the new.

### GLOSSARY OF ROSE TERMS

**Basal cane.** A stem that arises from the plant's crown or, in a grafted plant, from above the bud union.

**Bud union.** The point (usually swollen) where a graft meets its understock.

**Deadheading.** The practice of removing spent blooms, prompting the rose to produce more flowers instead of ceasing to bloom and forming hips.

**Double.** A bloom with many petals, generally between 24 and 50.

**High-centered.** Often used to describe hybrid tea blossoms; the middle petals are longest.

**Hip.** The fruit of the rose plant, usually red or orange, that follows the bloom; contains seeds (but unless the plant is a species rose, they will not produce a similar plant when germinated).

**Single.** A bloom with few petals, generally between 5 and 10.

**Sucker.** A stem arising from below the graft (it will resemble the understock variety and should be pruned off).

**Very double.** The term for rose blossoms that have more than 50 petals.

### BATTLE GEAR

- **Hand pruners or long-handled loppers.** These are the best tools to use on your roses.

- **Heavy leather gloves with long cuffs.** Even a single thorn in the flesh is no fun, and you are likely to promptly get several punctures without proper coverage.

- **Protective clothing.** A heavy jacket and long pants aren't usually necessary when working with roses unless you are working with tall shrub types, but you may want to avoid shorts.

*Disease resistance and large, profuse blooms make 'City of York' a favorite choice when you need a climbing rose.*

# CLASSES OF ROSES

The following are abbreviated descriptions of rose classes about which entire books are written.
Rose nomenclature is complex, even for experts, so we suggest that you consult a book on roses for more detailed information.

| TYPE | DEFINED | SPECIAL CARE | CULTIVARS |
|---|---|---|---|
| CLIMBERS AND RAMBLERS | Long, sometimes pliable canes, suitable for training to grow up and over a support, for example, a trellis or pillar | Need attention to train as desired (tying, pruning); many are not winter-hardy in very cold regions | Bright pink 'American Pillar', white 'Climbing Iceberg' |
| FLORIBUNDA | Low-growing bush roses, often with hybrid tea–quality blooms; blooms in clusters | Ordinary maintenance; dead-heading prolongs blooming | Purple 'Angel Face'; Simplicity series: red, white, pink, yellow, purple |
| GRANDIFLORA | Similar to floribunda, but flowers in clusters spring open all at once | Ordinary maintenance; dead-heading prolongs blooming | Tall pink 'Queen Elizabeth', yellow 'Gold Medal' |
| GROUND COVER | Low-growing, spreading bushes, generally no more than 2 feet (60 cm) high | Keep after weeds so they don't mar the display | Flower Carpet series: red, pink, white; pink 'Max Graf' |
| HYBRID TEA | Bush roses with long stems and refined-looking blossoms | Need annual pruning and fertilizing to look their best; in cold climates, many benefit from winter protection | Multicolored 'Peace', red 'Ingrid Bergman' |
| MINIATURE | Small in every way: stature, leaves, buds, and blooms | In cold climates, need winter-protection; some are vulnerable to insect pests | White 'Popcorn', apricot 'Jean Kenneally' |
| OLD GARDEN | The oldest roses still in cultivation today, including many old European varieties; many bloom only once each season; some have rough-looking foliage and informal profiles | Cut out old, damaged, and winter-injured wood at any time. Cut back tall-growing types to from 1 to 2 feet (0.3 to 0.6 m) in the fall for better shape and bloom the following year. | Creamy 'Sombreuil' (climbing tea), peppermint-striped 'Rosa Mundi' (Gallica) |
| SHRUB | Category includes many bushy roses, including old-fashioned polyanthas and modern "English roses" | Pruning necessary to keep in bounds; some are very thorny | Pink 'Carefree Wonder', yellow English 'Graham Thomas' |
| SPECIES | Old, unhybridized, naturally occurring roses; most are "single-flowered" (few petals, only five to ten) | If you don't prune, they eventually become unmanageable | Pink *Rosa eglanteria*, yellow *Rosa banksiae lutea* |
| TREE | These are usually familiar hybrid teas and floribundas that have been grafted atop a plain, stout stem, which in turn is grafted onto a rootstock (also called "standard" roses) | Need careful staking; not winter-hardy; grow well in pots | Many cultivars. Shop the rose nurseries, perhaps even arrange to have one custom-grafted for you if you cannot find what you want |

# Special Needs of Each Class of Rose

Because each class of rose has a different growth habit, each type of rose requires a different approach when you prune it.

## Hybrid Teas

These roses should bloom on stiff, erect stems rather than arch over toward the ground. Take off any horizontal branches and remove all the weak stems, which are unlikely to produce good blooms and steal energy from the stronger canes. Cut the remaining canes to 1½ to 2 feet (45 to 60 cm). This heavy pruning will encourage fewer blooms but they will be larger and more perfectly shaped.

In Zones 4 and colder, protect hybrid teas over the winter. The most reliable method is to cut them back to about 12 inches (30 cm) and mound soil over them, just as the ground begins to freeze in fall. Uncover as you do tree roses (see page 108).

## Floribundas and Grandifloras

These roses, all close relatives of the hybrid teas, should be pruned in the same way as hybrid teas.

## Climbers and Ramblers

Prune off any dead, damaged, or diseased branches, and thin out those that remain if they are weak or too thick. Cut away any suckers coming from below the bud graft. You can recognize the suckers because their leaves are noticeably different from those on the good part of the plant. Do not shorten the remaining canes any more than necessary because the flowers generally come on the previous season's growth. Clip as necessary throughout the summer to keep them within the bounds of the trellis or arbor where they are growing.

*When pruning climbers and ramblers, begin by removing canes that are crowding or crossing others.*

In cold climates, help them slow down for their winter rest by reducing water and withholding fertilizer. In the fall, take the canes off the trellis or arbor, and lay them down on the ground just before the ground begins to freeze lightly at night. Cover them with soil, evergreen boughs, or some other protective cover. Wait until all hard frosts are over in the spring before uncovering.

## Shrub Roses

Many shrub roses have tall, vigorous growth habits. If you want these types for a hedge or barrier, simply prune out the dead and injured branches and cut them back so they won't get too floppy.

Unless you want them to grow tall, late in the fall or early each spring cut them to 1 to 1½ feet (30 to 45 cm) from the ground. They will quickly grow back, but this drastic pruning keeps them low and bushy and prevents them from bending over under the weight of their numerous blooms. Thin out all weak, damaged, and aging branches at the same time.

Although shrub roses are not as susceptible to insects and diseases as are the more delicate hybrid teas, they too may be attacked by blights and insects and suffer from snow or ice breakage. They need very little fertilizer to keep them growing well and, if overfed, make rank growth at the expense of blooms. They appreciate mulch and the frequent removal of any weed competition.

## Tree Roses

Cut out any weak or damaged branches when the plant is dormant, prune it lightly to get it into a good tree shape, and insert a sturdy stake if there is none there. Snip off any sprouts coming from the trunk below the branched area, and keep them removed from the lower wild stem all season. Prune the top part, mostly to thin out branches that are old or too thick and to keep it in a good form.

In all but mild climates, bend the entire rose over and bury it in the ground for the winter. Dig it from its underground storage only after all danger of frost is over in the spring. Straighten it up carefully, restake it, and prune away any dead or winter-injured canes. Mix a tablespoon of rose plant food into the soil to help it recover from hibernation.

*Each spring when the tree rose is emerging from dormancy, clip off the top third of each branch.*

# Planting New Roses

If you need to replace roses, or want to add new ones to your garden, choose the kinds that will best fit into your landscape. Each hybrid tea, grandiflora, floribunda, tree, or climbing rose really consists of two plants — the part above ground that produces the gorgeous bloom and the part beneath, which is a vigorous rootstock. The top is attached to the root by a process called bud grafting. If you buy a bare-rooted rose you can see this fat graft between the roots and the stems of the plant. When planting in cold climates, set rose so graft is about an inch (2.5 cm) below ground level; those of roses planted in mild climates can remain at or slightly above the soil surface. Shrub roses are usually on their own roots.

## Choosing and Preparing a Site

Although wild roses and the more vigorous shrub roses are able to thrive under relatively poor growing conditions, most roses do best when planted in full sun and good, rich garden soil. Roses like a pH of from 5.5 to 6.5.

Spade the soil thoroughly for a single rose, or till the area for a rose garden before planting, to provide loose earth for the roots to grow easily. Mix compost and rose fertilizer into the soil.

### BARE-ROOT VS. CONTAINERIZED ROSES

**Mail-order bare-root roses** must be planted early in the spring. They need cutting back unless it has been done before shipping. Don't expect them to get off to as fast a start as potted roses.

**Containerized roses** are available at local stores. They will be leafed out and sport a few buds or flowers; examine the plant carefully for signs of insects or disease. When you get your rose home and out of the pot, if the roots seem rootbound from the confined life, knock off as much of the potting soil as possible without injuring the roots, and tease them apart.

# 3 STEPS TO PLANTING A BARE-ROOT ROSE

Most roses sold in nurseries and garden centers are growing in pots. Remove them from the pot with the ball of soil intact and plant them anytime the ground isn't frozen.

Roses bought by mail are usually bare-rooted, with their roots wrapped in sphagnum moss or other material. Plant barerooted roses early in spring before their growth has started.

**Step 1.** Dig a hole a bit larger than the rootball of the rose, and fill the hole with water to which you've added the recommended amount of liquid fertilizer (see package). Set the rose so the graft (the fat bud just above the roots) is just beneath the soil. If there is no visible graft, set it with the roots about 2 inches (5 cm) below the surface.

Step 1

**Step 2.** Pack the loose, enriched soil around the roots, and leave a depression to collect future waterings. Continue to water every few days for at least two weeks. Add liquid fertilizer to the water once a week for two or three weeks.

Step 2

**Step 3.** Spread shredded bark or other mulch material around the base of each rose after planting to protect soil from erosion and to retain moisture. Mulch will also keep the soil temperature more stable when air temperatures fluctuate. Renew it each spring.

Step 3

## Ongoing care

Feeble roses are more susceptible than healthy ones to insects and diseases, winter damage, and other problems, so coax your roses into the best of health by providing them with excellent soil, plenty of sunlight, and adequate moisture and nourishment.

If you conclude that they have been lacking nourishment, add rose fertilizer (available at most garden centers) or other complete fertilizer to the soil early each spring so the plant can begin to utilize it early in the growing season. Don't overfeed your roses, however. If they grow too fast, they are likely to be susceptible to insect and disease damage, and if they continue to grow too late in the season, they may get early frost injury. Renew the mulch over the roots each spring.

Rose care may seem like a formidable job, but it really isn't. If you are discouraged with the plants you have inherited, and restoring them to a worthwhile status seems daunting, you may want to start over with only a few plants and gradually get used to their culture. The rewards of even a small planting can be enormous.

# Rose Pest Control

After you have cleaned the area around your long-suffering roses and pruned them, inspect them for insects and diseases. A magnifying glass is a good investment for a serious rose grower; some insects are so tiny they are difficult to detect, though Japanese beetles are an obvious exception. The list of possible invaders is long. Aphids, Japanese beetles, leafhoppers, mites, thrips, rose chafers, sawflies, and slugs are common insect pests. Blackspot, mildew, canker, and rust are all diseases that are likely to discover your roses.

Most all-purpose rose sprays and dusts are effective in controlling these pests, and it is well to be prepared to take action at the first sign of trouble. Follow the directions on the package carefully. If pests are a serious problem in your area, you may want to consider mixing a rose systemic pesticide into the soil each spring. The plant absorbs the chemical, and then it is able to fight off many of the common pests all season.

Careful pruning, removal of diseased and dying canes, and keeping the area around the plants mulched and free of weeds are all practices that help to prevent rose troubles.

## COMMON ROSE PESTS

| PEST | DESCRIPTION | ORGANIC CONTROLS | SYNTHETIC CONTROLS |
|------|-------------|------------------|--------------------|
| APHIDS | Minute greenish, reddish, or brown insects that suck plant juices and coat unopened buds and leaves with honeydew, resulting in deformed flowers and foliage (sometimes accompanied by ants that eat the secretions) | Try dislodging them with a stiff spray from the hose. Import or encourage beneficial insects. | Spray with insecticide labeled for use on roses. |
| JAPANESE BEETLES | Hard-shelled, colorful beetles that chew on rose foliage | Pick them off by hand and drown or squash them. | Spray with insecticide labeled for use on roses. |
| SCALE | Small insects that tend to congregate on stems and suck plant juices, which stunts growth; may have waxy shells | Remove all affected plant parts and destroy. Release lacewings. | Spray with horticultural oil or other insecticide labeled for use on roses. |
| SPIDER MITES | Tiny red or yellow spiderlike creatures that scrape and suck on leaves, which subsequently lose color and drop | Try to dislodge them with a stiff spray from the hose. Release predatory mites. | Spray with insecticide/miticide labeled for use on roses. |

## COMMON ROSE DISEASES

| PEST | DESCRIPTION | ORGANIC CONTROLS | SYNTHETIC CONTROLS |
|------|-------------|------------------|--------------------|
| BLACKSPOT | Black circles on leaves, edges fringed; leaves eventually yellow and drop | Remove and destroy all affected plant parts. Water only at base of plant. Prune plant and surrounding plants to improve air circulation. | Spray with copper sulfate fungicide or neem. |
| POWDERY MILDEW | Powdery white substance coating leaves | Cut off and destroy all affected plant parts. Wash plant weekly with a jet from the hose. | Spray with Bordeaux mixture, neem, or sulfur. |
| RUST | Powdery orange spots and blotches on leaves, especially undersides | Cut off and destroy all affected leaves, including those that have fallen at the base of the plant. Water only at base of plant. Prune plant and surrounding plants to improve air circulation. | Spray dormant plant with lime-sulfur. Spray actively growing plant with neem. |

# 8 Evergreens for Year-Round Glory

It may seem like only yesterday when the arborvitae now towering above your rooftop was a small, tight, compact specimen, or you decorated the blue spruce in the front yard with only one set of Christmas lights instead of the five strands it now needs. Evergreens, particularly forest-type species trees, quickly grow upward and outward, and if unsheared and uncrowded, they become the large, beautiful specimens they were destined to be.

In spite of the speedy growth of these evergreens, they can be wonderful landscape trees when properly cared for. The dwarf cultivars are ideal in a home setting. They all provide stability of form and color throughout the changing seasons.

While deciduous trees and shrubs transform their colors and lose their foliage, the pines, firs, spruces, yews, hemlocks, arborvitae, and junipers remain green, as do the broadleaf evergreens — rhododendrons, hollies, and their ilk. The latter grow more slowly than the needled types, and many provide colorful blooms and berries.

*An evergreen planting not only provides a variety of shapes and sizes, from the traditional stately pyramidal types right down to creeping ground covers, but it also offers a wide range of colors and textures, from gold through many shades of green to blue.*

**111**

| PROBLEM | POSSIBLE CAUSE | SOLUTION | PAGE |
|---|---|---|---|
| LARGE BROWN AREAS HIGH IN THE TREE | Insect or disease trouble; heavy cone production | Use binoculars to get a better look. If cones are the cause, enjoy them. | 118 |
| DEAD LOWER BRANCHES | Lack of sunlight; part of the natural aging process (pines and firs especially) | There is no way to stimulate new branches to grow. Trim off dead lower branches and enjoy the tree's canopy of cool shade. | 116 |
| BROWN AND DEAD-LOOKING BRANCHES | Winter road salt damage (both that which seeps into the ground and spray that is kicked up onto the foliage by speeding cars) | Spray small specimens with Wilt Pruf (an organic liquid that seals needle pores against salt). Replace with more resistant evergreens (spruce, juniper, fir) or deciduous plants. | 171 |
| BROWNING NEEDLES | Windburn | Water well before ground freezes; mulch; protect plants with coverings such as burlap wraps and wooden lean-tos. | 171 |
| BREAKAGE OVER THE WINTER | Snow damage | Shear trees to narrow form, with pointed or rounded tops (avoid flat tops). Keep hedges narrow. | 99 |
| | Ice damage | Clean up what you can now; salvage what you can in spring. Prune to smooth up wounds and remove breakage. | 129 |
| ROOTS HEAVED OUT OF THE GROUND | Alternate freezing and thawing over winter | Apply mulch prior to winter. | 164 |
| YELLOW NEEDLES, WEAK GROWTH | Soil not acid enough | Most needled evergreens need acidic soil to stay healthy. If the soil around them tests above pH 6, use an acid fertilizer such as cottonseed meal or one recommended for broadleaf evergreens and blueberries. | 117 |
| YELLOW NEEDLES | Temporary discoloration due to older needles dropping off over a period of many weeks or months | Be patient; new needles will replace those that have fallen. | — |
| TWISTED GREEN SPROUTS | New sprouts are a sign that your evergreen is producing new growth. | Let them unfurl and grow naturally. | — |
| LARGE UNWANTED TREE | Years of unchecked growth and/or neglect | Unless you are a skilled woodsperson, hire professionals to cut and dispose of it. According to whatever agreement you make, they may either carry off the remains or chip it on the spot and leave you with a pile of organic mulch. Let it age for a few weeks before putting it around plants. | 130 |
| UNKEMPT OR OVERGROWN DWARF TREE | Neglect; improper or no pruning | In spring, begin a program of pruning and shearing. | 117 |

# Trees and Shrubs

If your evergreens are only moderately overgrown and are still healthy, you can probably operate on them successfully and get them back within bounds without killing or even disfiguring them. When they have been neglected for many years, however, it may be impossible to transform them into compact, attractive plants that are in proportion to your home and the rest of your landscape. If cut back heavily, they will appear truncated and misshapen — not a happy sight. Consider removing and replacing them with something more suitable (see page 119).

## Controlling Evergreens

You can usually cut back junipers, hemlocks, arborvitae, and yews, as well as dwarf cultivars of other tall-growing evergreens, to some degree without harming them (see page 114). If spruce, pine, fir, or other forest-type trees have been growing unrestrained for several years on your property, they have probably become large, beautiful sights to behold and need no cutting back, as long as they are in the right location. But if any of these vigorous plants has been growing alongside the foundation of your home, it probably has become a nuisance and an eyesore. Most trees growing in a foundation planting require regular shearing to keep them small.

## JUST WHAT IS AN EVERGREEN?

Many folks refer to all evergreens as pines, which, of course, they are not. The term *evergreen* is a conundrum. It usually refers to trees with needles but not always. Arborvitae have flat, leaflike foliage, for instance. Many evergreens bear cones, but the word *conifer* does not include all evergreens, since junipers and yews enclose their seeds in berries instead of cones. Larches bear cones but are deciduous, often surprising their new owners when the foliage turns golden yellow and falls off in autumn. (Some of the newcomers to our area thought their larch trees had died when this happened and had them cut down.) Most broadleaf evergreens hold their green leaves year-round, including those that actually have broad leaves, such as rhododendron, and the smaller-leaved plants, such as holly and boxwood. In the North, however, some lose their leaves in winter. Small wonder people are confused about evergreens. As Kermit the Frog sings, "It's not easy being green."

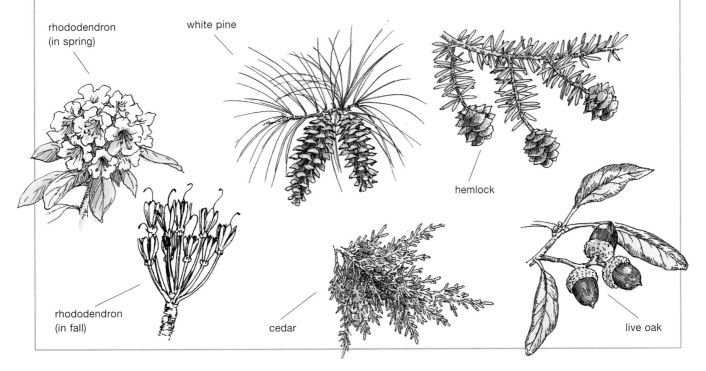

rhododendron (in spring)

white pine

hemlock

rhododendron (in fall)

cedar

live oak

## WHEN IS PRUNING NECESSARY?

- Wind, snow, or ice breaks off or cracks limbs.

- Diseases or insects disfigure a tree. If budworms attack the foliage of an evergreen for several years in succession, for example, it will be greatly weakened and you'll find many dead branches. Rusts, galls, and other pests also kill limbs and sometimes the entire tree.

- Tall-growing trees reach up toward power lines, endanger the siding or roof of a building, or hide views of sunsets.

- A large-growing pine becomes mature. Pines reach their majestic splendor only after someone removes their lower limbs or the limbs die and fall naturally. Pruning displays the beauty of their impressive trunks.

- Someone neglects annual shearing for many years or has done it carelessly, so the trees have outgrown their allotted space.

### Pruning Pointers

**What is pruning?** Pruning is the cutting of mature, woody portions with hand clippers, long-handled pruners, or a saw.

**When should I prune?** This heavier work is best done when the plant is dormant. You can prune safely nearly all winter in mild climates, but only in fall or early spring in areas with chilly winters, because you should avoid cutting wood when it is frozen.

**Should I seal the pruning wound?** Even though the evergreen doesn't bleed noticeably when dormant, enough pitch (the thick saplike substance that emerges from the bark) will form to seal the wound, making tree paint unnecessary. This pitch effectively protects the wound from the ravages of weather and helps it heal over rapidly.

### Pruning How-To

Your tall-growing evergreens will probably be the most challenging to prune, but even low growers can grow out of shape in time. Certain yews, mugho pines, and junipers sometimes spread a dis-

tance of 20 feet (6 m) or more after a few decades, and pyramid conifers may stretch up disproportionately tall for a small lot. Unless you want them for a tall screen or windbreak, you will likely want to either cut them back drastically or replace them.

Don't leave any dead stubs that will later rot. Cut branches close to either the trunk or a live limb with one exception: If you are cutting a large branch with a "collar" (a fat growth around it where it joins the trunk), cut it just outside the collar instead of making the cut close to the trunk.

When you cut back an evergreen, always take off a little more wood than would be necessary to get the plant to the size you want, so that the tree's new growth will hide the ugly pruning cuts you have made. Never remove too much of the green area in any one year, however. Arborvitae, yews, hemlocks, and junipers can tolerate more cutting back than spruces and pines, but be conservative, even with them. The best guideline is the old pruning rule: Never remove more than one-third of the wood for the first pruning on a small to medium-size healthy evergreen. For the next few years, remove less each time. On larger trees, prune much less.

*The secret to shaping and controlling evergreens is shearing off some of the new growth as soon as it appears in spring.*

If you need to prune a large evergreen into a smaller shape, spread the operation over several years by cutting back a small amount every other year. Unfortunately, you may be stuck with a weird-shaped tree until it regrows and you can start shearing.

In warm planting zones you are free to prune more severely than in the North, but even if you live in Zone 6 or a warmer climate, common sense should determine the amount you remove. As with shearing, always cut so that the bottom of the tree is at least slightly wider than the top. Otherwise the lower limbs will be shaded and gradually die.

### Shearing Basics

Shearing an evergreen tree or shrub is different from pruning it. Shearing, the removal of the plant's soft new growth, is much like clipping the fleece from a sheep. It should be done when the plant is actively growing, usually in spring or early summer. Hedge shears or power clippers are good tools for this operation.

Keep an eye on your evergreens to determine when they are growing. Firs, pines, spruces, and yews make nearly all their top growth during a few weeks in late spring, but arborvitae, hemlocks, and junipers start to grow a bit later. Yews often make a second spurt of growth later in the year, if the growing season is long enough, so they may need another clipping at that time.

*To keep evergreens in good shape, shear off the soft new growth (lighter in color) in late spring or early summer, depending on the type of tree.*

During the growing period, soft new growth appears along the sides and tips of the branches. The amount a tree grows in a single season depends on many things, including the habit of the species, the plant's vigor, and the moisture and nutrients it has available. At the end of the growing period the soft growth becomes hardened but the tree roots may continue to grow for much of the summer.

When you shear at the right time, new buds will form at the cut ends, and after a few days the bush won't look as if it has been sheared. If you wait to shear until after the plant has stopped growing, on the other hand, the ends will not heal and produce buds. The cut stubs will be obvious for the rest of the year.

If you want a young ornamental evergreen to grow larger and still stay in a tight form, wait until the new growth is about 4 inches (10 cm) long. Then snip off about 2 inches (5 cm) of this soft, light green growth, shaping the plant to the form you want as you shear.

### PRUNING AND SHEARING TOOLS

Pruners are fine for cutting smaller limbs, but a fine-toothed pruning saw is a better choice for limbs that are more than an inch (2.5 cm) in diameter. It leaves a smoother cut than a coarse-toothed bow saw, and carpenter saws tend to "gum up" badly. A chain saw can be dangerous to nearby limbs — those of both the tree and operator — so save that tool for cutting down the entire tree when its time has come. Here's a list of the basic tools you'll need, depending on the project:

Pruning saw
Bow saw
Pole saw
Hand pruners, anvil and scissors type
Long-handled pruner
Pole pruner
Chain saw (for removing trees)
Long-handled hedge shears
Electric clippers
Gasoline-powered clippers

## Keeping Your Tree to the Size You Want

You have several options for keeping evergreens to a manageable size.

**Annual shearing.** After your evergreen has reached the size you want, annual shearing can keep it that size indefinitely, as long as you cut off all the new growth each year while it is still soft. This treatment will not only stop its expansion upward and outward, it will also force new sprouts to form in the interior. This will make the shrub thicker, improving its appearance and making a secure place for birds to nest. Even a Norway spruce that might otherwise grow 150 feet (45 m) tall can be held at a neat, tight, 4-foot (1.2 m) height almost indefinitely, if you persevere, but it will take dedication. (You can't go on vacation for a couple of weeks during shearing season!)

We kept a white spruce growing at a compact 4 feet (1.2 m) in our back yard for 40 years by frequent, close clipping, and when we finally cut it down, we were surprised to find how large the trunk had become.

To prevent your new trees or newly shaped trees from becoming overgrown again, begin a program of annual shearing. It is a mistake to wait until an evergreen reaches the size you want before you stop its growth, because to develop a really tight plant, you must start when the tree is young. Even when you want a single evergreen to grow into a large specimen, or a row of them to become a tall screen or windbreak, you should shear them lightly every year during the first three or four years of their life. This treatment will encourage them to grow in a compact form and develop a growth habit that will continue.

If you want your evergreens to have a natural, informal appearance, one shearing a year is enough; but if you prefer more formal-looking, compact plants, trim them at weekly intervals during the short period when the new sprouts are appearing. Don't worry that such tight shearing might harm the plant because, like frequent haircuts, it will not do any damage if you do it before the growth hardens. If you are doubtful, visit botanical gardens, Disney World, or some other spot where beautiful, artistic topiary plants are tightly clipped to resemble animals, geometric forms, and other extraordinary shapes.

---

### MAKE ROOM FOR A VIEW: BASAL PRUNING

You can use a technique called "basal pruning" to open up the area under a large tree to provide a view or access to lower-growing plantings beyond. Here are some tips for how to do it successfully:

- Cut off only a few limbs during any one year, so that you don't shock the tree too much. Usually a third of the height of the branched part of a tree can be basal-pruned at one time with no severe setback to the tree.

- Wait two or three years before you attempt the next basal pruning.

- Remove dried-out limbs at any time. The lower limbs of evergreens are often dead or nearly so. All of these can be cut off, in any season, without damage to the tree.

- Always cut a large limb back to living wood, either a branch or the main trunk of the tree, so that no stub is left to rot away.

*Before basal pruning*

*Pruned tree, with a third of lower branches removed*

**Root pruning.** Another way to slow down the growth of a small tree or shrub is to sever all the roots around the plant each year with a spade, cutting at the outside spread of the branches. (See page 88.) This root pruning, combined with close shearing, will effectively dwarf nearly any evergreen for decades.

## Dwarf or Unusual Evergreens

Horticulturists have introduced many dwarf varieties of arborvitae, spruce, pine, hemlock, and other naturally large-growing trees that are good choices for homeowners who want to replace their larger cousins. These trees require far less shearing to keep them looking nice for many years, but the term *dwarf tree* usually means slow-growing rather than indicating that the plant will be permanently small.

Dwarf and other unusual-shaped evergreens are often created by grafting fine specimens on wild rootstocks; sometimes limbs grow from the vigorous wild understock and crowd out the good tree. If you notice that this has happened to one of your trees but some of the good cultivar is still alive, cut out all the sprouts coming from below the graft.

It usually works best to prune and shear all your evergreens to conform to the shape they would grow naturally, but it is possible to create a small globe-shaped dwarf specimen from a tree that would otherwise grow into a tall-growing, spreading white pine, for example. Be aware that this can be a demanding and time-consuming process.

## Feeding Evergreens

Large trees with deep, spreading roots are adept at finding what they need in the soil, and they are unlikely to need additional nutrients. The same may be true of smaller lawn trees that benefit from the fertilizer you apply to the grass. Whenever an evergreen tree is not growing well, however, feed it a complete organic or chemical fertilizer, such as a 5-10-10 formula, in early spring. Dig slits with a shovel or make holes with a bar a bit beyond the spread of the branches.

If the tree is small, one hole on each side of the tree is enough; larger trees need several, depending on their size. Add ½ cup (12 ml) of dry fertilizer to each opening and close the hole or slit tightly with your foot to prevent evaporation of the nitrogen.

### KEY TO EVERGREEN TERMINOLOGY

Species and cultivar names of evergreen trees are usually descriptive, which will help you when you are shopping, or if you have a young plant and are wondering what is in store.

*The botanic names of evergreens often tell you what form the tree will grow into. For instance, the species name of this plant is "pendula," which means weeping. "Globosa" indicates a round-shaped tree and "fastigiata" a tall, slender, upright pyramid.*

# PESTS AND DISEASES OF EVERGREENS

| PEST OR DISEASE | DESCRIPTION | MOST SUSCEPTIBLE PLANTS | SOLUTION |
|---|---|---|---|
| APHIDS | Suck juices from stems and needles; vary in color from green to brown | Different aphids attack different trees. | Spray with insecticide. |
| BEAVERS | Sometimes cut down evergreens (although they are not their favorite food or building material) | Many needled evergreens | Call game warden for advice. |
| BIRDS | Break off fragile new top growth as they perch/roost | Young "Christmas trees" and ornamentals | No good solution. |
| BUDWORMS | Nibble on needles, often first decimating the limbs at the top of large trees, then moving on to smaller ones | Fir and spruce | Spray with insecticide. |
| CATERPILLARS | Nibble on needles | Many needled evergreens | Spray with Bt (Bacillus thuringiensis) or insecticide. |
| DEER | Strip or scrape bark and devour foliage | Yews, arborvitae, hemlocks | Get dog or erect fence; hang strong-smelling soaps (such as Irish Spring). |
| ENVIRONMENTAL POLLUTANTS IN SOIL, AIR, RAIN | Sick trees, browning of needles | Pines, arborvitae, and hemlocks are especially susceptible | Difficult to control. |
| PORCUPINES | Devour bark | Prefer to chew on hardwood trees, but may hit evergreens | Humane trap. |
| RED SPIDERS | Nibble on needles | Many species of needled evergreens | Spray with insecticide. |
| RUST | Weakens tree, makes it unsightly; on junipers, shows as galls and thick growth on twigs | Junipers, pines, and balsam fir are susceptible | Remove host plants for rusts. Apples are host for cedar apple rust that affects some juniper; wild currants and gooseberries host the white pine blister rust that affects white and other five-needled pines; sensitive ferns host the uredinopsis rust that causes needle drop on balsam fir. |
| SAWFLIES | Nibble on needles | Spruce (European spruce sawfly) and pine (pine sawfly, red-headed pine sawfly) | Spray with insecticide. |
| SCALE | Nibble on needles | Juniper, pine | Spray with insecticide. |

Try to identify the cause of any damage you find, and if you cannot figure out what is wrong and it appears widespread and dangerous, consult your Cooperative Extension Service or a gardening expert for advice. They usually know which pests and diseases are prevalent in the area and can advise you about the currently recommended controls. Both organic and chemical insecticides are available.

## POPULAR EVERGREEN TREES

In addition to the many different genera of evergreens, in each genus there are many species. The pine genus, for instance, includes Austrian, black, mugho, red, Scotch, Swiss, white, and more. Each species also often has a number of distinctive varieties and cultivars, which may be dwarf, weeping, tall and slender, or with distinctive needle color. In order to make the best selection for your spot, visit a local nursery or garden center, or study a plant catalog carefully.

**American arborvitae, white cedar *(Thuja occidentalis)*.** The various cultivars are ideal for hedges, specimens, foundation plants, rock gardens, windbreaks, and screens.

**Dawn redwood *(Metasequoia glyptostroboides)*.** Too tall for most landscapes, but a striking tree. Hardy to Zone 6, and possibly colder regions. Fast grower in moist places.

**Douglas fir *(Pseudotsuga menziesii)*.** Not a true fir, but a striking specimen tree with beautiful, distinctive cones.

**Fir *(Abies)*.** Most have soft green foliage and smooth bark, and all have upright-growing cones. Many species and cultivars are available.

**Hemlock *(Tsuga)*.** One of the most beautiful evergreens. It can be easily sheared. The dwarf kinds are best for foundations and small landscapes. Taller kinds can be kept small for decades by heavy shearing and are ideal for hedges and topiary.

**Juniper *(Juniperus)*.** Rather prickly foliage and blue to black berries. Many different forms make them useful in a variety of locations. Some varieties are prone to diseases.

**Larch, tamarack *(Larix)*.** Deciduous conifer, good for moist (or damp) places. Golden orange fall color.

**Pine *(Pinus)*.** Most kinds have long needles, but different species vary in foliage color and growth habits. Many cultivars are available.

**Spruce *(Picea)*.** Sharp needles. Trees come in a variety of sizes and shapes. Dwarf forms are good for foundation plants.

**Yew *(Taxus)*.** The variety of forms and mature heights offers homeowners a wide choice for home plantings. Canadian and Japanese yews are the most hardy.

# Broadleaf Evergreens

An important group of evergreens, the broadleafs, has leaves rather than needles. Most are green throughout the year but, as we've mentioned, not all retain their foliage year-round in every part of North America. A few lose it during the winter in the North, and others, though they may retain their leaves, become discolored until spring.

*Azaleas are among the most brilliant-flowering of the broadleaf evergreens. Their spring display in all shades of red and white, and even orangey yellows, can be breathtaking and memorable.*

## BROADLEAF EVERGREEN TROUBLESHOOTING

| PROBLEM | POSSIBLE CAUSE | SOLUTION | PAGE |
|---|---|---|---|
| STUNTED OR ANEMIC-LOOKING GROWTH | Wrong cultivars for the climate | Pull them out, research suitable replacements. | 123 |
| | Soil may not be acidic enough, or lacking in essential nutrients | Have a soil test done and follow recommendations. | 166 |
| PLANTS NOT THRIVING | Old age (like all living things, these plants have a limited life span), poor soil, wrong pH, wrong choice of tree for location, windburn, salt damage | Determine cause. If old age, replace them rather than attempt to renew them. | 121 |
| LEGGY GROWTH ON OLDER PLANTS MAKE THEM LOOK TOP-HEAVY | Old age | Begin a several-year renewal pruning program, starting in early spring. | 121 |
| PLANTS NOT FLOWERING OR FLOWERING POORLY | Light conditions wrong; pH too high; pruned at the wrong time | Follow cultural directions for each plant. | 122 |
| YELLOWING FOLIAGE | Not enough fertilizer, pH too high, azalea leaf miner | Add fertilizer and trace elements to soil. Spray for miner. Adjust pH. | 120 |
| CURLED LEAVES | Drought; rhododendron wilt; aphids; cold weather | Mulch while soil is wet. Water when needed. Dig and destroy any with wilt disease. Check for aphids. If you find them, spray with insecticide. | 122 |

## Soil Requirements for Broadleaf Evergreens

Unlike many other shrubs you might grow, most temperate-zone broadleafs need an acidic soil with a pH between 4.5 and 5. If a soil test shows that your soil has a pH of 6 or more, the subsoil may be alkaline, and lime from this soil can percolate upward to the topsoil easily with each rain. We have this kind of alkaline soil and have sadly come to the conclusion that we should give up trying to grow these beautiful broadleafs and instead concentrate on the worthwhile plants that appreciate our higher pH.

If the pH of your soil is very high, you may want to use a combination of several organic products to help make it more acid and apply an acidic mulch as well.

### SOIL ACIDIFIERS

To dig into the soil:

- Compost made from oak leaves, hemlock or pine needles, or the shavings or sawdust of these trees
- Cottonseed meal
- Peat moss (moisten it first)
- Sphagnum peat moss
- Sulfate fertilizers, ammonium sulfate, used sparingly to avoid injuring plants
- Sulfur (powdered)

To use as mulch:

- Oak leaves, pine or hemlock needles
- Shavings, shredded bark, chips, or composted sawdust from oaks, pines, or hemlocks

## How to Prune

You may face a serious pruning job if your broadleaf shrubs have been left to their own devices. Although they grow more slowly than most conifers, like all plants they become overgrown after years of neglect. Although certain rhododendrons, including azaleas, still look good when they reach full size and may continue to bloom well, most broadleafs need cutting back eventually.

As you start to prune, visualize how you want the plant to look and prune with that vision in mind. Don't attempt to get a huge rhododendron to a smaller size in one season. Spread the job over several years if necessary, and be prepared to sacrifice the plant if it appears that whittling it down to the size you want isn't worth the risk or trouble.

If you live in a cold zone, keep your pruning to a reasonable amount each year so you don't encourage a fast regrowth of the plant, which would most likely cause it to be winter killed. (See below.) Where winters are mild, however, you should be able to safely remove a third of the shrub the first season, with no danger.

Cut back the branches that are growing too long to a bud or small shoot, and gradually thin the plant by removing some of the older branches that no longer bloom well or are growing too close together. Also remove any limbs injured by weather or damaged in any other way.

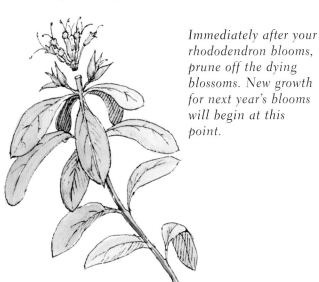

*Immediately after your rhododendron blooms, prune off the dying blossoms. New growth for next year's blooms will begin at this point.*

## When to Prune

Always prune when the plant is dormant. Early spring is a good time, because you can clip off any winter-injured twigs at the same time. Do not feed the plants for a year or two after any major pruning so they will not be stimulated to grow too rapidly, which could cause them to break off easily or suffer winter injury.

After the plants have recovered from their surgery, give them a light pruning early each subsequent spring (when they are still dormant) to ensure that no drastic action will be necessary in the future.

## Drastic Pruning to Rejuvenate

If your rhododendrons (including azaleas), hollies, and laurels have grown too large and are showing signs of age but still don't appear to be on their last roots, it is possible to safely thin out the old and wounded stems, and cut back healthy ones to rejuvenate the plants. To avoid shock, feed plants a generous dose of manure and cottonseed meal for a year or two before heavy pruning. You can cut them nearly to the ground in Zones 6 and warmer. In cooler zones, do it more gradually, cutting out a few overgrown branches each spring over a period of several years. Though you can do cosmetic pruning of the old blooms and deadwood anytime, cut to renew the bush only when plants are dormant.

---

### REPLACING AN OLD PLANTING

After you have cut down the old plants, dig out as many of their roots as possible. Then, before planting new shrubs, rebuild the nutrient-depleted soil with acidic plant food and sphagnum peat moss, or humus or compost made from plants that are naturally acidic.

---

## Pests and Diseases

Broadleaf evergreens have their share of pests, and it isn't always easy to discover what is wrong because of the tight growth of the plants. Since many species are natives of another area, in their new climatic zone they may have little resistance to unfamiliar diseases and insects. Fortunately, most of their ailments are not lethal.

To prevent problems, keep your plants mulched (they are shallow-rooted), well fed, uncrowded, and watered when necessary. Be wary of buying new plants from doubtful sources or accepting gift plants. If you hear of insect or disease problems in your region, inspect your plants often and be prepared with the proper controls.

## PESTS AND DISEASES OF BROADLEAF EVERGREENS

| PEST OR DISEASE | DESCRIPTION OF DAMAGE | SOLUTION |
|---|---|---|
| FLOWER SPOT | Small spots appear on petals. Spots may enlarge, causing flower to collapse. | Promptly remove the infected blooms. |
| CANKER | Lesion often with dead tissue at center. | Spray with a fungicide. |
| WILT | Drooping of a plant sometimes caused by a lack of moisture, and sometimes by a disease such as fusarium or verticillium. | Water the plant. If it doesn't recover, cut away wilted branches. If problem continues, remove entire plant. |
| VIRUS | Often begins by the sudden dying of a few limbs, discoloration of the leaves, poor growth. Eventually the plant dies. | None. Remove and discard affected plants. |
| BORERS | Small holes appear, usually near the base of the trunk. | Cut out infected branches. If in trunk, kill by poking with wire and seal up hole with tree-sealing compound. |
| SCALE | Small insects that suck plant juices from leaves and stems. | Spray with an insecticide labeled for the plant. |
| LACE BUGS | Pests that live on the lower side of leaves and suck out their juices. | Spray with insecticidal soap or other insecticide labeled for the plant. |

# POPULAR BROADLEAF EVERGREENS

Each of the species listed has numerous varieties and cultivars that vary in hardiness and appearance. A few azaleas, hollies, rhododendrons, and others have named cultivars that can survive in cold zones in a sheltered location, provided that the soil is sufficiently acid.

**Abelia *(Abelia).*** A shrub, abelia grows about 5 feet (1.5 m) tall. Different species are either evergreen or semi-evergreen. Flowers are showy, ranging from lavender to pink and red. The glossy abelia is one of the hardiest. Most are suitable for Zones 5 through 9. Pinch or clip back anytime to shape. Do heavy pruning when dormant.

**Barberry *(Berberis).*** A large number of cultivars can tempt the gardener in this genus. Foliage color ranges from glossy green to red, and some have attractive flowers. Hardy from Zones 3 to 8. Shear in summer for tight specimens and hedges. Cut back heavily when dormant to renew.

**Boxwood *(Buxus).*** A wide choice of cultivars makes it necessary for the buyer to shop carefully to get the right plant for the location. Some *microphylla* cultivars are among the hardiest. Shear to shape all season for tight hedge or specimen. Cut back when dormant to renew.

**Camellia *(Camellia japonica).*** Popular flowering, glossy-leaved evergreen in Zones 7 to 9. Many cultivars. Prefers partial shade and acidic soil. Cut off fading flowers and prune directly afterward.

**English laurel *(Prunus laurocerasus).*** Excellent hedge plant. Many cultivars of this attractive shiny, leathery-leafed shrub. A vigorous grower, so cut back frequently to keep in shape and prevent crowding of other plants. Clip when needed all season, but do heavy pruning when dormant. Zones 6 to 8.

**Holly *(Ilex).*** Since holly plants are either male or female and only the females produce berries, you'll need at least one of each sex growing near each other. If yours are not bearing fruit, one of the pair may be missing. Blooms on the male plants have stamens covered with pollen, but females have only a single pistil in the center of each flower. Most holly species will pollinate each other as long as they bloom at the same time, which makes it possible to grow many different kinds of females with only a few males to pollinate them. Prune in late fall or early winter.

**Chinese holly *(Ilex cornuta* and its various cultivars).*** Chinese hollies are exceptions to the rule and produce fruit without a partner, so they are valuable in locales where they will grow (Zones 7 to 9). When they are dormant, use hedge shears to cut back any that are growing out of shape to make them more symmetrical. Since the plants grow slowly, they need only occasional pruning to correct growth problems and remove old or damaged wood. An ideal pruning time is when you harvest the berries and greenery for holiday decorations.

**Magnolia *(Magnolia).*** The magnolia family is huge, with species and cultivars ranging from low-growing shrubs to large trees. The showy blooms are their crowning glory. Some have evergreen foliage, others are deciduous in the North. Some are strictly southern trees, others grow well in Zone 5. Prune to remove old flowers and to shape plants directly after the blooms fade. Do heavy cutting back only when plants are dormant.

**Mountain laurel *(Kalmia latifolia).*** A colorful, tall growing plant, mountain laurel has a variety of cultivars with colorful blooms. Most are hardy in Zones 5 to 9. Clip or shear when growing to encourage tighter growth. Remove faded blooms. Renew plants when necessary by cutting back when dormant.

**Pieris *(Pieris).*** These are shrubs or small trees varying in hardiness. Most have clusters of white or pink-white blooms. Needs little pruning. Clip anytime to keep neat.

**Rhododendron *(Rhododendron).*** This family also includes azaleas, which are among the most widely planted broadleafs. Horticulturists have successfully extended the hardiness range of these plants in recent years, so that several beautiful cultivars now thrive in Zone 4. So many new cultivars are now available, there are almost unlimited choices. Prune back new growth throughout the summer. Cut back heavily to renew when dormant.

# chapter 9

# Deciduous Trees That Thrive

Magnificent deciduous shade trees on your property can be your pride and joy. A mature maple, beech, oak, or other tree provides spring magic as the leaves emerge, then summer shade, autumn color, and winter warmth as it allows the sun to shine through its branches. It can be a home for nesting birds, a tree house, swings, or hammocks, and it can provide a canopy for picnics and other pleasures.

When shade trees become mature they are usually quite self-sufficient, and their problems, unlike those of many other plants, do not often stem from neglect. Nevertheless, if such a tree is in the wrong place, it can become a colossal headache as it ages. Some attention is necessary when branches begin to crowd power lines or hang over a roof, if its weak limbs threaten to fall on people or cars below, or if gaping holes appear in the trunk. The prospect of performing major surgery, or even first aid, can be daunting — a giant is not an easy patient.

Before attempting to fix the problem, try to determine the cause (see chart on page 125). It is tempting to attempt to save any tree, but if it has come to the end of its life span or is struggling to survive where road salt runoff is chronic, for instance, it may make more sense to have it cut down and plant a new one rather than to repeatedly remove deteriorating limbs. On the other hand, you may be able to cure certain problems by simply cutting off limbs that overhang a roof or eliminating insects that are attacking a trunk.

*Tall shade trees, combined with spring-blooming understory trees such as dogwood, provide beautiful, year-round enjoyment.*

## DECIDUOUS TREES TROUBLESHOOTING

| PROBLEM | POSSIBLE CAUSE | SOLUTION | PAGE |
|---|---|---|---|
| BRITTLE BRANCHES SPLINTER AND/OR FALL IN WINDS | Problem is species-related (locust, poplar, and willow are especially susceptible) | Keep tree well-pruned; replace with a less vulnerable species; feed less. | 127, 129 |
| TREE FOLIAGE HAS BURNED EDGES | Drought | Water slowly and thoroughly. | 38 |
| | Fertilizer has not been watered in well | Water tree prior to and after feeding. | 125 |
| | Overfertilized | Cut back on fertilizer. | |
| BROWNING OF FOLIAGE; TREE BECOMES WEAK AND MAY BE DYING | Salt damage | Move tree, to a spot away from roadside. Divert or runoff away from tree roots. | 171 |
| | Leaf blotch | Spray regularly in spring with fungicide. | 125 |
| TREE IS LEANING | Improper planting or support while tree was young | If tree is still young, it may be possible to straighten it out using ropes and pegs. | 128 |
| CAVITY IN TRUNK | Canker, insect, or animal damage | Clean out well and fill with tree sealer. | 130 |

## Determining the Problem

Although pests sometimes attack perfectly healthy trees, if a tree is stressed by weather, poor nutrition, crowding, or other adverse conditions, its roots, stems, and leaves become easier targets for preying insects and circulating diseases. Native trees have their share of problems, but those imported from another part of the country or world often must put up with unfamiliar environmental conditions, including a hostile climate, unfamiliar soil conditions, and insects and diseases that are foreign to them.

Refer to the box on page 126 to assess whether insects or disease may be causing your trees harm.

### SAVVY SPRAYING

Spraying a large tree safely is not easy, and you must be sure the spray will not drift where it can harm people or pets. Fortunately, spraying with chemicals, once considered a general panacea for insects and diseases, is no longer automatically recommended as the best way to handle every tree problem, so always investigate safer alternatives, such as Bt (Bacillus thuringiensis). Cooperative Extension Service personnel usually know which insects and diseases are affecting an area and are able to offer the safest and most effective remedies.

## Feeding a Tree

Because the roots are so spreading and far-reaching on a large tree, they are often able to obtain the necessary nutrients and need little extra fertilizer from you. Lawn trees benefit from the plant food that you give the grass, so if the leaves on your trees look healthy during the summer, they probably don't need extra food. If they seem bedraggled, however, applying more nutrients will be helpful in improving both young and mature trees. Put it in holes you make with a bar or spade in a circle outside the leaf spread in early spring, and just before a lawn sprinkling or a rain, if possible.

# INSECT PESTS AND DISEASES OF DECIDUOUS TREES

| PROBLEM | POSSIBLE CAUSE | SOLUTION |
|---------|----------------|----------|
| CURLING, DISCOLORED, OR DEFORMED LEAVES | Various pests and leaf diseases | Spray only if numerous enough to weaken tree. *Note:* Many leaf problems are cosmetic only, and not cause for alarm. Maple leaves often develop colored spots or small upright growths, for example, but neither is likely to threaten the health of the tree. |
| HOLE(S) AT BASE OF BRANCHES | Borers | Prune out infected limbs. Kill by punching a wire into the hole. |
| LESIONS ON THE BARK | Cankers | When tree is dormant, cut out canker, and apply lime-sulfur fungicide. |
| FOLIAGE NIBBLED ON | Caterpillars | Handpick; spray with *Bt* (*Bacillus thuringiensis*) |
| TREE DRAMATICALLY DEFOLIATED, WEAKENED, MAY EVEN DIE | Gypsy moths | Spray twice in early summer with *Bt*. Collect and destroy egg cases in winter. Place bands coated with petroleum jelly around trunk in spring. |
| FOLIAGE NIBBLED ON | Japanese beetles | Pick off or spray with neem as insects are appearing. |
| FUNGAL GROWTH ON FOLIAGE | Leaf spots (various fungus diseases) | Spray early in spring or summer with garden fungicide; several sprays may be necessary. |
| HOLES IN THE LEAVES | Chewing insects such as caterpillars, worms, gypsy moths, bagworms, leaf rollers, sawflies, and others | Apply appropriate insecticide. |
| BROWNING OF LEAVES IN LATE SUMMER | Leaf miners | Spray with the insecticide neem early to prevent insects from entering leaves. |
| RED OR BROWN SPORES ON LEAVES | Rusts (various kinds) | Rusts are difficult to control. Eliminate host plant, if possible (see page 130). Destroy diseased foliage as it falls. |
| SERIES OF SMALL HOLES (SIZE OF A PENCIL OR SMALLER) IN TRUNK | Sapsuckers (birds) | Hard to control, but usually not too damaging to the tree. Chase the birds away when you see them. |
| TREE PARTLY OR COMPLETELY DEFOLIATED IN SUMMER | Sawflies | Apply insecticidal soap or neem when pests appear. |
| LEAVES, BRANCHES, FRUIT DISFIGURED BY FUNGUS; TREE WEAKENED | Scab (crab apples are especially vulnerable) | Fungicides control the condition, but frequent spraying is necessary during a wet summer when fungus is most prevalent. When you buy a new tree, get a scab-resistant one. |
| WEBS ON BRANCHES IN SPRING | Tent caterpillars | Cut off webs and burn, apply *Bt* when webs are small. |
| WEBS ON BRANCHES IN FALL | Webworms | Spray with *Bt* as soon as worms appear. Repeat if necessary. |
| LEAVES THAT SUDDENLY WILT; DEAD BRANCHES | Wilt disease | Cut off affected parts and burn. |

Fertilizer needs to become dissolved and make its way deep into the soil, and then be absorbed by the roots and transferred up to the limbs. It is not a speedy process, so don't feed a tree after July 1 in temperate zones. If you follow this guideline, the tree can make use of the nutrients during its growing season and will not experience new growth in late summer that might be winter-killed.

Fall frosts that come before the new growth has hardened cause much of the "winterkill" that is usually credited to the cold temperatures later in the winter. Controlling late summer growth is especially critical in areas where the growing season is short or if you have trees of marginal hardiness.

Fertilizer is expensive and easy to waste if not applied wisely. It can also damage a plant if you simply dump it on the nearby soil.

**Step 1. Prepare the area.** Water the area first. Beware of applying synthetic fertilizer during a dry period because it can "burn" the tree, sometimes badly enough to kill it. When there is not enough moisture in the soil to dissolve the fertilizer, it will steal moisture from the roots, resulting in a sudden browning of the leaves. If this should happen, and there isn't a hard rain soon, you can often revive the tree by running sprinklers on the turf around the tree for an extended period.

**Step 2. Provide access.** Make a series of holes well outside area of the limb spread (see Where to Feed, above right, for more details).

**Step 3. Apply the fertilizer.** Insert into each hole a handful of a balanced granular or powdered fertilizer, natural or synthetic (formula 5-10-10). Tree food is also available in pellets and as fertilizer spikes, as well as in soluble form. Follow the directions on the package if you use any of these.

## Don't Overfeed

Various trees respond differently to fertilizer. Young pines, for example, sometimes grow badly out of shape when they are overfed. An underfed

### WHERE TO FEED

It is important to place fertilizer in the right locations for it to work well. Instructions nearly always tell you to feed a tree directly under the "drip line" of the branches or just outside that imaginary line, "because the feeder roots are located there." This is true for small trees but larger trees need their fertilizer even farther out, beyond the branches. The feeder roots of larger trees reach far beyond this circumference because in most locations the soil is too shallow for roots to reach deeply into it. Consequently, they grow sideways for long distances in every direction, searching for the nourishment that they need. The roots of a large maple or oak sometimes spread over a quarter acre or more. If you feed such a tree close to the trunk, the fertilizer will reach only the large roots near the trunk and be of little use. Feed a tree 2 or 3 feet (0.6 or 0.9 m) outside the branch spread.

Never feed a small tree too close to the trunk, because it may encourage the roots to grow there rather than to spread out so they can anchor the tree firmly as it gets larger. Trees with small root systems can easily blow over in a windstorm.

young maple may grow only a few inches a year, but when adequately nourished with plenty of fertilizer and water, your tree may grow 3 to 4 feet (0.9 to 1.2 m) during one season. If the tree is growing well, feed it sparingly, if at all.

Trees that are overfed and grow too quickly are likely to become weak, with fragile branches that break in the wind. They are also more susceptible to stress from adverse weather and attacks from diseases and insects. Naturally fast-growing trees, such as poplars and willows, have weak wood that can be further weakened by fertilizer overstimulation.

# First Aid for Trees

When a tree begins to have problems or to show signs of deterioration, try to determine the cause of its condition. You may need to seal up cracks, repair gashes from broken limbs caused by lightning, or deal with any of the following problems:

➤ **Life span.** Has it reached the end of its natural life? Although oaks (and the evergreens hemlock and sequoia) can live for centuries, many trees have much shorter life spans. Some, such as certain types of willows and poplars, may succumb after fewer than 30 years.

➤ **Location.** Was it planted in a bad location, perhaps by someone more concerned about the view or appearance than the soil or light exposure? If so, it may be struggling to survive in a thin layer of worn-out soil over rocks, hardpan, or in a swamp; it may be located too near a building, driveway, or the neighbor's swimming pool; or it may be leaning badly and require straightening.

➤ **Sickness/damage.** Has it been attacked by insects, animals, or a disease? Although healthy trees are often able to fend off predators, sometimes there is no known antidote, as in the case of Dutch elm disease, which killed off nearly every American elm in the mid–20th century.

➤ **Natural disaster.** Has it been hit by strong winds, ice storms, or lightning? Devastating weather can strip off large healthy limbs or topple entire trees while you stand by helplessly, wondering what to do with the mess.

➤ **Environmental conditions.** Road salt runoff, traffic fumes, or other pollution may weaken or otherwise adversely affect a tree, as can paving, leakage from an oil tank, or heavy traffic over the roots.

➤ **Malnutrition.** Lack of nutrients is a common cause of stress in trees.

➤ **Graft failure.** Some of the newer hybrids, such as some with colored leaves, are grafted and may be short-lived. The 'Crimson King' maples are often short-lived in the colder zones, although we discovered that, grown on their own roots, they live much longer.

## Straightening a Leaning Tree

A tree leans for a variety of reasons. Sometimes one begins to tip because it wasn't set deeply enough when planted, or it may not have had enough soil to spread out its roots and anchor it firmly. If someone neglected to stake it properly during its first years, the wind may have tilted it, or it may have become crowded by other trees or buildings and needed to lean to reach enough light. If the tree is young and has grown no more than 12 to 15 feet (3.6 to 4.5 m) tall, you can often straighten it with little trouble.

**Step 1.** In spring or early summer, dig a hole at the base of the trunk opposite the direction of the lean. Loosen soil all around the trunk, as near roots as you can get without damaging them.

**Step 2.** Wrap burlap or cloth around the trunk, up about two-thirds the height of the tree, and tie a long rope around it.

**Step 3.** Gently pull rope, nudging tree gradually into an upright position. If it is too large to budge by hand, use a truck, tractor, or come-along, a ratchet device that is used for moving heavy objects such as cars that are stuck in the mud.

**Step 4.** When the tree reaches a vertical position, anchor the rope to a stake driven into the ground at a slant, like a tent peg.

Step 4

**Step 5.** Fill the hole around the tree with water containing liquid fertilizer (mix according to the directions on the package). This solution will help ease the shock from damage done to the roots by the operation.

**Step 6.** Shovel the soil back into place, and carefully firm it down all around the trunk.

**Step 7.** Leave the rope support on the tree a few months until you are certain the roots have become completely established in their new position. Water the tree heavily once every two or three days for two weeks, and include some liquid fertilizer in the water once a week.

## Routine Pruning

Late winter is a fine time to prune most trees, but late summer or early fall is a better time to cut limbs from trees such as maples and birches that would bleed heavily in early spring and often in late fall. (See page 115 for suggested pruning tools.)

Remove any branches that show signs of disease or insect injury, and those that are dead or broken. Prune out any limb that is rubbing against another one, and shorten those that are out of balance with the rest of the tree. Cut out any branches that are forming extra tops on young trees; these could develop into weak forks that could eventually split apart the tree.

## PAINT OVER WOUNDS?

Some tests have shown no advantage to painting, but many tree surgeons contend that such experiments were carried out on young, healthy trees. They argue that sealing is beneficial on older trees to prevent weather damage, but less necessary on young, vigorous ones. We have no strong feelings on the subject, but since paint does no harm and does keep moisture and weather from entering, we usually paint any cut larger than 2 inches (5 cm). Most any paint will seal the wound, but commercial tree paints are antiseptic and therefore a better choice. You may need to apply a second coat after the original has weathered a couple of years, unless the opening has mostly healed.

## Storm Damage

Take care of storm damage as quickly as possible. Cut all jagged wounds smooth to minimize sap loss, and paint any large cuts with tree sealer to keep out weather. Make all cuts back to the trunk or a live branch to avoid leaving a dead stub.

## CUTTING A LARGE LIMB

If you were to cut off a large, heavy limb close to the trunk without first supporting it, it would be likely to break off when only partially cut and tear big hunks out of the trunk. The resulting wound would not heal easily and would be difficult to repair. To avoid this calamity, perform the operation in three stages.

**Step 1.** Cut into the limb about 1 inch (2.5 cm) on its lower side, at a spot about 1 foot (30 cm) from trunk.

**Step 2.** Take off the limb, sawing from the top down, at a point 2 or 3 inches (5 or 7.5 cm) farther from the trunk than the first cut.

**Step 3.** Cut off remaining stub close to the trunk.

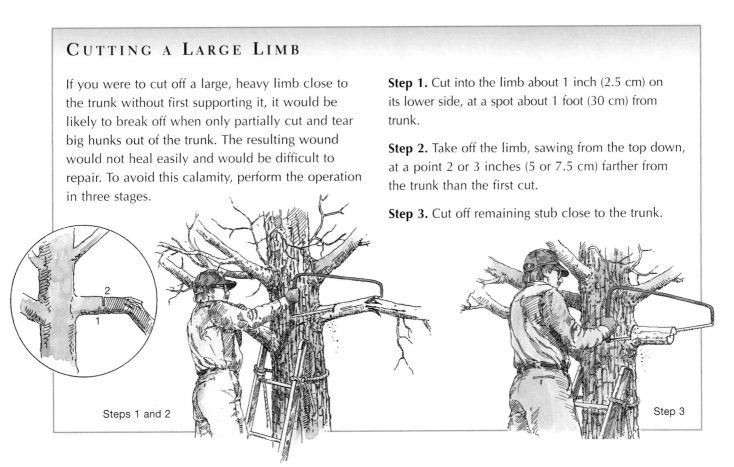

Steps 1 and 2

Step 3

## Cavities

A tree can develop a cavity or receive a wound at any stage of its life, but older trees are most vulnerable. Cavities begin as wounds — where a limb has been torn off, where something has struck the trunk and injured it, or after animals have chewed the bark or deer have rubbed their antlers over it. Unless a wound heals quickly, it can become infected and will grow larger.

If possible, fill any cavity before it becomes infected or begins to rot. Clean out all the dirt, old bark, insects, and rotten wood, and smooth up the rough edges with a rasp (heavy file). Then, like a dentist, fill the opening with a tree sealer. Follow the directions on the can and smooth the surface when finished. Check it often to be sure the sealer hasn't slipped out during hot weather.

# Taking Out an Entire Tree

Unlike taking out a juniper or rose bush, removing a tall tree that has grown for a half century or more is a massive chore and not a job for an amateur. In rural areas, if there are no power lines or other hazards nearby, a local lumberjack can often safely remove it for you more cheaply than a tree service. If there could be problems — a tree threatening a building, for instance — by all means hire an expert.

Although you may be happy at the prospect of getting rid of most trees that are falling apart, it can be very sad to lose a favorite tree, even if it is obviously dying or becoming dangerous. It can be like losing an old friend, but you can ease the blow by planting a new tree to replace it.

## Dealing with the Stump

After your tree has become firewood, you will have a stump to contend with unless you have also contracted for its removal. Don't try to dig out a big stump yourself with a shovel, or attempt to pull it out with the family car. Someone with a stump grinder can shred it into mulch, or you can feature it as part of the landscape by digging out the center and using it as a planter. We once planted a potentilla in an old stump; it looked quite attractive for a decade before the stump collapsed. Then we converted the stump to mulch. Alternatively, you could set a pot on a solid stump and plant ivy or other trailing plants in it, which will partially cover it in an attractive way. Always water any plants regularly that are not in direct contact with the earth.

Be aware that huge roots take many years to rot. You can speed up the process by adding nitrogen fertilizer each spring. To hasten the rotting of a stump, cut it level with the ground and keep it moist with mulch.

# Replacing a Lawn Tree

If you decide to replace a tree that you remove, select a pest-resistant, long-lived species. If you aren't sure what you want, study the trees in other people's yards, in parks, and in arboretums. Nurseries and garden centers now supply mostly balled and potted trees that you can plant all season.

When you are making your selection, avoid any that are badly shaped, have pale-colored leaves or needles, or appear stunted.

As for siting, keep it away from wires, buildings, and roads. Don't set your new tree too close to the old stump either. After many years of supporting the former tree, the soil in that spot will be depleted of nutrients and humus. Provide some good topsoil for your new tree to get its roots into, and feed it with a fertilizer rich in nitrogen to replace that which the rotting roots are absorbing for their decomposition.

## Criteria for Selecting a New Tree

➤ Avoid shallow-rooted species as lawn trees. For instance, the balsam poplar *(Populus balsamifera),* a large-growing poplar, is relatively long-lived, but its shallow roots often grow through the grass, which not only wrecks the appearance of the lawn, but also presents a hazard to walkers and lawn mowers.

➤ Match the tree size to your lot size. Even though you may admire oaks and maples, if your yard is small, a single tree could dominate it; a smaller tree is likely to be a better choice. Flowering trees such as mountain ash, redbud, flowering crab, and tree lilac are good lawn trees for a small area.

➤ Beware of excessive shedding. Avoid shade trees that would create a mess on their lawns. Poplars, willows, black walnuts, and horse chestnuts dump leaves, cotton, or nuts.

➤ Think twice about trees that shed acidic foliage, mainly oaks and evergreens. It is difficult to grow anything, even grass, beneath them. Oaks shower acorns, which are difficult to rake up. And pines cast heavy shade and drop an abundance of acidic needles.

➤ Does it fruit? The flowering trees that also produce fruits or berries later are especially nice. We enjoy another bonus our fruiting trees provide: Uncommon birds migrating south stop by every fall to feed for a few days. More than once we have seen them inebriated and flying with difficulty because the fruit had started to ferment slightly.

➤ Do you want colorful fall foliage? All maples are wonderful. The amur maple *(Acer ginnala)* is especially vivid.

➤ How much shade do you really want? Oaks and maples, in time, cast dense shade. If you envision dappled shade below (and prefer it for the sake of good lawn growth), choose trees without a canopy of heavy foliage, such as birch, ash, or linden.

➤ How fast does it grow? Shade trees take time to grow large. If you want shade or a screen quickly, choose a fast-growing type such as willow, poplar, or gray birch, or perhaps a large treelike shrub, such as the Russian olive. Most of the fast growers are short-lived, so you may want to set a longer-lived kind nearby.

*One thing to consider as you shop for a new tree is the density of the shade the tree will ultimately cast, especially if you hope to have a good lawn or garden in the vicinity.*

## Buying a Tree

Though garden centers sell both balled and potted plants that are usually larger and invariably get off to a faster start, mail-order nurseries often offer a much wider choice of varieties. If you order a tree by mail, it will probably arrive bare-rooted in the spring or late fall. Unless the tree comes already pruned, you will need to cut all the limbs back about one-third, or if there are no limbs, cut back the trunk about one-third. This will compensate for the injuries the tree suffered while being dug. Whether you purchase a tree locally or order it by mail, plant it as soon as possible.

If it is bare-rooted and wrapped in paper or plastic, unwrap it and soak the roots in a tub of water for a few hours before planting. If the roots are growing in a ball of soil wrapped in burlap or plastic, unwrap the plastic and remove it or loosen the burlap; give the roots a good soaking, but don't disturb the soil

## CARING FOR THE NEWLY PLANTED TREE

Water heavily at least twice a week, adding fertilizer to the water once each week for the first month if you plant in spring or early summer. If mice could be a problem, install a tree guard, and if deer roam the premises, put up a fence to keep them at bay. Check frequently to be sure that protective devices are working.

rootball. If the tree is growing in a large pot or basket, before removing it soak the soil thoroughly while you prepare the hole.

## PLANTING A NEW TREE

**Step 1.** Prepare a supply of compost, dried manure, and a bucket of water. Mix some liquid fertilizer such as fish emulsion or balanced fertilizer into the water, according to the directions on the package.

**Step 2.** Spread out a sheet of plastic, so the lawn will remain clean. Dig a hole half again the volume the roots or rootball will require, so the roots can start growing quickly in loose soil. Oaks, nut trees, pines, and certain other trees have long taproots that need deep, loose soil to get started in. Maples and many other trees tend to have more spreading root systems, so holes for them should be wider. Make two piles of soil: one of the topsoil you dig from the top foot (0.3 m)

or so of earth, and another of the poorer subsoil. Mix the compost and manure with the pile of topsoil to make a rich mixture that will encourage the tree to get off to a fast start when you pack it around the roots.

**Step 3.** Put enough of the topsoil mixture in the bottom of the hole so you can set the tree just slightly below the level where it grew originally. Slit burlap before putting tree in place (if the burlap is plastic, remove it entirely).

**Step 4.** Check the bark to find the soil line. Position the tree, and get someone to hold it firmly in place while you pour in the full bucket of water with fertilizer added.

Step 3

Step 4

**Step 5.** Carefully pack the remaining soil mix around the roots, so no air can remain to dry them out. Firm it carefully, leaving a slight depression in the soil around the trunk to catch future waterings and showers. Use any extra soil to fill in depressions. Spread a 2- to 3-inch (5 to 7.5 cm) layer of bark or other mulch around the tree, extending 2 to 3 feet (60 to 90 cm) out from the trunk, to help prevent the soil from drying out. The mulch will also keep the lawn mower a safe distance from the fragile bark.

**Step 6.** Stake the tree or put up guy wires or heavy twine to keep it from bending in the wind.

Step 5

Step 6

## Pruning a Young Tree

When you replace an old, overgrown, unsatisfactory tree with a new, young one, this is your chance to do things right from the outset. Don't neglect good and frequent pruning to get the shape you want.

If you bought your tree already growing in a ball of earth or in a pot, do not prune it when you plant. If it was bare-rooted, cut off all the weak branches and part of the others until you have removed about a third of the branch area. If there are no limbs, cut the stem back about one-third. This pruning will delay top growth until the roots have developed enough to support it. Keep in mind how you want the tree to grow and shape it accordingly.

## Maintenance Pruning

Always snip off branches growing too low on the trunk, or any suckers forming around the base of the tree. By starting to prune early you will not need to remove large limbs later. If your tree is on a lawn, "head" it high enough so you can walk and mow comfortably beneath it.

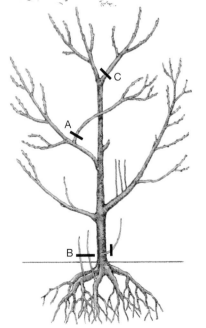

*Some routine maintenance pruning will keep your young tree growing the way it should. (A) Cut off any branch that crosses another. (B) Cut off "suckers" that develop at the base of the tree. (C) Encourage a strong central leader by cutting off any side branch that would produce a weak crotch as the tree ages.*

# RECOMMENDED SHADE TREES

Some tree species listed below have named cultivars that vary in hardiness from the species. If you are interested in one of these special cultivars, check with your nursery to see if the tree is suitable for your planting zone.

| NAME | FEATURE(S) | GROWTH | HARDINESS ZONES |
|---|---|---|---|
| ASH, GREEN (*Fraxinus pennsylvanica*) | Fast-growing shade tree. Cultivars 'Patmore' and 'Summit' have rich gold fall color. | To 60 feet (18 m) | 3–9 |
| ASH, WHITE (*Fraxinus americana*) | Attractive fernlike foliage; a good lawn tree. | To 80 feet (24 m) | 3–9 |
| BASSWOOD, AMERICAN LINDEN (*Tilia americana*) | Fragrant flowers that are attractive to bees; good wood for carving. | To 80 feet (24 m) | 3–8 |
| BEECH, AMERICAN (*Fagus grandifolia*) | Smooth gray bark that is attractive all winter. | To 70 feet (21 m) | 3–9 |
| BEECH, EUROPEAN OR COPPER (*Fagus sylvatica*) | Many cultivars, some with purple leaves. Long-lived, handsome tree. | To 60 feet (18 m) | 5–7 |
| BIRCH, EUROPEAN WHITE OR WEEPING (*Betula pendula*) | White bark; available in many cultivars, giving a wide selection in size, leaf shape, and weeping habits. | To 50 feet (15 m) | 3–7 |
| BIRCH, GRAY (*Betula populifolia*) | White bark that hangs tighter to the tree than other species, with black triangular markings. | To 40 feet (12 m) | 3–6 |
| BIRCH, PAPER OR CANOE (*Betula papyrifera*) | Loose white bark. | To 50 feet (15 m) | 3–6 |
| BIRCH, SILVER OR SWEET (*Betula lenta*) | Reddish black bark; the bark on the young twigs has a wintergreen taste when chewed. | To 75 feet (22.5 m) | 3–6 |
| CORK TREE (*Phellodendron amurense*) | Small whitish flowers in panicles, followed by small black berries; leaves that come out late in the season, turning yellow in the fall; corklike bark; large limbs. | Small tree, to 30 feet (9 m) | 4–7 |
| CUCUMBER TREE (*Magnolia acuminata*) | One of the hardiest species, large leaves; pink to red cucumber-shaped fruits; attractive massive shape. | To 50 feet (15 m) | 4–8 |
| GINKGO (*Ginkgo biloba*) | Fruit can be stinky; plant only male trees. | To 80 feet (24 m) | 4–8 |
| HORSE CHESTNUT, BUCKEYE (*Aesculus hippocastanum*) | Interesting flowers and nuts, but can be messy on lawns, dropping twigs, flowers, leaves, and nuts. | To 75 feet (22.5 m) | 4–7 |
| LARCH, EASTERN LARCH, TAMARACK (*Larix laricina*) | Deciduous conifer with yellow fall color, tiny pink blooms and brown cones. | To 60 feet (18m) | 2–5 |

# RECOMMENDED SHADE TREES *(cont'd)*

| NAME | FEATURE(S) | GROWTH | HARDINESS ZONES |
|------|-----------|--------|------------------|
| LARCH, EUROPEAN (*Larix decidua*) | Longer needles and larger cones than those of *L. laricina;* cones hang on for several years. | To 75 feet (22.5 m) | 3–6 |
| LINDEN, LITTLE-LEAF (*Tilia cordata*) | Good lawn and street tree. | To 70 feet (21 m) | 4–7 |
| LOCUST, THORNLESS HONEY (*Gleditsia triacanthos* var. *inermis*) | Good lawn or street trees; brightly colored young leaves on some cultivars. | To 70 feet (21 m); many cultivars grow in various shapes and heights | 4–9 |
| MAPLE, RED (*Acer rubrum*) | Leaves turn a bright red in fall. | To 100 feet (30 m) | 3–9 |
| MAPLE, SILVER (*Acer saccharinum*) | A fast grower; tall and spreading. | To 100 feet (30 m) | 3–9 |
| MAPLE, SUGAR (*Acer saccharum*) | Massive tree; yields sap that is made into maple syrup; one of the best trees for colorful fall foliage. | To 100 feet (30 m) | 4–8 |
| OAK, RED (*Quercus rubra*) | Leaves turn a rich red shade in autumn and hang on for many weeks. | To 75 feet (22.5 m) | 4–8; sheltered parts of Zone 3 |
| OAK, WHITE (*Quercus alba*) | Long-lived, rugged, spreading tree with purple red fall color. | To 100 feet (30 m), with an 80 foot (24 m) spread | 4–9 |
| POPLAR, ASPEN, COTTONWOOD (*Populus*) | Most are fast growing, but, unfortunately, short-lived. Some turn a rich yellow color in autumn, and many rattle musically in a breeze. Leaf shape varies widely. White poplar *(P. alba)* has leaves with white undersides, that are shaped like those of a maple. | 50 to 100 feet (15 to 30 m) | 2–9, depending on species |
| TULIP TREE (*Liriodendron tulipifera*) | Fast-growing, sturdy tree with attractive foliage. | A massive tree, to 150 feet (45 m) | 5–9 |
| WILLOW, BABYLON WEEPING (*Salix babylonica*) | The best of the weeping forms, widely grown in the South. | About 30 feet (9 m) | 6–8 |
| WILLOW, CORKSCREW (*Salix matsudana* 'Tortuosa') | Twisted branches, an interesting novelty. | To 30 feet (9 m) | 4–8 |
| WILLOW, GOLDEN (*Salix alba* 'Tristis') | Fast-growing, but often short-lived. Weeping form. Can grow in damp spots. Golden bark and branches. | To 40 feet (12 m) | 3–8 |

As the tree grows taller, cut off a few of the lower limbs each year until the bottom ones are 8 or 9 feet (2.4 to 2.7 m) above the ground. The basal pruning you do should be higher than might seem necessary when a shade tree is young, because its lower branches tend to tip upward then, but as it grows, the limbs become heavier and gradually begin to bend toward the ground. If your tree is not branching where you want it to, cut back the top to force growth in those spots.

*Small, deciduous ornamental trees are often the best choice for a small lot. They provide shade, some produce flowers and berries or other fruits, and a few have colorful foliage. For the best choice you may have to order from a specialty catalog or large nursery. Treat most the same as shade trees. They need fertilizer, occasional pruning, and sometimes pest control.*

## RECOMMENDED SMALL ORNAMENTAL TREES

| NAME | DESCRIPTION | GROWTH | HARDINESS ZONES |
|---|---|---|---|
| ASH, MOUNTAIN (Sorbus) | Pretty (sometimes edible) orange or red berry clusters attract birds in late summer and fall. | To 45 feet (13.5 m) | 3–7 |
| CRAB APPLE, FLOWERING (Malus) | Short blooming season; often produce abundant showy fruits later. Some have red or purplish foliage all season; susceptible to scab. Many different cultivars and shades of blossoms. | Various sizes | 3–8 |
| DOGWOOD, FLOWERING (Cornus florida) | Popular spring-blooming tree, mostly with white flowers, although some cultivars have pink or red ones; blooms sometimes wrecked by late frosts. | 40 feet (12 m) | 5–9 |
| LILAC, JAPANESE TREE (Syringa reticulata) | White flowers in June; tends to bloom heavily every other year; brittle wood tends to break in the wind; subject to borers and scale; may need spraying. | To 30 feet (9 m) | 3–7 |
| ORNAMENTAL PEAR (Pyrus) | One-inch (2.5 cm) white flowers early in the spring, followed by tiny russet-colored fruits; nice shape, red leaves in the fall; susceptible to fireblight and storm damage. | To 30 feet (9 m), unless grafted on dwarf rootstock | 4–8 |
| REDBUD (Cercis canadensis) | Purplish pink buds opening to pink flowers in spring, depending on cultivar; heart-shaped leaves that turn yellow in autumn. | 20 feet (6 m) | 5–9 |

# 10 Reclaiming Fruit Crops

Mature fruit trees and berry patches make a landscape particularly appealing by virtue of their homestead connection. They indicate that someone has grown fresh food there, which makes a house feel more like a home. If you have food plants that need to be rejuvenated, you have both a challenge and a treat in store.

The advantages of investing effort in growing your own fruit are many. You can't beat the taste of fresh fruit. While you may not be able to grow everything 100 percent organically, you can at least have complete control over the sprays and fertilizers. You can raise your favorite kinds, including berries that are extremely perishable. You can save money. Last but not least, you have the fun of doing it yourself.

## Fruit Trees

When our nursery specialized in fruit trees, we were often asked, "I just bought a new place with an old orchard. Are the trees worth saving? Can I get them to produce good fruit again?" Without seeing the trees, our safest answer was, "It depends."

The condition of a tree depends on many variables, but not necessarily on its age. Many fruit trees planted a century ago are still producing, yet others only a third their age are struggling along on their last roots. Never sacrifice a tree just because it appears old. Old age can be a sign that the tree is rugged and has survived the ravages of time. Quite likely it may be capable of bearing good fruit for years to come.

*When you grow your own raspberries and other fruits, small and large, you can control the amount of pesticides and fertilizers used to maintain the plants, and you'll enjoy a fresh, abundant harvest at much less cost than if you were to buy it.*

| PROBLEM | POSSIBLE CAUSE | SOLUTION | PAGE |
|---|---|---|---|
| DISCOLORED LEAVES | Plant is diseased or being attacked by insect pests | Get a proper diagnosis; consult chart on pages 143–44 for treatment options. Plant may be too ill to save. | 139 |
| DEAD OR DYING LIMBS | Disease, the results of a pest attack, or storm or winter damage | Remove all dead and dying limbs. This can be done at almost any time of year except winter. Assess what remains to see if it is succumbing or worth saving. | 139 |
| GAPING HOLES OR CAVITIES IN TRUNK OR BRANCHES | Disease, insect, or weather damage | If they are not too big, you may be able to clean them out and fill; if the plant is debilitated by this damage, it may not be worth saving. | 139 |
| SMALL FRUIT LACKING IN FLAVOR | Neglected plant or inferior variety | Prune at proper time; prune adjacent plants for better light and air circulation. Water and feed regularly. | 140 |
| FRUIT WITH POOR COLOR AND FLAVOR | Too much fertilizer (probably too much nitrogen) | Cut back amount of fertilizing; avoid plant's general area when fertilizing nearby plants or the lawn. | 141 |
| LITTLE OR NO FRUIT, OTHERWISE HEALTHY | Too young or no pollination; frost damage to blossoms | If too young, try to be patient. Plant a pollinator tree or bush, if needed, and/or coax bees to the yard. | 139 |
| MOST FRUIT DROPS WHILE IMMATURE | Fruit "set" too large or soil pH too high or too low | Thin the fruits of apples, apricots, nectarines, pears, peaches, and large plums when they are about marble size. Don't thin crab apples, cherries, or small plums. Get soil tested and correct pH accordingly. | 141 |
| LARGE FRUITS DROP EARLY | Soil lacks nutrients or pH is incorrect | Test soil and adjust pH and/or add nutrients, as indicated. | 141 |

Unfortunately, certain varieties of fruit trees have acquired many viruses over the years, and many are already infected when they are sold, even though symptoms may not appear for more than a decade. Bacterial and fungal diseases, weather damage, hungry animals, and insects may also force fruit trees into early retirement. We have seen many relatively young trees so suffering from neglect that the only practical use for them was as firewood.

## Determining Fruit Ripeness

There are early, midseason, and late varieties of most fruits, and different cultivars ripen at different times. You may have a variety of kinds, so do not be impatient if they don't all turn color at once. Don't even be surprised if some lack bright color. 'Greening' and 'Yellow Delicious' apples never turn red, of course, but we know of people who have let them spoil on the tree while waiting for them to change color. Late or "winter" fruits, such as 'Delicious' apples and 'Anjou' pears, should be picked in the fall before they are ready to eat, and stored in a cool place until they reach their peak of ripeness and flavor during the late fall and winter.

Most fruits are ready to pick when they separate easily from the branch; apples and pears are ripe when their seeds have turned a dark color. You'll find that plums take on a rich "bloom" when ready. Pears are the most tricky fruit to pick at the right time, and after years of growing them we are still mostly guessing. We try to pick them a bit before they are completely ripe and let them ripen further indoors. If you wait until they get soft, they are likely to rot on the tree.

- **Are you willing to invest the time needed?** It may be more of a commitment than you initially envision.

- **What kind of tree is it?** If possible, get the plant identified. You may be persuaded to work on it if you are lucky enough to have one of the fine old varieties of fruit that were prized long ago.

- **Does it have gaping cavities** or a hollow center? If so, it may be too far gone.

- **Are many limbs dead or dying?** If so, even pruning these out may not bring the tree back from the brink.

- **Are the leaves discolored** rather than green and healthy looking? This is not a good sign; the tree may be too sickly or weak to save.

- **How does the fruit look,** and perhaps more important, taste? Realize that pruning can increase fruit size. Also, letting additional sunlight into the interior of the tree can improve both color and flavor.

- **Has the tree sprouted in an old orchard** and is it growing in a haphazard way with others of similar size and age? If so, they are likely to be wild seedlings, inferior to the original plant.

- **Is it crowding other trees?** Crowded trees block out light, most soils are not deep enough to support all of the root systems. Do not hesitate to sacrifice a tree if it is crowding better ones. Wait until they bear, so you can identify those worth saving.

- **How old is the tree?** It takes many years for a newly planted young fruit tree to bear a large crop of fruit. It is worthwhile to expend a bit of work and money to urge an existing tree into better production. Plus, aging trees have charm. The fringe benefits, in addition to its beautiful, gnarled appearance, are to walk beneath it in spring when it is blooming, to sniff its heady fragrance, and listen to thousands of buzzing bees at work.

## Operation Rescue: 8 Steps in Reviving Fruit Trees

Dwarf or semidwarf trees are much easier to revive than large, full-size (standard) trees. When standard trees are tall, they are more difficult to prune, spray, and harvest. If your trees have grown up out of reach and have no lower branches, pruning them may not be worth the work and risk involved. If there are numerous lower branches, you may be able to cut back the top to lower it. Lacking this branch area, it is difficult to lop 10 feet (3 m) off a 25-foot tree (7.5 m) without killing it.

**Step 1.** Begin by cleaning the orchard "floor" so you can move around easily and see clearly what to do next. Do this at any time of year. Cut out any brush, wild seedlings, and suckers growing around the base of the trees, and chip or burn them. Clip off tall weeds and mow the grass. Cut to the ground any vines gone wild.

**Step 2.** Examine each tree. Be sure it is solid without large cavities or a hollow center. If there is either,

the tree still could live several years longer, but may not be worth a lot of repairs in the meantime.

**Step 3.** Check the base of the trunk for small holes that may have been made by borers.

**Step 4.** Are there broken and dead limbs? Prune these off anytime. Make all cuts back to the trunk or a live limb so you don't leave any stubs.

**Step 5.** If there is apparent disease or insect damage, see page 143 for treatments.

**Step 6.** Patch any small cavities with tree-sealing compound, available from hardware stores.

**Step 7.** Mark trees worth salvaging and turn the others into firewood. Unless you are skilled with a power saw, get an expert to do the job, since cutting off a large limb or felling a tree can be dangerous both to the saw operator and to other trees.

**Step 8.** Remove cut wood from the vicinity so disease and harmful insects cannot reproduce there.

# Pruning Fruit Trees

Orchardists prune their trees for maximum production, not beauty. Naturally, you would not prune as drastically if your trees are part of your home landscape. If you want them to be productive as well as beautiful, try to achieve a happy medium between appearance and productivity.

Don't try to get your orchard into tip-top shape immediately. Cutting too much wood the first year can be a great shock to a tree that has not been pruned for years. Instead, spread the job over several years, and the tree will forgive you. A good rule is to not remove more than a quarter of the wood on a mature fruit tree over a period of two years.

**Step 1.** Thin out the bearing branches to reduce the number of fruits produced, so more of the tree's energy can go into those that remain. After thinning, the tree should bear a medium-size crop of larger fruits and, having conserved its energy, it is more likely to bear annually rather than every other year.

**Step 2.** Prune to let more light into the interior of the tree, which will ripen the fruit better and increase its vitamin content. If you have seen a commercial orchard when the leaves are off, you've probably noticed that the trees usually look butchered.

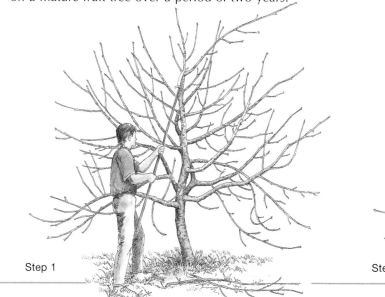

Step 1

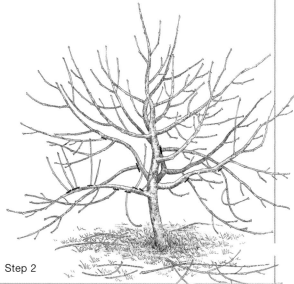

Step 2

## When to Prune Fruit Trees

Prune the trees when they are dormant, in late fall or very early spring, so sap does not bleed. Never prune when the wood is frozen because the wood cells may rupture. Use the right tools for pruning (see page 115) and, avoid using chain saws unless you are highly skilled. It is too easy to cut into yourself or a healthy branch.

Remove limbs that are dead or weather–damaged at any time of the year. Make all cuts close to the main trunk or to a live limb. If the limb is heavy, cut it off in three stages (see Cutting a Large Limb page 129). Use a saw to smooth any stubs left behind when limbs are broken.

*What to Prune*
- ❏ Cut out any large, older branches that are past their prime.
- ❏ Remove all water sprouts (limbs growing vertically from a nearly horizontal branch), since they are unproductive and weaken the tree.
- ❏ Cut out any limbs that rub against other limbs.
- ❏ Thin out branches in areas where they are too thick.
- ❏ Some stone fruit trees develop long, floppy branches that droop to the ground. Cut these back to get them out of the way.
- ❏ Cut back the top to let more light into the tree and make it more spreading (provided there are plenty of lower limbs).

## Feeding Fruit Trees

Neglected trees are likely to be suffering from malnutrition, but if you have recently done major pruning, don't apply fertilizer right away. The removal of many live branches is likely to stimulate the tree enough to make it grow rapidly. A dose of fertilizer can make it grow even faster, and the resulting new growth will be weak and subject to damage from frost and other harsh weather conditions. If you notice that the growth is poor the summer after pruning, add a small amount of fertilizer the following spring.

Where growing seasons are short, fertilize only in early spring so the trees will make their growth early, stop growing in late summer, and harden up their wood before the first frost. Timing is not as critical in warmer areas, but even there it is wise to stop all feeding by early July.

On a small tree, apply the fertilizer just outside the spread of the branches, where the small roots that feed the tree are located. If the tree is larger, it has more spreading roots, so feed it even farther away. For best results, dig a slit with a shovel or make a hole with a bar, insert the plant food, and close the hole so the nitrogen in the fertilizer will not evaporate before the tree can use it. Space the holes about 6 feet (1.8 m) apart around the perimeter of the circle, and put about ½ cup (12 ml) of a complete fertilizer, organic or synthetic (formula 5-10-10, for instance), in each hole, or follow the directions that come with the fertilizer. If you are fortunate enough to have a good supply of compost or manure, spread it around the perimeter of the branch area. It is one of the best things you can do for your fruit tree.

## Correcting Soil pH

Too much or too little lime makes it difficult for a tree to make effective use of the nutrients in the soil, resulting in poor growth and an increased risk of premature fruit drop. Trees always drop excess fruits when they are small if the fruit "set" is too large, but when large fruits drop early, either the supply of nutrients in the soil is low or the pH balance is incorrect.

Many soils lack lime, but if you are not sure about the pH of the soil supporting your trees, do a soil test. Apples and pears prefer a pH of 6 to 7, but apricots, nectarines, plums, and peaches do best when it ranges from 5 to 6. (See pages 166–67.)

## Disease and Insect Control

If your trees have been neglected for a long time, insects may have invaded and diseases may lurk there. Unfortunately, fruit trees have collected so many pests over the centuries that it is almost impossible to grow perfect fruits without some sort of pest control.

If you are not fussy and do not mind imperfect fruit, and if you have only a few trees, you may be able to get by without using pesticides. We prefer to do a minimum of spraying, using the safer sprays. Unless a surprising invasion of summer bugs appears, we spray only in early spring before any fruit develops.

Three types of disease affect fruit trees: bacterial, fungal, and viral. Fungicides control fungus; antiseptics and antibiotics fight bacteria. The best remedy for more-difficult-to-control viruses is prevention.

Insects from all over the world have discovered North American gardens and orchards. Many are harmless; some are beneficial. The bad guys are destructive only when their numbers increase too much. Spray only if necessary, so you won't harm the beneficial bugs. Use an all-purpose orchard spray to control most insects, and follow the directions on the package for the kind of fruit you are growing.

## ORGANIC VS. SYNTHETIC FERTILIZERS

You can choose either an organic or a synthetic fertilizer. We prefer to use the organic kinds on all our food plants for many reasons. They act slowly and feed the trees evenly throughout the season with no danger of "burning" them. Synthetics furnish a quick shot of readily available nutrients that give the trees a spurt of growth that may be weak and break easily in the wind. Too much can also "burn" the tree. Overfeeding when using a synthetic fertilizer can provide too much nitrogen, resulting in fruit with poor color and flavor.

## Orchard Sanitation

A tidy orchard makes caring for the trees easier and more enjoyable, and it also cuts down on pests of all kinds.

➤ Pick up all fallen fruit. Bury it in the compost pile or destroy it because bugs and diseases overwinter in old fruit. If you have grazing deer, they will probably take care of this chore for you.

➤ Prune trees annually, and thin the branches to allow more sunlight to enter the interior of the tree. This also permits air to circulate better, which helps control mildew and scab. Burn the prunings if it is permitted, or take them to a landfill.

➤ Keep the orchard mowed to discourage insects and mice from reproducing in the tall grasses.

➤ Rake up dried fallen leaves in the fall, since these are favorite overwintering spots for scab and other diseases.

➤ Remove any loose bark from older trees so insects cannot breed there.

➤ If you are planting several different kinds of trees, mix up the different kinds — apples, pears, or other fruits. Like isolation, separation of the different kinds makes it tougher for any attacking insects and disease to find the next tree of their choice.

➤ Choose disease-resistant cultivars when you plant new trees.

## Spraying Fruit Trees

Nobody likes to spray, even with "natural" sprays, but we don't relish finding tunnels throughout the fruit, biting into a fat worm, or having to throw away most of our crop. To protect your fruits from pests, use an all-purpose mixture of fungicide and insecticide, either organic or synthetic. For the first spray of the season (see the box on this page, Fruit Tree Spray Schedule), dormant oil works well. It is often available in stores that sell organic products, but if not, make your own by mixing 2 quarts (1.89 L) of light motor oil with a ½ cup (12 ml) of detergent. When you are ready to spray, mix 1 part dormant oil spray with 20 parts water.

## FRUIT TREE SPRAY SCHEDULE

**1. Dormant spray.** When tips of buds are swelling and turning green. (Use dormant oil for this one, if you like. Use a prepared orchard or fruit spray for later sprays.)

**2. Bud spray.** When leaf buds (those that are thin and pointed) are just beginning to open.

**3. Pink spray.** When blossom buds (the fat ones) show pink and are nearly ready to burst open.

*To avoid harming pollinating insects, do not spray when flowers are in bloom.*

**4. Petal fall spray.** When nearly all petals are off the tree. This is the most important spray because insects are most likely to be hatching at this time.

These first four applications may be all the control you need in an isolated home orchard, unless you want absolutely perfect fruit or summer pests are a serious problem.

**5. Later sprays.** Space these 7 to 12 days apart if it becomes necessary to control mites, sawflies, curculios, apple maggots, or summer diseases such as brown rot and scab. Discontinue all spraying, including the organic sprays, at least two weeks before harvest, or follow the recommendations on the package, if they are different.

It is best to spray trees early with a dormant all-purpose orchard or dormant oil spray to control scab, a fungus that floats around the orchard in early spring. This spray also controls early flying insects such as codling moths. It may be necessary to combat later arrivals, such as brown rot and late scab, with additional sprays or other controls.

Since trees bloom at different times, the second, third, and fourth sprays should be done according to the flowering period of each species. Most organic sprays tend to wash off easily and may need to be repeated if it rains soon after spraying. If additional sprays are needed after the fourth, you can spray the entire orchard at the same time.

# PESTS AND DISEASES OF FRUIT TREES

| PEST | DESCRIPTION | SOLUTION |
|------|-------------|----------|
| APHIDS | Leaves curl from ends; tiny insects are often visible on undersides of leaves; plant becomes obviously weak. Aphids, suck the juices from leaves and bark, and spread viruses and other diseases. | Use insecticidal spray or dust. |
| APPLE MAGGOTS | Flies that resemble houseflies lay eggs under the skin of developing apples in midsummer. They develop into larvae that tunnel through the fruits. | All-purpose orchard sprays control them. Artificial apples covered with various sticky materials, available at garden stores, trap them and reduce their numbers. |
| BLACK KNOT | An ugly-looking substance that oozes out of stone fruit trees in summer, turning black as it ages. | Cut off the affected portion as soon as you notice it. Fungicides in early spring help control its spread. If you plant new trees, choose those that are resistant, and keep them at least 500 feet (150 m) from infected trees, particularly the susceptible wild cherries and plums. |
| BORERS | Small holes appear near the ground. Borers weaken and sometimes even topple trees. | Kill borers by poking a wire in each hole, then fill the hole with a tree sealing compound. |
| BROWN ROT | Stone fruits rot on the tree before they ripen. Brown rot is worse in wet summers. The fungus overwinters in fruit and leaves on the ground. | Keep the area as clean as possible. Treat with a fungicide when tiny fruit is forming, and repeat if necessary. |
| CANKER | Open wounds appear on trunk and limbs of fruit trees and bush fruits. | Cut out the wound as soon as you notice it and seal the hole with tree dressing. To help prevent canker, always make pruning cuts close to a trunk or live limb, and remove any dead stubs or branches immediately. |
| CATERPILLARS | Masses of cobwebs appear on the plant, spun by various caterpillars, including the tent caterpillar, webworms, and cankerworms, to protect their eggs and hatching larvae. | Cut away and burn webs, or tear them open and soak with insecticide. |
| CODLING MOTHS | Night-flying moths lay their eggs inside the blossoms, and the larvae hatch into large gray grubs inside the fruits of pears and apples. | Control by spraying dormant oil or fungicide early in the season, after the moths have laid their eggs but before any fruits form. |
| CURCULIOS | The adult beetles feed on and puncture the skin of stone fruits and lay eggs that hatch into larvae and ruin the fruits, much as maggots do apples. | Insecticides are an effective control if applied in early summer. |
| LEAF SPOT | Leaves of stone fruit trees become discolored. | Spray with fungicide whenever it appears. |
| MICE | Trees are girdled, usually over the winter. | Protect young trees with plastic tree guards, but remove them in spring to keep the tree trunks from moisture that invites disease. |
| MITES | Small insects attack fruit and leaves. They may appear in larger numbers in dry summers, but are not usually a problem in home orchards. | When the infestation is heavy, control with miticide. |

| PEST | DESCRIPTION | SOLUTION |
| --- | --- | --- |
| PEACH LEAF CURL | Leaves of peaches and nectarines curl up. | Control with a fungicide and by picking up old fruit in the orchard, where spores could overwinter. |
| PEAR PSYLLA | Leaves are stripped from the tree in a short time and fruits are covered with a black, sooty secretion. These tiny insects are a common problem for pear and quince trees. | Garden insecticides applied in midsummer provide good control. |
| POWDERY MILDEW | White, powdery fungus spreads over the branches, leaves, and fruit of grapes and many tree and bush fruits. | Control with fungicide in early spring and summer. Choose resistant kinds whenever possible. |
| ROOT GALL OR CROWN GALL | Fleshy growths on roots. | There is no cure, but galls rarely cause great damage. |
| RUSTS | Cedar apple rust is a common disease on apples and flowering crabs. The virus spends part of the year on some species of juniper, where it causes galls or swelling on the twig, but it can be fatal to apple trees. White pine blister rust travels between white and other five-needled pines, and *Ribes* (currant and gooseberry) plants. It is sometimes fatal to the pines but does not usually greatly affect the berry plants. | Choose resistant plants, or keep the two host plants separated by several hundred feet (30 or more m). |
| SAN JOSE SCALE | Hard scale appears over branches. Insects are so small you need a magnifying glass to identify them, but they can suck so much juice from branches that they weaken and may even kill a tree. | Control with orchard insecticides. |
| SAPSUCKERS (BIRDS) | Small orderly holes are drilled in tree trunks in early spring. | No good controls available except to scare them away. Plastic owls and noisemakers may help. |
| SAWFLIES, EUROPEAN | Circular raised ridges appear on the skin of developing apples and other fruits. | Use all-purpose orchard spray early, or control with bug traps. |
| SCAB | Branches, leaves, and fruits are covered with dark, hard blotches, and sometimes open cracks appear on the fruit. Spores of this fungus overwinter on the ground in fruit and leaves, and they spread during early spring rains. | Use dormant oil sprays and fungicides in early spring to help control it. Repeat in early summer, if necessary. |
| VIRUS | Trees usually start to die, a few limbs at a time, then all at once. Berry plants become stunted and eventually die. | No cure as yet. Remove infected plants. If you replant, use virus-free or virus-resistant cultivars. Keep new plantings a few hundred feet (30 or more m) from other plants of the same species that may be infected. |
| WILT | Various diseases cause wilts. Leaves and sometimes entire branches of trees and berry plants suddenly wilt and die. | Cut off the affected limbs. If it strikes small fruits, dig out the entire plant and remove it from the area as soon as possible. The disease can spread from plants such as potatoes, tomatoes, and strawberries. Sprays are of little use. |

# Small Fruits

Berry plants are easier to care for than tree fruits and are ideal for a small lot, because they produce so much fruit in a small space. They are delicious, rich in vitamins, and by growing them, you can be sure that they are free from toxic pesticides and preservatives.

Don't be discouraged if time has taken its toll on the small fruit bushes growing on your property. With a bit of first aid, many of your ailing plants can have a new lease on life, because most small fruits are tough. We have discovered gooseberry and currant plants bearing good fruit near the cellar holes of farms abandoned a century ago. Blueberry plants can still produce after years of neglect. Beds of raspberries and blackberries often become junglelike, but they too can be tamed. Last but not least, grapevines need regular pruning to yield good, large fruits, but even when they have been neglected, they often bear small grapes.

## First Aid for Ailing Berry Bushes

Competing vegetation probably has diminished the nutrients available to fruit-bearing bushes, but a weeding job, together with fertilizer and pruning, should bring them back to productivity. We once were shown a row of 10-foot-tall (3 m) blueberry bushes growing among a jungle of young wild cherry trees, thorny rose plants, dogwood, and poison ivy. Rescuing the blueberry plants was a challenge for the new owners of the property, but their hard work was worth the trouble. Once the plants had sunlight, fertilizer, and pruning, they produced buckets of berries, resulting in delicious blueberry pies, jams, and other delicacies.

If you face a similar situation, wear a heavy jacket and gloves to clean out the patch, even if poison ivy is not part of the picture. Summer is a good time to clear out overgrown bushes because you can easily identify the weed plants then. But wait until the berry bushes are dormant to prune them.

If you are dealing with a patch, aim to cut out enough plants so that those remaining will be in a manageable row. If you have more than one row, space the rows 6 feet (1.8 m) apart.

## RESCUING RASPBERRIES AND BLACKBERRIES

- **Raspberries.** Wild ones sometimes join a neglected patch and make a real hodgepodge. Their leaves are slightly different, and the fruit smaller. Try to identify and mark the good berries when they are ripe. Dig them in early fall or spring and plant them in rows.

  If you didn't plant them originally, don't be alarmed if you discover the fruits are not red, since there are wonderful yellow, purple, and black kinds as well. You may also have some of the fall bearers that produce one crop in midsummer and another in September.

- **Blackberries.** Reclaim an overgrown blackberry patch the same way as raspberries, but wear even heavier clothing, since the thorns are sharper and more painful to touch. Blackberry plants are also biennial and are harder to control than raspberry bushes; they are very vigorous and can quickly spread over a wide area.

  You may find that some of your husky blackberry plants are bearing few berries, if any. Over the years some plants produce seeds that grow into sterile plants. If this has happened, the best thing to do is dig out the patch and start again with new plants.

## Pruning Berry Bushes

**Dewberries, boysenberries, youngberries, and other vine blackberries.** Tie to an overhead wire to keep the long, limp canes off the ground. Shorten the canes that are too long, and cut out the old ones each fall after harvesting.

**Blueberries.** Your bushes may look rather scraggly after the weeding job. Begin to get them in shape in either late fall or early spring before growth starts. We emphasize "begin." Do not remove more than a third of the branch area of each bush in any one year. Cut out limbs that appear diseased, insect infested, or winter damaged. Then clip out those that are showing signs of age. If the plants are tall with few branches, cut the tops down to 5 or 6 feet (1.5 or 1.8 m) to encourage them to branch. When plants are more bushy than tall, however, thin out any limbs that are within 2 or 3 inches (5 or 7.5 cm) of each other. If you live in a cold region (Zones 3 to 5), limit pruning mostly to removing injured branches and cutting off their twiggy ends. In those areas, an overpruned bush may take several years to get back into full production. In Zones 5 and warmer, after the bush gets into full production, prune out some of the old wood each year. By faithfully doing this you can completely renew the bearing surface over a period of several years.

*In early spring, cut out all wood on bush fruits that is more than three years old.*

**Gooseberries and currants.** Prune out the oldest branches, then fertilize and mulch them. Thin out gooseberry branches during early summer, which makes it easier to safely pick the fruit and is likely to result in larger berries. After your initial pruning, early each spring when the plants are dormant, cut out all wood more than three years old. Feed and mulch each year.

**Raspberries.** These are perennial shrubs that bear biennial canes, which means that they grow one year, produce the following year, and then die.

The new canes that are growing that season are green; the older ones have brown stems. Those with brown stems will bear fruit that summer and die shortly after, but those with green stems will overwinter and bear the following year. Leave both kinds in place until after you have finished picking the berries. Either then or later in the fall, cut out the dying canes that bore fruit, and take them to a landfill or burn them to prevent any disease or insects from spending the winter near your patch. Cutting and disposing of dead canes will be an annual fall chore. Leave those with green stems to produce next year's crop. Before winter, cut all the canes back to about 5 feet (1.5 m) in height so they will be stiff and won't tip over during a wind or heavy snowstorms. At the same time, thin out weak canes and any that are closer than 6 inches (15 cm) to each other, to ensure that the remaining ones produce larger berries.

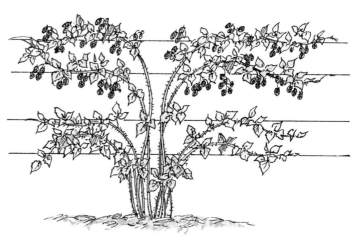

*Raspberry canes are biennial. In the fall, cut out the old canes that bore fruit that season. The new canes will bear fruit next year.*

## Aftercare

Plant grass between your reclaimed rows and mow between them, or keep the rows closer together and mulch with shavings, bark, or wood chips.

**Fertilizing.** The first summer after the rescue operation and initial pruning, allow the plants to grow without feeding them. Early the next spring and every spring thereafter, fertilize them. Use a complete plant food and follow the recommendations on the package.

**Mulching.** Since many berry plants, including blueberries, have shallow roots, spread a mulch 2 or 3 inches (5 or 7.5 cm) thick around them. Use shredded leaves or other organic materials. (See Marvelous Mulch Materials, page 164, for ideas of what to use.) Mulch protects them from drying out during droughts and from suffering in cold winter temperatures. If you find that weeds grow right through it, try a heavier mulch.

## Landscaping Uses of Small Fruits

Whether you're reclaiming an overgrown patch, moving plants around your property, or shopping for new berry plants, you can employ these landscaping ideas to take advantage of the plants' ornamental qualities:

➤ Plant berry plants as a hedge. Just don't plant them too close together — they spread!

➤ Use thorny types along your property line to deter unwanted visitors (animal or human).

➤ Add one or two plants to the perimeter of a vegetable garden.

➤ Train plants with arching canes onto a trellis against a wall, or let them swoop over a low fence (realizing that if you cannot or choose not to do the "by-the-book" pruning, the plants will be less productive).

➤ Grow an individual bush solo, as a specimen plant, and give it superb care in order to get a bountiful harvest.

➤ Prune a plant or plants to a single stem (cordon); this allows you to fit more plants in less space.

# GRAPES: THEIR SPECIAL NEEDS AND CARE

Whether you have neglected a grapevine you planted a few years ago, or you've found one on your newly acquired property, it may be creeping over walls and climbing up trees. In only a decade a grapevine can cover a large area, sending down roots and creating new plants as it progresses. It may take a lot of pruning to reclaim it, so first check the ripe grapes to see if they are of good quality. If not, cut it back to the ground and plant a new one somewhere else if you want to grow grapes.

If you have decided to keep your vine, and it is in a good location, it will need some severe pruning. When it is dormant, cut it back to about 5 feet (1.5 m) from the ground. Then you will need to decide whether you want it for fruit, beauty, or both.

When the primary function of a grapevine is to cover an arbor, trellis, or fence, and to provide shade or block off a view, you'll need to prune it back only enough each year to get and keep it within bounds. It must be cut back annually, however, because mature grape plants grow with such vigor. It is important to prune only when the vine is dormant.

To grow quality fruit, you will need to prune the vine severely each year. The distance the canes are growing away from the roots and main stem affects production: If they are far away, production will be poor. Therefore, you will want to keep your vine very compact. Consult with someone familiar with grapes on how to best do this, or read a book about growing fruits. It will tell you how to set up a support system, and how to prune and fertilize each year for maximum production.

If you want your vine to do double duty, you can make it both produce good fruit and offer aesthetic shade over an arbor or trellis. Prune it enough to let in plenty of sun to ripen the fruit, and thin out the old canes each year, but leave enough vines for plenty of shade.

*A healthy grapevine not only promises a harvest of good fruit, but grown on an arbor or trellis, it also provides cool shade.*

# 11 Water in Your Landscape

If you have a water garden that has gone untended for a number of years, it may now look as if nature is completely in charge. Soil-bottom ponds are likely to be overcrowded with vegetation and algae. If you have a man-made pond, the water may have evaporated completely and the plants are very likely in plant heaven. Because certain types of water gardens need only minimal care, they are often completely neglected. With a bit of attention, however, they can once again become a beautiful asset to the landscape. A water garden is an exciting way to add a focal point to your backyard. It is also a way to transform a defect such as a swampy back corner into a special garden containing a collection of beautiful plants.

The term *water garden* encompasses many different types of wet and moist spots where you find aquatic plants (those that must live in water) and semi-aquatics (those that grow in either wet soil or shallow water). In nature, you find these plants growing in shallow ponds, slow-moving streams, bog areas that are covered with water part of the year and swampy the rest, and wet areas surrounding a pond or bordering a stream. When landscapers discuss water gardens, however, they're likely to mean a shallow pool constructed expressly for water lilies and other ornamental aquatic plants. You can even construct a water garden in a large tub placed on your deck or patio.

*The peace and serenity of a water garden is the perfect focal point for a sunny spot in many backyards.*

| PROBLEM | POSSIBLE CAUSE | SOLUTION | PAGE |
|---|---|---|---|
| UNHEALTHY PLANTS | Water unclean or inadequate | Clean and refill unit. | 155 |
| | Plants crowded | Thin and divide overgrown plants. | 154 |
| | Plants undernourished | Add soluble fertilizer tablets. | 154 |
| | Inadequate sunlight (less than 4 to 6 hours per day) | Remove light obstructions, if possible. | 150 |
| | Disease or insect problems | Identify and treat. | 155 |
| | Soil-bottom pool filling in with silt | Remove sick or dead plants, thin and/or divide remainder. If silt is heavy, remove all plants and remove silt. | — |
| PLANTS PRODUCE FEW AND/OR SMALL BLOOMS | Plants crowded (foliage covers more than 70 percent of water surface) | Thin and divide overgrown plants. | 154 |
| | In a bog-type garden or wet area surrounding a pond, crowded by cattails and other rushes | Remove aggressive plants by hand-pulling or by hiring a bulldozer, dragline, or backhoe. | 152 |
| | In soil-bottom or bog garden, water table has changed since garden was planted, resulting in inadequate or excessive moisture | Get expert hydrological advice; if water too low, add water or build higher dam; if water too high, drain or build dikes to divert water. | 151 |
| ALGAE PRESENT | Ecological balance upset | Treat to restore balance. | 155 |

# Installing a New Water Garden

If your water garden is in hopeless shape, you may want to install a new one on the same spot or in a different area of your landscape. Before you start, consider the type of terrain you have and the kind of plants you want to grow. On a small lot, you may decide to confine your growing to a large tub on a deck or terrace, but with more space you could install a shallow pool or use a swampy spot to grow water plants.

## A Shallow, Lined Pool

**Siting.** If possible, situate your pool within reach of a garden hose for filling. If you plan to use a pump, you'll also need an electrical outlet. Avoid locating the pool under deciduous trees, not only because of the shade they produce, but also because when the leaves fall they cover the pool and necessitate a clean-up job. To bloom well, hardy water lilies and many other water plants need at least 4 hours of full sun each day; tropical water lilies need 6 hours.

**Pool type.** Concrete pools are durable, but in the North, frost heaving often damages them. Because concrete pools should be installed by professionals, they are also expensive, and they must

---

### A TIP FOR A CLEANER POOL

To help keep the water clean in a shallow, lined pool, grow all the water lilies and other aquatic plants in submerged plastic pots, instead of covering the bottom with soil.

be treated to make them safe for fish. "Instant" preformed pools of fiberglass or plastic are available in a multitude of different shapes and sizes, but are advisable only in warm climates because, in the North, frost easily damages them, too.

Where winters are cold, lining the hole with a PVC liner, between 20 and 32 mils, or a more expensive and longer-lasting 45 or 60 mil thick rubber liner, is a better choice. All are available in different sizes. You may want to sandwich the liner between two layers of protective felt to protect it.

**Excavation.** The hole you dig for your pool, whatever liner you use, should be 18 to 30 inches (45 to 75 cm) deep, depending on the type of plants you want to grow. The size of the pool is a matter of personal preference, but 8 X 12 or 10 X 14 feet (2.4 X 3.6 or 3 X 4.2 m) works well for most "first" water gardens. Since different plants need to be sunk at different depths, the pool should have different levels if you plan to grow a variety of plants. To adjust the depth of containers, set them on plastic crates, concrete blocks, or overturned containers. Some gardeners build a ledge about 8 inches (20 cm) deep around the perimeter. This is a good time to invite friends for a pool party, especially if they are muscular!

**Water source.** Fresh running water is not necessary in a pool garden, but after you have filled it initially, usually with a garden hose, you will need to add water now and then as it evaporates. Some gardeners install plumbing, which makes it easier to fill and refill the pool. A drain in the base facilitates emptying the pool for cleaning. If your water contains chlorine, allow it to sit for a week until the chlorine evaporates. Or, if you don't want to wait, pool supply houses sell products that remove the chlorine instantly.

---

## WATER LILIES NEED STILL WATER

Water lilies, as well as many other water plants, cannot tolerate moving water, so if you have a waterfall, be sure your pool is large enough for both a waterfall and plants.

---

To circulate the water for aeration, a waterfall or fountain connected to a pump is not only useful, but adds a welcome, relaxing sound. A mechanical or biological filter system is another helpful addition.

## A Soil-Bottom Pond

Instead of a commercially made backyard pool into which you sink potted container plants, you may decide to have a shallow water garden with the plants rooted in soil. Obviously it is not possible or important to keep the water perfectly clean there. Many native aquatic plants, as well as hardy water lilies, thrive in such a pool. Some grow in shallow water only 8 inches (20 cm) deep, but others, such as water lilies, need water from 1 to 1½ feet (30 to 45 cm) deep. If it is deeper, you can build piles of soil here and there in the bottom so that the aquatic plants will not be rooted too deeply. Most farm ponds and those built for swimming, fire protection, or for raising fish are too deep and cold to grow water lilies.

**Siting and water source.** If you want to build a new soil-bottom pond, you'll need a naturally swampy area that has some standing water all year or an area in which you find springs. After excavation, the water that is naturally present should keep your pond filled.

**Excavation.** Hire someone with a bulldozer or drag hoe to dig it for you. (Before you begin, be sure to check local and state regulations to see if you need a permit to construct a pond.) Damming up a stream usually does not work well, because during heavy rains, flooding can easily damage or wash away the plants. It may also be against regulations to alter the flow of a brook.

**The plants.** To keep an ecological balance in a soil-bottom pond, experts recommend that for each square yard (m²) of water surface you should plant two bunches of oxygenating grasses to prevent algae formation. (These grasses absorb nutrients through their underwater leaves and stems and produce oxygen, giving algae less opportunity to develop.) Also add two goldfish or koi to eat bugs and algae, as well as twelve snails for algae control.

## A Bog Garden

A swampy area is not unusual on a large country lot, and you may find such spots in suburbs, as well. These spots are sometimes offensive to owners who consider them mainly breeding places for mosquitos and other pests. People often spend large sums trying to drain them, or they fill them in, a practice that is frequently not successful and may also be illegal.

Instead of filling a soggy, swampy piece of land that is poorly drained, you may want to transform it into a bog and pond garden where you can grow both aquatic and semi-aquatic, or transitional, plants. To create an environment for both, hire someone with a bulldozer or dragline to gouge out part of the area. Water will collect in the basin, and you'll have a small pond where you will be able to plant true aquatics. Semi-aquatics should be able to thrive in the surrounding soil.

If you don't want to bother with a pond, just enjoy your wet area as a bog and grow semi-aquatics such as golden marsh marigolds *(Caltha palustris)*, blue flag *(Iris versicolor)*, and other colorful, attractive plants. (See page 157 for other suggestions.)

## A Brook Garden

Another place where you might grow aquatic and semi-aquatic plants (such as watercress for your salads) is in a shallow stream. We have seen native water lilies growing in the outlet of a pond where the stream moved very slowly. Before you plant, be certain that the stream is not subject to heavy seasonal floods that would wash away the plants. Check, too, to see that it isn't too deep and that there is enough soil to support the plants.

## A Container Water Garden

If you don't have the space, energy, or money to install an in-ground water garden, you can get many of the same benefits in miniature, by planting a large container, such as a half–whiskey barrel or even more simply a generous-size bowl with water plants.

# Growing Aquatic Plants

One of the fascinations of water gardens is the wide variety of plants now available for home gardeners. You can choose from many different types of water lilies and lotus, among others.

## Water Lilies

When most people think of aquatics, water lilies *(Nymphaea)* are at the top of the list. You may envision Monet's paintings of water lilies in his famous water gardens at Giverney. Water lilies are of two types, hardy and tropical, and both have numerous varieties. Pink, red, yellow, and white blooms of the easy-to-grow hardy plants float on the surface along with their foliage. The flowers of the exotic tropical water lilies stand above the surface of the water on 2- to 4-inch (5 to 10 cm) stems and bloom in those shades as well as purple, blue, and violet. They are usually fragrant and more showy than the hardy types.

Most water lilies are day bloomers, but many of the tropicals are night blooming. Each blossom lasts approximately three days and then sinks, to be replaced by another. The hardy types endure the winter safely outdoors as long as the roots do not freeze. You must treat the tropicals as annuals in areas cooler than Zone 10, unless you protect them by removing the containers and storing them in a frost-free basement, greenhouse, or garage.

## Lotus

Another popular aquatic is the lotus *(Nelumbo)*. Instead of floating on the water like hardy water lilies, lotus grow 2 to 5 (0.6 to 1.5 m) feet above the surface with enormous leaves and large, fragrant, yellow, white, red, or pink flowers that are followed by showy seed pods. Since they need deep soil and shallow water, these vigorous growers are best suited for ponds with earth bottoms, where there is room for their huge root systems. For a small pool, you can find cultivars that grow only 1 to 2 feet (30 to 60 cm) tall. Most species need winter protection in northern climates. Lotus cutivars are available in water plant catalogs. Follow the directions that

*Water lilies and water hyacinths are two dependable — and favorite — plants for backyard ponds.*

come with the plants, and don't crowd too many into the same pool.

## Other Water Plants

Water lettuce and water hyacinth are plants that need no soil or planting because they float on top of the water. These were once widely used in water gardens, but are so invasive that it is now forbidden to plant them in Texas and South Carolina, and laws forbid interstate shipment.

Refer to the chart on page 156 for many other interesting water plants.

# Caring for Water Plants

You can plant hardy aquatics in early spring, but wait to plant tropical water lilies until the water temperature reaches about 70°F (21°C). When you receive your aquatic plants from a mail-order company in the spring, follow the potting directions.

Water garden supply houses offer many sizes of containers for water plants, or you can use your own large plastic pots or even a plastic water pail with holes punched in the base. The type of plant should determine the size of the container. Each hardy lily needs at least a 12-inch (30 cm) container that holds 2½ gallons (9.48 L) of soil. A tropical lily needs 4 gallons (15.16 L) of soil, and a lotus, 8 gallons (30.32 L). The more soil a plant has for its roots, the more vigorous it will be and the larger the blooms. The best medium is a mixture of clay and loam, plus a handful of commercial organic or synthetic fertilizer; or you can insert fertilizer tablets from a supply house. Avoid using manure, peat moss, or compost, as these muddy the water. They also make it more acid, which does not suit either plants or fish.

## PLANTING WATER LILIES

**1.** Fill the appropriate size container (see page 153) with a clay-loam soil, to which you've added a handful of fertilizer or slow-release fertilizer tablets.

**2.** Set the crown of the plant just above the soil surface, and then cover with 2 inches (5 cm) of sand or fine gravel to keep the water clean. (Be sure not to cover the crown, however.) Before submerging the pot in the pool, soak the plant well, so the soil doesn't mix with the pool water.

**3.** Initially, set the container on a plastic crate so that its rim is approximately 6 inches (15 cm) below the water surface. After the plant begins to grow, lower it so the rim rests about 12 inches (30 cm) below the surface.

**Nutrition.** Water lilies are heavy feeders so fertilize them about twice a month. Fertilizer for container-grown plants is available in tablet form, and an injector is available to place it in the pot without removing the container from the pond. Continue to feed plants until early fall, when the water temperature has fallen below 60°F (16° C).

**Winter care.** Once the plants stop growing and the foliage yellows, prune plants to within a few inches of their crowns. After the first killing frost, remove all foliage except the tiny leaves beneath the water near the crown. You can purchase a pruning device with a long handle, so that you can snip off the leaves from the edge of the pool, without entering the water.

**Leave the hardy plants in place.** If you decide to winter over the tropicals, remove them from the pool after a frost or two. The water should reach about 50°F (10°C) before you remove the plants, so they will become dormant. Follow the directions that come with the plant for wintering over in a frost-free garage or basement.

**Dividing plants.** Divide the plants when necessary. If water lilies growing in pots appear crowded, split apart the rhizomes of hardy plants (or the tubers of tropicals) in the spring. The hardy types usually need dividing every two to five years when they are growing well, but the tropicals should be split up each year. Hardy plants in a soil-bottom pond can be left alone, as long as their roots have plenty of soil for expansion. Water lilies and most bog plants are long-lived and should last for half a century. The soil in the pots should be changed every three to four years, whether you divide or not.

## HOW MANY PLANTS DO YOU NEED?

Set containers of hardy, standard-size water lilies about 5 feet (.9 to 1.5 m) apart, and count on about 6 to 10 square feet (.56 to .93 m²) of water surface for each mature plant. Miniature lilies, such as pygmy cultivars, have only a 6-foot (1.8 m) spread. Each tropical plant may cover up to 30 square feet (2.79 m²) of water surface, so miniature cultivars are most suitable for small pools. Plant foliage should never cover more than 70 percent of the water surface.

Submerged oxygenating plants, available at pool supply houses, help control algae and keep the water clear. Plant at least one clump for every 2 square feet (.19 m²) of water surface.

If you prefer to avoid the mathematics, pool suppliers often offer collections of aquatic plants to suit various sizes of pools.

# Pest Control

Aquatics and semi-aquatics are not likely to be bothered by diseases or insects. Occasionally, however, in hot, humid weather, you may see signs of a fungus disease on the leaves, particularly if the plants are crowded. Pick off the infected leaves and thin out the plants.

Control the water lily aphid, the most likely insect to infest aquatics, by hosing them off and letting fish eat them, or by trimming off and destroying affected leaves. If more control is necessary, use a mixture of kerosene, detergent, and water. (Pour equal amounts of kerosene and water into a container and then add enough detergent to combine the oil and water.)

Pool supply firms sell floating repellent cakes that control mosquitos.

---

## SOME PITFALLS TO AVOID

**Enough is enough.** Beware of an overpopulation of fish. One of our friends had a beautiful, large earthen pond filled with koi. The fish census exploded, and because they didn't have enough food, they fed on the plants and tree roots around the edge of the pond. The banks eroded and trees slid in, filling up the pond and creating an unsightly ecological disaster.

The best prevention against such a disaster seems to be to continually fish out the extras. You may even be able to sell them to other pool lovers.

**Beware of chemicals.** If your water source is chlorinated, it could harm fish unless you add a product that neutralizes the chlorine. Alternatively, let the water stand for a week before putting it into the pool. Some municipal systems treat water with other chemicals that are harmful to fish. If your water is treated, use a neutralizing agent. (Neutralizers are available at pool supply houses.)

It's also important to keep all pesticide use away from water gardens, as these can harm your fish and other aquatic organisms.

---

## FALL CLEANUP

In the fall you may need to do a thorough pool cleaning to remove leaves and other debris that have collected in the bottom of a lined pool:
1. Remove the plant containers and place them in tubs of water, so they won't dry out.
2. Catch any fish and place them in water.
3. Siphon off or otherwise drain the water.
4. Clean the base, and then refill the pool.
5. Cover the pool to keep leaves and twigs from falling into the water over the winter months, if they are a problem.

---

# Pool Maintenance

Water gardens need less care than earth gardens, but they must have regular attention if they are to look spiffy.

**Neaten up.** Pick off fading flowers and discolored leaves frequently. Water garden supply companies sell a variety of cleaning aids, from pond vacuums to brushes that loosen algae. A long-handled pond skimmer is indispensable for gathering foreign debris that collects on the pool. If you have excess leaves and other matter falling into the water, you can get chemical formulations designed to make pond debris clump together and fall to the bottom. You can then clean it with a pond "vacuum cleaner."

**Control algae.** To keep the water in a shallow lined pool clean and free of algae, for every 1 to 2 square feet (.3 to .6 m$^2$) of water surface, plant one bunch of oxygenating grass and add one Japanese black snail and two goldfish or koi.

Sunlight is vital for the growth of algae. Do not be dismayed if algae covers the water initially, because it will probably disappear when leaves grow to shade the water. You can also help prevent its spread by using algae blockers, which are black or blue-green dyes that you mix with the water to block out the sunlight. These are formulated to be safe for plants, fish, and other wildlife, and actually enhance the appearance of a pond.

# Wildlife in Your Water Garden

Water attracts all sorts of wildlife, and we thoroughly enjoyed the frogs that relaxed on the lily pads in our tiny water garden. They helped keep the plants free from bugs, added color and style to the garden, and serenaded us with delightful froggy songs on warm spring nights.

If your pool doesn't already have fish in it, you may want to add them. They eat mosquitos and their larvae, as well as other insects and algae. Although you will need to feed them periodically, the benefits are worth it. Goldfish are beautiful, but as they become larger they tend to make the water muddy and are not winter hardy in the North. Japanese carp, known as koi, are better choices for northern ponds.

A variety of birds are attracted to water, which is desirable, but be careful about importing ducks, geese, or swans, if you want to grow plants successfully. They appreciate water plants only as food and will digest your garden in short order. They also make the edges of the pond muddy as they dine, and their droppings can be a problem.

Turtles and other water lovers may also enjoy dining on your plants, but great damage from them is unlikely.

*The wildlife that your water garden is likely to attract, from frogs to birds, provide entertainment of their own.*

## PLANTS THAT LIKE WATER

### *Aquatic Plants: Those That Must Live in Water*
American lotus *(Nelumbo lutea)*
Arrow arum *(Peltandra virginica)*
Arrowhead *(Sagittaria)*
Water hyacinth *(Eichhornia)*
Water lettuce *(Pistia)*
Water lilies *(Nymphaea)*

### *Semi-Aquatic Plants: Those That Grow in Wet Soil or Shallow Water*
These plants do well in bogs.
Arrow arum *(Peltandra virginica)*

Arrowhead *(Sagittaria)*
Blue flag *(Iris versicolor)*
Cattail *(Typha latifolia)*
Giant reed *(Arundo)*
Golden club *(Orontium)*
Narrow-leafed cattail *(Typha angustifolia)*
Pitcher plant *(Sarracenia purpurea)*
Royal fern *(Osmunda regalis)*
Sweet flag *(Acorus calamus)*
Water clover *(Marsilea)*
Yellow flag *(Iris pseudacorus)*
Yellow pond lily, bullhead lily *(Nuphar)*

# PLANTS FOR WET AREAS

Instead of draining a swampy spot, consider planting some of the following. Specialty nurseries offer these plants, and you may find some growing wild that you can get permission to move.

Bee balm *(Monarda)*
Blue bog violet *(Viola cucullata)*
Blue lobelia *(Lobelia siphilitica)*
Boltonia *(Boltonia asteroides)*
Boneset *(Eupatorium perfoliatum)*
Cardinal flower *(Lobelia cardinalis)*
Cattail *(Typha)*
Closed gentian *(Gentiana andrewsii)*
Culver's root *(Veronicastrum virginicum)*
Ferns, cinnamon, royal, and sensitive varieties
Forget-me-not *(Myosotis)*
Joe Pye-weed *(Eupatorium maculatum)*
Lanced-leaf goldenrod *(Solidago graminifolia)*
Marsh marigold *(Caltha palustris)*
New England aster *(Aster novae-angliae)*
Plantain lily *(Hosta)*
Ragged robin *(Lychnis flos-cuculi)*
Rose mallow *(Hibiscus moscheutos)*
Siberian iris *(Iris sibirica)*
Summer phlox *(Phlox maculata)*
Swamp buttercup *(Ranunculus)*
Swamp candles *(Lysimachia terrestris)*
Swamp milkweed *(Asclepias incarnata)*
Virginia bluebells *(Mertensia)*

## Ornamental Grasses for Bog Areas

The ornamental grasses that like moisture are colorful in fall and winter, but some kinds are so aggressive, they can crowd out other plants. Many of these are good for planting around the perimeter of an earthen pond or stream.

Bowles' golden sedge *(Carex elata)*
Bulbous oat grass *(Arrhenatherum elatius* var. *bulbosum)*
Feather reed grass *(Calamagrostis acutiflora* 'Stricta')*
Japanese silver grass *(Miscanthus sinensis)*
Quaking grass *(Briza media)*
Switch-grass *(Panicum virgatum)*
White-striped ribbon grass *(Phalaris arundinacea* 'Picta')*
Zebra grass *(Miscanthus sinensis* 'Zebrinus')*

# Part 3

# A Healthy Foundation for Your Lawn and Garden

Advertisements in garden magazines and catalogs often imply that all we need to do to get beautiful flowers, luxurious trees, prize-winning vegetables, and lush lawns is to buy and use their superb plants and seeds. We gardeners soon learn, however, that even if lawns, gardens, and landscape plantings start with good seed and plant material, they flourish only if we give them healthy, fertile soil and maintain vigilant pest protection. Few of us are blessed today with the deep humus and nutrient-rich soil the earliest settlers enjoyed. Too often we have inherited a thin layer of topsoil, sadly lacking the elements and organic matter that make for productive growth. We also have received a legacy of troublesome insects, diseases, and weeds that, like the human population, increase annually. Fortunately, there are ways to improve the soil and safely combat pests so that anyone can have excellent gardening results. The following chapters will help you do just that.

# 12 Upgrading Your Soil: The Secret to Good Plant Growth

During a garden club talk we once used the word *dirt* to refer to the spot where plant roots dwell. A member immediately protested. "Dirt is something to sweep off the floor," she said. "Soil is what you are talking about."

She was right. We sometimes use the words interchangeably, but the top layer of the earth's surface is far more than dirt. Although we tend to consider soil a permanent part of our landscape, of course it is not. The great deserts of the world were once fertile soil, covered with fields and forests. The virgin soil that newcomers to North America found was deep and very rich in nutrients, but over the centuries in most places it has worn thin from use and misuse, and now needs regular attention to keep it productive.

When our plantings deteriorate, whether they are petunias, magnolias, or an oak tree, we are likely to blame their age, disease, or insects, when often the fault is a soil that no longer provides for their needs. Take good care of your yard and garden soils, and you will be richly rewarded.

## Well-Balanced Soil

Good soil consists of a well-balanced mixture of sand, clay, silt, and humus, an organic material made up of partially decayed plant or animal life. Humus not only adds fertility to the soil but it holds moisture and nutrients and releases both to the plant roots. It also encourages earthworms, which keep the soil loose so roots can grow readily. Unless soil is maintained with a supply of humus, it deteriorates into a mixture of rock and clay particles.

The ideal soil for most horticultural purposes has approximately 30 percent each of clay, sand, and silt, and 10 percent humus (organic matter). If the soil is unbalanced, with more than 50 percent clay or sand, for instance, many plants will have difficulty growing in it. Also, the soil structure — arrangement of the clay, sand, and silt particles and the spaces between them — must be such that air and water can move through it effectively. Unless your soil is hopelessly poor, you can usually improve its structure.

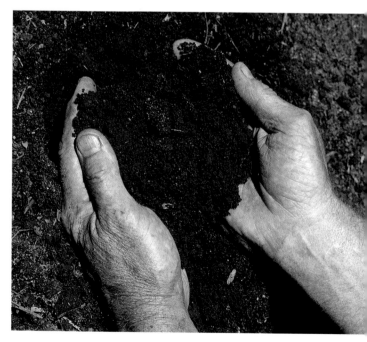

*Vigorous plants depend on healthy soil, the reservoir that holds the moisture and nutrients they need.*

# Fertility

Fertility is crucial to plant growth, and nature enriches the soil in many ways. Animal and bird droppings supply both nutrients and humus, as do fallen leaves and decaying woody materials. Earthworms add nutrients to the soil via their rich castings. Winter snows offer a protective cover that prevents erosion for several months in snowy regions. (In fact, New England farmers describe snow as "poor man's fertilizer," but its main benefit is that it shields, rather than enriches, the soil.) Interestingly, lightning adds nitrogen to the soil with every thunderstorm, making the grass greener and stimulating a spurt of growth to gardens, trees, and shrubs.

To supplement nature's offerings, gardeners have a wide choice of fertilizers, both organic and chemical, in liquid and granular forms. Which are best? Talk to 10 gardeners and you are likely to get 10 different recommendations. Everyone has favorites.

## SOIL NUTRITION

| NUTRIENT(S) | DESCRIPTION | ORGANIC SOURCES | CHEMICAL SOURCES |
|---|---|---|---|
| NITROGEN (N) | A gas in its pure natural form, nitrogen can become unstable when exposed to water, air, or high temperatures, even when it is in a compound such as ammonium nitrate. Because it dissipates so rapidly it is always likely to be in short supply in soil. | Animal manure; cottonseed meal; dried blood; blood meal; grass clippings; leaves; and plant legumes, plants that manufacture nitrogen from the air and add it to the soil through their roots. Use a nitrogen-fixing bacteria sold by most garden stores and in catalogs. | Balanced, granular chemical fertilizers, such as 10-10-10, and liquid chemical fertilizers contain nitrogen, usually in a form more concentrated than organic fertililzer. They become available to the plants rapidly, sometimes too rapidly, so must be used with care or they may "burn" the plants. |
| PHOSPHORUS (P) | Critical for good plant growth and likely to be scarce in most soils. Available in varying amounts in most fertilizers. Moves through the soil well. | Hard rock phosphate; colloidal rock phosphate; bonemeal, a by-product of the meat industry ("steamed" bonemeal works faster than regular bonemeal). | Balanced commercial fertilizers; superphosphate, a fertilizer that has been treated with acid to make it available faster. (Organic gardeners feel superphosphate discourages earthworms and other beneficial soil life.) |
| POTASSIUM (K) | Critical for good plant growth and likely to be scarce in most soils. Available in varying amounts in most fertilizers. Moves through the soil well. | Greensand, granite dust, wood ashes, seaweed, and composted wood and leaves. | Balanced chemical fertilizers. |
| CALCIUM (CA) | Plants need calcium to grow well, and though it is usually available in most soils, in some it may be lacking. | Lime, hardwood ashes, and calcitic and dolomitic limestone (dolomitic also contains 8 percent magnesium). Use gypsum if you don't want to raise the pH of your soil. | No chemical sources, but lime may be included in chemical fertilizers. |
| TRACE ELEMENTS, including boron, iron, copper, and zinc in minute amounts. | Healthy soils usually contain enough of these for most kinds of plants, but certain crops require additional amounts of one or another. When the soil does not provide enough, the plant growth is poor and the leaves are pale green or various light shades of other colors. | Compost and manure; composted sawdust, bark, shavings, and leaves. Earthworms deposit trace elements throughout the soil in their castings, and organic fertilizers sometimes contain seaweed meal and dried fish products, both of which are rich in these elements. | Often available in chelated form, which makes them available more slowly to plants. Use commercially produced trace elements sparingly, since some are toxic to the soil if they are applied in even slightly excessive amounts. |

## Necessary Nutrients

The most important nutrients that plants need are nitrogen (N), phosphorus (P), and potassium (K). On bags of fertilizer you see the percentage of these elements designated in the order of N, P, and K. For example, 5-10-10 means that the fertilizer has 5 percent nitrogen, 10 percent phosphorus, and 10 percent potassium (by weight). Most of the remaining 75 percent is an inert filler called ballast. Sometimes a fourth number also appears, which represents a trace element such as iron, boron, or manganese.

You can buy soil kits that test for nutrients. These are more complicated to use than those that test for pH, and Cooperative Extension Services will often do these tests for you, for a fee. In the tests we have made, we nearly always have found that the soil, unless recently fertilized, needed almost every nutrient.

## Organic vs. Synthetic Fertilizers

**Organic fertilizers** tend to be lower in nutrients than synthetic fertilizers and cost more per unit of nutrient, but they last longer in the soil and are safer to use. They are also excellent soil conditioners. Many growers feel that when they use organic fertilizers on vegetable gardens and orchards, the soil is maintained in better condition, the plants are healthier, and the flavor of the crop is better.

"Organic fertilizer" is a tricky term. Strictly used, it refers only to fertilizers produced from animal and vegetable matter. Yet rock phosphate, gypsum, and sulfur, which are considered "natural" products and used by most organic gardeners, were mined from the earth and are therefore not organic. On the other hand, most organic gardeners do not approve of nitrate of soda, a naturally occurring material rich in nitrogen.

## POPULAR ORGANIC FERTILIZERS

**Animal by-products, tankage, and dried blood.**
Available from slaughterhouses, these contain a lot of nitrogen. Drawbacks are their strong smell (dried blood is also used as a deer repellent) and high cost. They work speedily and continue to feed the plant for longer periods than synthetic fertilizers. They are also less likely to burn plants than are synthetic fertilizers.

**Manure.** Poultry manure and guano (bat manure) are particularly rich in nitrogen. Other less rich but still excellent fertilizers are cow, sheep, pig, rabbit, and goat manures, either direct from the farm or in dried form. Animal manures from zoos, when available, are also good sources of nutrients. In addition to farms and zoos as a source, don't overlook horse stables and racetracks, which often have large amounts and no use for it. Most manures, in either farm-fresh or in dried form, are safe to use. Poultry manure can be harmful to plants when used fresh in excessive amounts, however, so compost it first. Guano is safe to use in any form, but it is expensive.

**Dried whey.** A by-product of the cheese industry, dried whey is a 5-9-1 formula. Spread 3 pounds (1.4 kg) per 100 square feet (30 m²).

**Composted sewage from commercial sewage plants.** This is a good source of nitrogen and makes fine topdressings for lawns and ornamentals. It may be smelly temporarily. Not everyone favors using sewage, even composted kinds, on food plants, however, since it may contain heavy metals and chemicals.

**Commercial compost made from plant sources.** This is an excellent source of nutrients and humus. It is usually finely screened and weed-free. It is made from vegetables and fruits discarded by stores, and kitchen wastes from restaurants, schools, hospitals, and other establishments.

**Plant products.** These include cottonseed meal and soybean meal, both good sources of nitrogen. (Be aware that some gardeners are concerned that the pesticides used for growing cotton may be toxic.) Less rich in nitrogen, but still good sources of humus, are citrus pulp, soybean and alfalfa meals, and the alfalfa pellets usually sold as animal feed. Dried seaweed and dried salt hay are good for mulches and also useful for making compost.

Synthetic fertilizers, especially those in liquid form, are the speediest way to add readily available nutrients to the soil. Synthetic fertilizers used alone provide no humus, however, and when used exclusively over a period of time, the humus in that spot is depleted and the soil suffers. Most are "complete," which means that they contain the primary essential nutrients — nitrogen, phosphorus, and potassium — in various proportions, depending on the crops for which they have been formulated. The most popular formula for a granulated fertilizer is 5-10-10, which is the only kind of plant food many gardeners ever use. If they need a stronger fertilizer, they simply use more of it.

Slow-release synthetic fertilizers are especially popular for plants grown in containers, but they are also widely used for those in the yard or border. These fertilizers are designed so that a percentage of the nutrients is water soluble and therefore released immediately, while the remaining portion is not soluble and releases slowly into the soil over a period of time.

## WHEN A PLANT IS UNDERNOURISHED

Neglecting to fertilize plants and trees is one of the most common causes of plant deterioration. To flourish, plants are likely to need many more nutrients than soil can provide if it has already been used for decades. Starving specimens not only look anemic (the leaves turn pale green or yellow), but they become stressed and in their weakened condition offer an open invitation to insects and diseases. Stressed plants are also far more likely than healthy ones to suffer from cold temperatures, high winds, and other weather-related injuries. Starving tree roots, searching for nutrients, sometimes grow close to the surface of the earth and heave up sidewalks or walls. Herbaceous plants with shallow roots dry out quickly during droughts.

When even those elements that are needed in minute amounts are lacking, their absence can affect growth. If you are not sure how to correct a nutrient deficiency, get advice from a Cooperative Extension Agent or some other professional about which elements are lacking and the best action to take.

# Improving Your Soil

If you examine the soil around plantings that are deteriorating, you are likely to find that it has become compressed or powdery, lifeless, and devoid of earthworms. Worn-out soil cannot be renewed by adding superphosphate or 5-10-10, although gardeners often try. If the soil is compressed, plant roots have trouble working through the hard earth to find the nutrients they need. Till some organic matter such as manure, compost, or peat moss into the soil to improve tilth and nutrients.

## Humus

Some of the best soil builders are decaying plant materials, including grass, roots, weeds, and wood in the form of shredded bark or decomposed sawdust, as well as various animal or poultry wastes. You can make your own humus in a compost pile or bin. The heat produced should kill any undesirable disease or pest organisms. Or you may have a municipal composting plant in your area that is a good source of ready-to-use organic matter that is weed- and odor-free. Other soil builders include the organic products that are mentioned on page 162).

Tree leaves are our favorite source of humus. We shred maple leaves in the fall and spread them on our vegetable garden, tilling them in thoroughly. Shredded leaves are also a fine material to layer in the compost pile, along with kitchen and garden wastes.

Leaf mold (composted leaves) is a valuable fertilizer as well as a superior humus, because it contains an abundance of useful soil bacteria, essential nutrients, and many trace elements. Earthworms like it, as do tiny plant roots. If your compost supply is limited, save leaf compost for your choicest plants or new seedlings.

## Compost

Homemade compost is excellent fertilizer and a good way to add humus to your garden. Layer garden wastes, garbage, leaves, and grass clippings with soil and manure (either dry or farm manure), and keep it moist. Within a year it will be converted into rich, odor-free, valuable humus. You can speed up the process by using compost activators, available at most garden supply stores, and by keeping the pile moist and turning it monthly.

## Cover Crops

A cover crop is one of the best ways to add humus and improve poor soil before starting a new planting, such as a perennial bed, vegetable garden, or berry patch. Till the land thoroughly in the spring, apply a complete fertilizer, add lime or sulfur, if necessary, and rake or till it in. Then sow a grain that will not live over the winter — millet, annual rye, or oats. If your land is unusually weedy, plant buckwheat, because it is competitive (a good weed fighter).

Let the crop grow during the summer and, as it starts to die down in the fall, till it in. Green manuring, as this method of soil renewal is known, is an excellent way to add both nutrients and humus. You can also keep the soil in your vegetable garden plot in good condition by tilling, fertilizing, and sowing winter rye after everything has been harvested in early fall. In most planting zones it will sprout and stay green throughout the winter. In the spring, after it has made additional growth, till it into the soil, which will be in good shape for planting within a few weeks.

Cover crops not only build soil but, like mulch, they keep the land covered when not in use, guarding it against torrential rains, baking sun, and eroding winds. Agronomists disagree about which cover crop is best, but for spring planting, oats usually get the most votes because their heavy root system adds a lot of humus to the soil. Because we need only a small amount of seed and farm stores don't like to sell small amounts, we buy several packages of millet birdseed and plant that, which works fine. Winter rye is the best choice for late summer or early fall planting because it stays alive over the winter. Mow both millet and winter rye before they go to seed, to avoid the proliferation of seedlings the following years.

## Mulches

Mulch is an invaluable aid in soil building and saves much time in maintenance. Its many benefits are impressive:

➤ It keeps the soil covered, which prevents erosion from sun, rain, and wind.

➤ It prevents drying out of the soil, ensuring that moisture is available to the plants over a longer period — and lessening your watering chores. It provides winter protection to plant roots.

➤ A thick mulch around a tree helps keep lawn mowers and other equipment away from it.

➤ As it rots, it enriches soil with humus and nutrients, and feeds earthworms working beneath it.

Many different materials are useful for mulching. We like organic materials because they protect the soil for a season and then decompose into a rich humus that earthworms love and fledgling plant roots appreciate as they work their way through the soil beneath them. (Just avoid using hay or other farm products that may bring a load of weed seeds into your garden.) If you use magazines or newspapers, shred them and then cover them with wood shavings or chips to keep them from blowing away. Inorganic mulches such as plastic sheets, landscape fabric, and stones may meet your needs, but they don't contribute humus or nutrients.

---

### MARVELOUS MULCH MATERIALS

| Organic | |
|---|---|
| Citrus pulp | Peat moss |
| Coarse wood shavings | Salt marsh hay |
| Cocoa hulls | Shredded bark |
| Farm wastes | Straw |
| Hay (chopped hay is by far the best) | Wood chips |
| | Wood shavings |
| Lawn clippings | |
| Leaves | **Inorganic** |
| Magazines and newspapers | Crushed rock or gravel |
| | Flat rocks |
| Peanut shells | Landscape fabric |
| | Plastic sheeting |

# Well-Fed Plants

Even the best plants won't flourish without proper nutrients. Fertilizer gives them vigor and helps keep them healthy. Choose a synthetic plant food for fast results, but an organic fertilizer is safer and longer lasting.

## Lawns

Feed most northern lawn grasses each fall and feed southern grasses in the spring and, if growth is poor, give the lawn a light feeding in the fall, also. Add lime too, if a soil test shows it needs it or if acid-loving weeds are creeping into the turf. (See page 166-67.) Mow often enough so you don't have to rake clippings; they will add humus to the soil if left on the lawn.

## Trees

A tree is a lifetime project, so don't try to hasten its growth too much, even if you want shade in a hurry. It is more important to get a strong, healthy, long-lived specimen. Organic fertilizers are safest to use. Feed trees early in the spring, if their growth has been poor.

Maples can tolerate more fertilizer than most other shade trees, but some evergreens, including pines, are sensitive to fertilizer; too much will result in weak, twisted growth. Overfeeding any tree can also make it weaker and more prone to insect and disease damage. Arborvitae tolerates extra nourishment better than other evergreens.

To feed trees, make a hole with a spade or a bar every 4 feet (1.2 m), beyond the outer spread of the branches, and fill each hole with ½ cup (12 mL) of complete fertilizer. Close the hole to protect the nutrients.

## Perennial Beds

When herbaceous perennial and annual plants are growing well in good, rich soil, feed them only if they appear to need it. Overfed plants tend to produce lots of greenery but don't bloom as well, and you'll just need to divide clumps more often. If the plants are not growing well in midsummer, give them liquid fertilizer, such as fish oil emulsion.

## Shrubs and Foundation Plantings

To keep shrubs and foundation plants in healthy condition, dig in plant food around the outside perimeter of the branch spread of evergreens and deciduous shrubs each spring, and then surround them with a mulch. Don't be too generous with the nutrients, unless the plants are not growing well.

The broadleaf evergreens, dwarf hemlocks, and pines do best in an acidic soil of 4.5 to 5.5 pH. If your soil is not acidic enough for them, give them a commercial acidic fertilizer or cottonseed meal, or treat the soil around them with sulfur (see page 165). Then mulch with oak leaves, pine needles, oak sawdust, or sphagnum peat moss. Avoid putting lime on evergreens.

## Fruit Trees

Fruit trees need nourishment every spring to prepare them to produce a crop of fruit that summer. Follow the directions given in chapter 10 for feeding. Do not overfeed young trees because if they are overnourished, they will concentrate only on growing taller and broader and will not bear fruit for many years. Overfed mature trees are likely to produce fruit that doesn't color well, and it may have an inferior flavor. They also may be more susceptible to aphid and other insect damage.

Don't give fruit trees more lime or wood ashes than the soil needs to maintain the pH that is right for them or a heavy fruit drop may result. (See pages 166-67.) For example, the soil on our property is about 6.5, and after years of trying to lower it to 4.5 in the spot where we wanted to grow blueberries, we finally gave up, and now raise the berry bushes in large pots where we can better control the acidity. Fortunately, most of the crops we grow do well with the higher pH.

If you doctor the soil pH to fit the plants you are growing, it is not a good idea to grow acid-loving plants, such as azaleas, close to those that prefer alkaline soil, such as lilacs. Some of the elements that affect pH can easily move through the soil and change the pH of neighboring plants.

# Coping with Other Soil Problems

**Thin topsoil.** If the topsoil consists of a thin layer over hardpan or rock, plant roots will spread out along whatever soil is available and are likely to dry out quickly. If you must grow large plants in such locations, spread enough topsoil over the area to have a soil depth of at least 12 inches (30 cm). Otherwise, grow a ground cover or tough strain of grass.

**Clay soils.** Heavy soil usually has a high percentage of clay particles and tends to compact easily, resulting in poor water drainage and lack of air. To improve such soil, add more organic matter. Perennial plants, trees, and shrubs grow better in soil that their roots can penetrate readily and fertilizer can permeate.

**Rocky soil.** Soil filled with large rocks is difficult to remedy. You can pick out small stones as they appear while tilling, but larger rocks are difficult to remove. The easiest solution we have found is to work around them. When large rocks and ledge lie close to the surface, it is an especially difficult place for trees to grow because there is not enough soil to support them adequately. Unless you want to add large quantities of topsoil, grow mostly small shrubs and plants with shallow roots in these locations.

# Soil pH

The pH of a substance is a measure of its alkalinity or acidity on a scale ranging from 1 (most acid) to 14 (most alkaline), with 7 as neutral. In soil, the pH is determined by the breakdown of water molecules into positive and negative ions. A soil rich in calcium compounds is likely to be close to neutral or alkaline, and one containing large amounts of decaying sphagnum moss or aluminum or sulfur compounds is more acidic. Most soils range from 4.5 to 7.

Although many plants, particularly weeds, grow well over a wide range of pH levels, some trees, shrubs, and herbaceous plants have a more limited tolerance. When soil is either too acidic (sour) or too alkaline (sweet), these plants cannot properly absorb the available nutrients, and poor growth results.

## SOIL pH TESTING

You can purchase kits for testing pH at garden centers and through mail-order catalogs. Both chemical kits and electronic testing devices are available. An electronic tester can be quite expensive, but it is useful if you are going to make a lot of tests. For accuracy, with both types of tests, follow the directions that come with the testers. If you don't want to do these tests yourself, your Cooperative Extension Service can do them for you. Some fertilizer companies also offer this service, as do many nurseries and garden centers.

Because there can be many different types of soil in the same yard or garden area, take samples from various spots, put them in small containers, and label them. Use dry soil for chemical tests, wet soil for the electronic ones. If the test kit directs you to moisten the soil, be sure to use water with a neutral pH, so it doesn't skew the results. Hard (alkaline) water affects the reading, as does acidic rain.

If you need to change the pH, test again each year to see if it has reverted to its former level. Lime can leach easily from some soils.

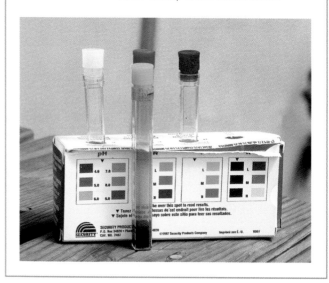

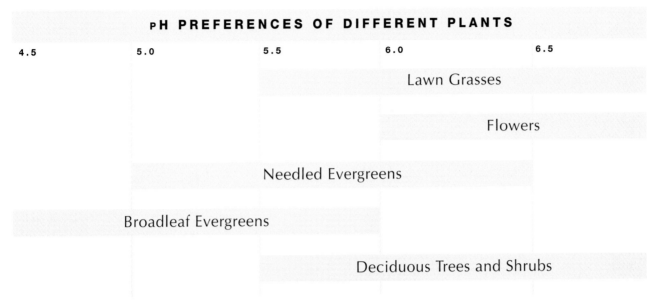

## pH PREFERENCES OF DIFFERENT PLANTS

| 4.5 | 5.0 | 5.5 | 6.0 | 6.5 |
|---|---|---|---|---|

Lawn Grasses

Flowers

Needled Evergreens

Broadleaf Evergreens

Deciduous Trees and Shrubs

These pH ranges indicate what is optimal for most plants of each type listed. Many plants adapt to soils with a somewhat higher or lower pH than what they prefer.

Most plants can grow well within a wider range of soil pH if the soil is buffered with an abundance of humus. Whether you perceive the pH of your soil as good or bad depends on what you want to grow in it. For optimum growth, most cultivated plants need a soil with a pH ranging from 5.5. to 6.5.

If your soil is extremely acidic or very alkaline, either you can decide to grow only the plants that like those conditions or you can change the pH. Though it is not difficult to raise the pH (see below), lowering it is harder, and more likely to be temporary because in many alkaline soils, lime from the subsoil tends to percolate upward with every rain, negating your attempts to make it acidic.

## Changing the pH of Your Soil

**To make soil more alkaline.** The material most often used to raise pH is lime. Ground limestone is widely available and the one most gardeners use. Calcitic lime contains a small amount of magnesium, and dolomite, a larger amount. Burnt lime, known as quicklime, is not pleasant to handle; slaked lime is produced by reacting burnt lime with water. In takes about 10 pounds (4.53 kg) of ground limestone per 100 square feet (9.29 m²) to raise the pH of ordinary garden soil (loam) one point.

Most hardwood ashes are alkaline, except those of oak, which are acidic. Ashes supply both calcium and potash. Spread them in early spring so that spring rains can push them into the soil before summer.

Make a special pile of compost from naturally alkaline products such as eggshells and oyster shells.

**To make soil more acidic.** Add sphagnum peat moss; composted leaves, sawdust, and bark of oak, pine, and hemlock trees; cottonseed meal; sulfur and sulfur compounds; and aluminum sulfate and similar compounds. You can also use an acid fertilizer, such as cottonseed meal. It takes about 9 pounds (4 kg) of elemental sulfur per 100 square feet (9.29 m²) to lower the pH of ordinary garden soil (loam) one point.

---

### WARNINGS!

- Never add lime and synthetic fertilizer at the same time because they sometimes react unfavorably to each other. Instead, wait for a good soaking rain between the two applications.

- If your soil is poorly drained, using sulfur is questionable, because it can be converted into toxic compounds.

---

# Hardpan

Hardpan is a layer of hard soil or subsoil, or clay with particles cemented together, present in moist soils, somewhere below the surface. In locations where the topsoil layer has become thinner and thinner through use, it is necessary to break up the hardpan to grow plants. Farmers use a knifelike steel subsoiler pulled behind a tractor to break up hardpan. In the past, orchardists sometimes used part of a stick of dynamite to fracture the subsoil when they planted fruit trees. Neither method is feasible for most of us, but deep tilling and adding humus and organic fertilizer will encourage earthworms that help break up this layer.

# Soil Moisture Solutions

Both too much moisture and too little moisture can threaten your plants' survival. Vagaries of weather often present challenges to gardeners from one year to the next, but persistently unfavorable conditions need a more long-term approach.

## When It's Too Wet

Most garden plants, shrubs, and trees don't do well in soil that is so wet it is soggy for more than short periods. Move such plants to a better location or, if the wet spot is small, you may be able to fill it in or grade it so it will have better drainage. Alternatively, grow only plants that thrive in moist conditions.

## When It's Too Dry

Only a limited number of landscape plants are happy in dry, sandy soils. Such soil does not hold water well, even when water is available, and it is not likely to store and release nutrients either. You can upgrade dry or sandy soil by adding compost, peat moss, manure, or other partially decomposed organic materials.

Bare soil loses moisture, nutrients, and humus rapidly, so protect it from erosion while it is absorbing its new humus by using a mulch or by planting a fast-germinating crop there until you plant the crop you want. If these measures don't work, switch to xeriscaping, a growing method that uses only plants that do well without an abundance of moisture.

# 13 Keeping Your Landscape Out of Harm's Way

Even with the best of care, bad things can happen to good gardeners. Wind, cold, floods, droughts, and septic systems that need digging up are beyond our control. Nevertheless, we can be ready to fight insects, diseases, and animals, and be careful with equipment that can damage plants. We may be able to animal-proof our gardens, choose the proper plants for our climate, and take other preventive steps. By learning to recognize the possible causes of damage, we can feel in control, rather than victimized, when our plantings are endangered.

## Environmental Contaminants

Often what appears to be a disease is actually a condition caused by some physiological factor that interferes with the proper functioning of a plant. A suffering plant growing near a septic drainage field, for example, may be adversely affected by chemicals used in washing and cleaning. The misuse of herbicides, even years ago, may mean they remain active in the soil, resulting in poor growth.

Weed killers, insecticides, and fungicides used in excessive amounts can affect the soil and make it difficult for plants to grow. Wood preservatives can damage adjacent plants.

Excess fertilizer or lime is also a possibility when a plant looks ill. In the North, road salt can be hard on plants, and by the seashore, ocean spray may also be lethal to salt-sensitive plants.

If you suspect chemical toxicity, move the plants to a new location and let grass grow in the damaged spot for at least two years to allow the toxins to leach out. If you need to use the space sooner, you can detoxify the soil by lifting out all the plants and raking or tilling in activated charcoal to absorb the chemicals. Wait a few months before replanting, so the charcoal will have time to work.

### TOO MUCH OF A GOOD THING

Overfeeding any plant with synthetic fertilizer at any time can be disastrous, but especially if the weather is dry. The fertilizer needs moisture to work, and if there isn't enough in the soil, it draws it from the plant roots, resulting in leaves with a brownish, burnt appearance. Unless rain or moisture is added promptly, the plant often dies.

Any overfeeding with either synthetic or organic fertilizer can cause a plant to grow so rapidly during the long days of summer that it faces life in a weakened condition. The branches can break readily in a wind or if brushed against.

## Machinery

Machinery often is hard on plants. Lawn mowers, weed whackers, garden tractors, motorbikes, and snowmobiles frequently scrub the bark off trees and stunt or kill them. Digging to repair a water or septic system can break off tree roots too — a common cause of tree infirmity.

Heavy equipment can also affect soil quality. It compacts the ground, making it difficult for plant roots to reach the necessary nutrients, air, and moisture. Wet clay soils are most vulnerable to compression, but any soil can be affected. Treat worn-out soils, such as dry ones, by building up the organic matter. Sometimes you'll need to apply large quantities of sand to lighten badly compressed soils.

# Hardiness Problems

Sections of a landscape sometimes look forlorn because someone goofed and chose plants that were better suited for a climate that is either warmer or cooler than where they live. For example, magnolias that thrive in Virginia are not likely to winter well in northern Michigan, and English holly, acclimated to the long, mild, moist growing season of the Pacific Northwest, often has difficulty growing in the East.

Guides that recommend plants for various planting zones are helpful, but within each planting zone microclimates exist that may be a zone or two warmer or colder than the region immediately surrounding it. A tree hardy in a valley in Zone 5 may have difficulty growing a few miles away on a windy mountaintop, even though both are assigned the same plant hardiness zone.

Some plants need a certain amount of cold to survive. White spruce, lilacs, and rhubarb, for example, need long, cold winters. Temperate-climate fruit trees, such as peaches and apples, must have a certain number of chilling hours each year, so most cultivars are not recommended for Florida or southern California.

To survive a winter in the North or in a high elevation, a plant must be able not only to endure the lowest temperature of the winter, but also to adjust to the short growing season there. It must stop growing long before the first fall frost so the new growth will harden enough to withstand the cold temperature. Many trees need a long growing season and cannot make this adjustment. Some imports may start growing too early in the spring, and spring frosts damage their new sprouts.

---

**BEING AT HOME**

A plant can become acclimated to a region that is listed as a zone or two different from its native home, especially if it has been moved gradually into its new climate. You may find, for example, that although a walnut tree that originated from a seed grown in your neighborhood will thrive in your yard, seedlings of the same variety imported from a warmer region may greatly resent the change in climate and protest by not growing.

---

# Winter Damage

Cold weather can injure plants, whether in Georgia or Quebec, and winter ice storms, wind, and hail have been known to damage plantings in places that ordinarily don't have winter. Certain types of winter damage are avoidable, however, and you can take steps to minimize such things as sunscald, plant heaving, and hedge breakage.

## Alternate Freezing and Thawing

In regions where snow doesn't cover the ground all winter, the soil can develop cracks that dry out roots. Perennials can be completely thrust out of the ground. To help prevent these problems, apply a heavy mulch in fall.

## Physical Snow and Ice Damage

Snow and ice can be just as devastating as low temperatures. Perennial shrubs and trees will be damaged if heavy snow or ice falls on them from a roof or if freezing rain covers their limbs. A metal roof often is hazardous to plants beneath it because snow slides off the surface so easily. Branches break in ice storms or when the frozen crust of deep snow settles as it melts beneath the surface. Pools of ice over low-growing ground covers, lawns, or perennials can seriously damage plants beneath.

If you are aware of possible dangers, you can avoid many of them. Grade your lawn and garden so water doesn't collect there and freeze. If possible, locate vulnerable plants where they are least likely to suffer weather damage. Don't plant under eaves or where snow drifts pile up. Trim your hedges so tops are tapered. Choose plants that are hardy for your climate, and mulch perennials and shrubs with shallow roots to prevent frost heaving over winter.

## Sunscald

Sunscald damages trees in both warm and cold climates. In warm climates, hot sun may blister exposed sections of tender growth. In cold areas, the damage usually occurs in late winter when the sun is especially bright, and it affects mostly young trees that do not yet have enough branch area to effectively shade their tender trunks. The sun heats up the dark-colored bark and then, if a cloud suddenly hides the sun, the temperature drops rapidly and the rising sap in the tree freezes, rupturing the bark. To prevent sunscald, paint the bark on the sunny east and south-eastern sides of tree trunks with diluted white latex paint. If you notice bark that is already split, tack it back in place immediately with thumb tacks or small nails, before it has a chance to dry out.

## Winter Road Salt

Sensitive plants and trees adjacent to heavily salted roads suffer considerable damage. You can divert salt runoff away from the roots, but even plants some distance from the road can be affected when salt spray is kicked up by vehicles and spread by the wind. If the plants are affected year after year, it's best to remove them before they die and replace them with salt-resistant species.

## Windburn

Windburn can result when plants, especially evergreens, run out of moisture during the winter and the wind dries out their branches and needles or leaves. It occurs if the soil was unusually dry going into winter or if the ground freezes hard. Wrapping sensitive plants (yews and hemlocks especially) in burlap may help, as can spraying with Wiltpruf or a similar product that seals needle and leaf pores and checks evaporation. Provide windbreaks.

# Toxic Plants

The roots of black walnut and butternut trees exude a substance into the soil that kills certain other plants. Grass and many deciduous trees and shrubs are not usually affected by this interaction, but some plants cannot tolerate it, including certain evergreens and paper birch. The culprits are not always living plants; the allelopathic effects of the roots of a black walnut long gone may still be present — this is sometimes the reason for the mysterious death of newly planted trees and shrubs.

# Animal Damage

Moles, mice, voles, deer, rabbits, other animals and even neighborhood dogs and cats can make life difficult for plantings. As animals have proliferated, even in suburbs and small cities, they have created many battered landscapes.

## DEERPROOFING

Deer are among the most hazardous pests of perennials, shrubbery, vegetables, annual flowers, and trees. And they are also among the most difficult to control. You can't count on repellents to be completely effective, and even replacing your plantings with other types that are not on their list of favorites may not be helpful, because hungry deer will eat almost anything.

Desperate gardeners have tried many tactics, from broadcasting blood meal to applying pepper sprays on foliage. Some controls that are reputed to be effective in small areas are bags of unwashed hair from a barber shop or beauty parlor, smelly soaps (one of our friends cuts cakes of Shield soap in small pieces and scatters them throughout his garden with good results), and lion or cougar manure from a zoo.

A high, tight fence around your property is ultimately the best protection against these marauders.

| DAMAGE | PROBABLE CULPRIT | ACTION |
|---|---|---|
| TREE BARK NIBBLED NEAR THE GROUND | Mice | If chewing doesn't go all the way around the trunk, paint the wound with tree paint. If the tree has been girdled and the tree is not grafted, save the best sprout that starts below the wound and train it to become a new trunk. If the girdled tree is grafted, however, the good top will die. Sprouts coming from below the graft will be wild trees and of little value. |
| BRANCHES CHEWED OFF A SHORT DISTANCE ABOVE THE GROUND | Rabbits | Trim the damage and, if bark is loose, treat the injury as you would that of mice (see above). |
| TREE OR SHRUB BRANCHES CHEWED OFF HIGHER THAN RABBITS COULD REACH; BARK SCRUBBED OFF ALONG TRUNK | Deer feeding or rubbing their antlers on the tree trunk | See Deerproofing, page 171. |
| TREE BARK CHEWED OFF AT VARIOUS PLACES ALONG TRUNK OR LIMBS | Porcupines | Encourage hunting or trapping. |
| TREES CUT DOWN WITH TRUNK CHEWED TO A POINT, AS ON A PENCIL | Beavers | Contact your state's Fish and Game officials, requesting that they trap and move perpetrators. |
| TUNNELS JUST BELOW THE GROUND SURFACE, IN THE LAWN OR THROUGHOUT THE GARDEN | Moles searching for grubs to eat | Sprinkle area with organic pesticide such as *Bacillus thuringiensis (Bt)* or beneficial nematodes to kill grubs; use castor-oil–based mole repellent. |
| HOLES DUG IN LAWN | Skunks searching for grubs, or other animals digging for bone meal used as fertilizer | Spray area with organic pesticide such as *Bacillus thuringiensis (Bt)* or beneficial nematodes, to kill grubs. Trap skunks in box trap. Refrain from using bone meal as fertilizer. |
| EVERGREENS TURNING BROWN AT THE BASE | Male dogs using trees or shrubs as fire hydrants | If it is your pet, use dog repellent on shrubs. If you catch him in the act or shortly after, flood the immediate area with water to dilute or wash away the acidic urine. |
| TOPS BROKEN ON EVERGREENS OR SHRUBS | Birds roosting on tender new growth | Try to provide roosting places with better views (though we admit this is not likely to be too effective) |
| BERRIES MISSING OR BITES TAKEN FROM TREE FRUITS | Birds or possibly squirrels | Use plastic snakes, fluttering pieces of foil, netting, plastic horned owls. Cats or traps are effective for squirrel control. |
| VEGETABLE AND FLOWER PLANTS NIBBLED OR EATEN TO THE GROUND | Deer, raccoons, rabbits, woodchucks | See Deerproofing, page 171. Control raccoons, rabbits, and woodchucks with box traps, a dog, or a low electric fence. |
| BROWN EVERGREENS IN THE SPRING | Windburn or salt spray | See page 171. |

# Appendixes

## USDA Plant Hardiness Zone Map

The United States Department of Agriculture (USDA) created this map to give gardeners a helpful tool for selecting and cultivating plants. The map divides North America into 11 zones based on each area's average minimum winter temperature. Zone 1 is the coldest and zone 11 the warmest. Once you determine your zone, you may use that information to select plants that are most likely to thrive in your climate.

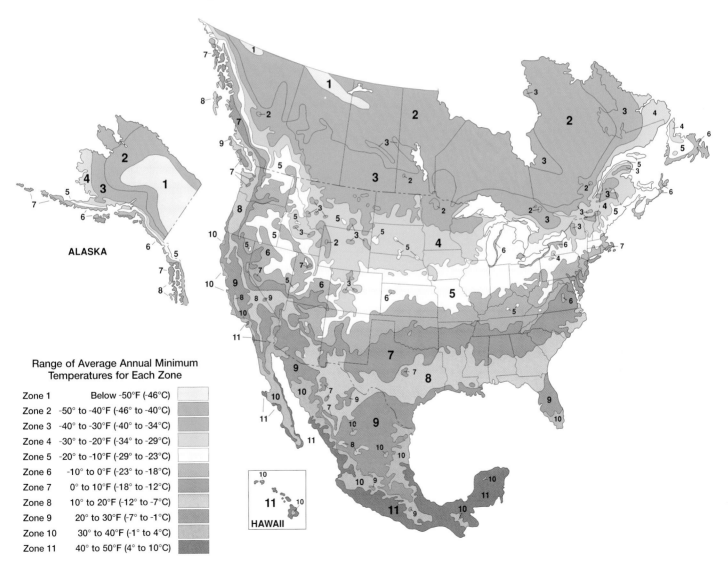

**ALASKA**

**HAWAII**

### Range of Average Annual Minimum Temperatures for Each Zone

|  |  |
|------|-------|
| Zone 1 | Below -50°F (-46°C) |
| Zone 2 | -50° to -40°F (-46° to -40°C) |
| Zone 3 | -40° to -30°F (-40° to -34°C) |
| Zone 4 | -30° to -20°F (-34° to -29°C) |
| Zone 5 | -20° to -10°F (-29° to -23°C) |
| Zone 6 | -10° to 0°F (-23° to -18°C) |
| Zone 7 | 0° to 10°F (-18° to -12°C) |
| Zone 8 | 10° to 20°F (-12° to -7°C) |
| Zone 9 | 20° to 30°F (-7° to -1°C) |
| Zone 10 | 30° to 40°F (-1° to 4°C) |
| Zone 11 | 40° to 50°F (4° to 10°C) |

# Resources

## Plants

### Brent and Becky's Bulbs
7463 Heath Trail
Gloucester, VA 23061
Phone: 877/661-2852
Fax: 804/693-9436
Website:
www.brentandbeckysbulbs.com
*Bulbs*

### Crescent Nursery
RR #4, Rockwood
ON N0B 2K0 Canada
Phone: 519/856-1000
Fax: 519/856-2712
Website: rdcrwfrd@ican.net
*Perennials*

### Gurneys Seed and Nursery
110 Capital Street
Yankton, SD 57079
Phone: 605/665-1930
Fax: 605/665-9718
E-mail: info@gurneys.com
Website: www.gurneys.com

### Jackson & Perkins
1 Rose Lane, P.O. Box 1028
Medford, OR 97501
Phone: 800/292-4769
Fax: 800/242-0329
Website: www.jacksonandperkins.com
*Roses, perennials, bulbs, garden supplies*

### Lake County Nursery
Route 84
Perry, OH 44081
Phone: 800/522-5253
Fax: 800/699-3114
Website: www.lakecountynursery.com
*Perennials, trees, shrubs, ornamental grasses, ground covers, roses, vines*

### Lilypons Water Gardens
6800 Lilypons Road, P.O. Box 10
Buckeystown, MD 21717-0010
Phone: 800/999-5459
Fax: 800/879-5459
E-mail: info@lilypons.com
Website: www.lilypons.com
*Water plants, pool supplies, fountains, pumps, filters, pools and liners, fish*

### Logees Greenhouses
141 North Street
Danielson, CT 06239
Phone: 888/330-8038
Fax: 888-774-9932
E-mail: logee-info@logees.com
Website: www.logees.com
*Perennials*

### Nichols Garden Nursery
1190 North Pacific Highway
Albany, OR 97321-4580
Phone: 541/928-9280
Fax: 541/967-8406
E-mail: info@gardennursery.com
Web site: www.gardennursery.com
*Seeds, herbs, garden supplies*

### Paradise Water Gardens
14 May Street
Whitman, MA 02832
Phone: 1-800-955-0161
Fax: 1-800-966-4591
Website:
www.paradisewatergardens.com
*Water plants and supplies*

### Park's Countryside Gardens
1 Parkton Avenue
Greenwood, SC 29647-0001
Phone: 800/845/3369
Fax: 800/275-9941
E-mail: info@parkseed.com
Website: www.parkseed.com
*Bulbs, ornamental plants, gardening supplies*

### Perry's Water Gardens
136 Gibson Aquatic Farm Rd.
Franklin, NC 28734
Phone: 828/524-3264
Fax:828/524-3264
Website: www.perryswatergardens.com
*Water plants and water garden supplies*

### Pinetree Garden Seeds
Box 300, 616A Lewiston Rd
New Gloucester, ME 04260
Phone: 207/926-3400
Fax: 207/888-52-SEEDS
E-mail: superseeds@worldnet.att.net
Website: www.superseeds.com
*Perennials, bulbs, seeds, garden tools, books*

### Van Dyck's
P.O. Box 430
Brightwaters, NY 11718-0430
Phone: 800/248-2852
Fax: 800-639-2452
E-mail: Jan@Vandycks.com
Website: www.vandycks.com
*Perennials and bulbs*

### Van Ness Water Gardens
2460 N. Euclid Ave.
Upland, CA 91784-1199
Phone: 800/205-2425
Fax: 909/949-7217
E-mail: vnwg@vnwg.com
Website: www.vnwg.com
*Water plants and water garden supplies*

### Wayside Gardens
1 Garden Lane
Hodges, SC 29695-0001
Phone: 800/845-1124
Fax: 800/457-9712
E-mail: info@waysidegardens.com
Website: www.waysidegardens.com
*Perennials*

West Coast Seeds
206-8475 Ontario Street
Vancouver, BC V5X 3E8
Phone: 604/482-8800
Fax: 604/482-8822
E-mail: mark@westcoastseeds.com
Website: www.westcoastseeds.com

Weston Nurseries
P.O. Box 186, East Main Street
Hopkinton, MA 01748
Phone: 800/322-2002
Fax: 508/435-3274
*Evergreens, trees, shrubs, vines, perennials, roses, garden supplies*

White Flower Farm
P.O. Box 50
Litchfield, CT 06759-0050
Phone: 800/503-9624
Website: www.whiteflowerfarm.com
*Perennials, bulbs, shrubs*

## Garden Tools and Supplies

### Gardener's Supply Company
128 Intervale Road
Burlington, VT 05401
Phone: 800/863-1700
Fax: 800/551-6712
E-mail:info@gardeners.com
Website: www.gardeners.com

### Langenbach
P.O. Box 1420
Lawndale, CA 90260-6320
Phone: 800/362-1991
E-mail: CustomerService@langen-bach.com
Website: www.langenbach.com

Lee Valley Tools
*US orders:*
12 East River Stree, P.O. Box 1780
Ogdensburg, NY 13669-6780
Phone: 800/871-8158
Fax: 800/513-7885
*Canadian orders:*
P.O. Box 6295, Stn.
Ottawa, ON K2A I24
Phone: 800/267-8767
Fax: 800/668-1807
E-mail: customerservice@leevalley.com
Web site: www.leevalley.com

A.M. Leonard
241 Fox Drive, P.O. Box 816
Piqua, OH 45356-0816
Phone: 800/543-8955
Fax: 800/433-0633
Website: www.amleo.com

Mellinger's
2310 W. South Range Road
North Lima, OH 44452-9731
Phone: 330/549-9861
Fax: 330/549-3716
Website: www.Mellingers.com

Troy-Bilt Manufacturing Co.
1 Garden Way
Troy, NY 12180
Phone: 800/828-5500
Fax: 518/391-7448
Website: www.troybilt.com

## Helpful Organizations

### American Rose Society
P.O. Box 30,000
Shreveport, LA 71130-0030
Phone: 318/938-5402
Fax: 318/938-5405
E-mail: ars@ars-hq.org
Website: www.ars.org

Canadian Rose Society
Anne Graber
10 Fairfax Crescent
Scarborough, Ontario M1L 1Z8
Phone: 416/757-8809
Fax: 416/757-4796
E-mail: crs@mirror.org
Website: www.mirror.org/groups/crs/

## Magazines of Interest to Gardeners

*Country Journal*
4 High Ridge Park
Stamford, CT 06905

*Flower and Garden*
4251 Pennsylvania
Kansas City, MO 64111

*Horticulture*
98 North Washington St.
Boston, MA 02114

*Kitchen Gardener*
The Taunton Press, Inc
63 South Main St.
Newton, CT 16470-5506

*National Gardening*
180 Flynn Ave.
Burlington, VT 05401

*Organic Gardening*
33 East Minor St.
Emmaus PA 18098

# Index

Page references in **bold** indicate charts; those in *italics* indicate photographs or drawings.

# Other Storey Titles You Will Enjoy

*Caring for Perennials,* by Janet Macunovich. A month-by-month approach to perennial gardening. Includes care charts for more than 130 perennials. 200 pages. Paperback. ISBN 1-88266-957-5.

*Daylilies: The Perfect Perennial,* by Lewis and Nancy Hill. How to create dramatic, colorful, and long-lasting daylily displays. 208 pages. Paperback. ISBN 0-88266-651-7.

*Landscaping Makes Cents,* by Frederick C. Campbell and Richard L. Dubé. A complete guide to adding substantial value and beauty to a home through careful landscape design. 176 pages. Paperback. ISBN 0-88266-948-6.

*Pruning Made Easy,* by Lewis Hill. A gardener's visual guide to when and how to prune everything, from flowers to trees. 224 pages. Paperback. ISBN 1-58017-006-4.

*Secrets of Plant Propagation,* by Lewis Hill. Techniques for those who want to discover the satisfaction of propagating their own plants. 176 pages. Paperback. ISBN 0-88266-370-4.

*Storey's Basic Country Skills: A Practical Guide to Self-Reliance,* by John and Martha Storey. More than 150 of Storey's expert authors in gardening, building, animal raising, and homesteading share their specialized knowledge and experience in this ultimate guide to living a more independent, satisfying life. Step-by-step, illustrated instructions for every aspect of country living. 544 pages. Paperback. ISBN 1-58017-199-0.

*Successful Perennial Gardening,* by Lewis and Nancy Hill. A user-friendly guide to the challenges and joys of perennial gardening. 240 pages. Paperback. ISBN 1-88266-472-7.

*The Vegetable Gardener's Bible,* by Edward C. Smith. Integrates four gardening techniques — wide rows, organic methods, raised beds, and deep soil — to grow high-yielding, healthy vegetable gardens. Contains all you need to know about pest and disease control, soil, compost, and how to grow more than 70 vegetables and herbs. 320 pages. 450 full-color photographs. Paperback. ISBN 1-58017-212-1.

*Watering Systems for Lawn and Garden,* R. Dodge Woodson. A complete handbook for anyone wanting to buy or install a small-scale irrigation system for the lawn, garden, or backyard. 144 pages. Paperback. ISBN 0-88266-906-0.

These and other Storey titles are available at your bookstore, farm store, garden center, or directly from Storey Books, Schoolhouse Road, Pownal, Vermont 05261, or by calling 1-800-441-5700. Visit our Web site at www.storeybooks.com.